THE WAR

OF

ORMUZD AND AHRIMAN

IN THE

NINETEENTH CENTURY.

BY

HENRY WINTER DAVIS.

Litora litoribus contraria, fluctibus undas
Imprecor, arma armis: pugnent ipsique nepotesque.

BALTIMORE:
JAMES S. WATERS, 244 BALTIMORE ST.
MDCCCLII.

JOHN D. TOY, PRINTER.

TO THE AMERICAN PEOPLE.

THE American People have passed the season of youth when withdrawn from the eye of the world their pleasures might blamelessly be their pursuits.

In the maturity of years and strength they are amenable to mankind for the conformity of their conduct to the higher motives of policy and duty.

They cannot if they would be silent and neutral in that great controversy of the age which they opened on the field of battle.

It concerns their safety that the part they play be adopted in full view of all the dangers that beset them.

It concerns their dignity that their part be worthy of their origin and pursued with manly fortitude to the end.

I have endeavored to develope some of the considerations which throw light on the path of safety and of honor.

On this great theme I invoke the judgment of the American People.

HENRY WINTER DAVIS.

8 March 1852.

CONTENTS.

Πρῶτον μέν, ὦ ἄνδδες Ἀθηναῖοι, τοῦτο παρ' ὑμῖν αὐτοῖς βεβαίως γνῶναι, ὅτι τῇ πόλει Φίλιππος πολεμεῖ καὶ τὴν εἰρήνην λέλυκε—καὶ παύσασθε περὶ τούτου κατηγοροῦντες ἀλλήλων—καὶ κακόνους μέν ἐστι καὶ ἐχθρὸς ὅλῃ τῇ πόλει καὶ τῷ τῆς πόλεως ἐδάφει, προσθήσω δὲ καὶ τοῖς ἐν τῇ πόλει πᾶσιν ἀνθρώποις, καὶ τοῖς μάλιστ' οἰομένοις αὐτῷ χαρίζεσθαι (εἰ δὲ μή, σκεψάσθωσαν Εὐθυκράτη καὶ Λασθένη τοὺς Ὀλυνθίους, οἳ δοκοῦντες οἰκειότατ' αὐτῷ διακεῖσθαι, ἐπειδὴ τὴν πόλιν προὔδοσαν, πάντων κάκιστ' ἀπολώλασιν), οὐδενὶ μέντοι μᾶλλον ἢ τῇ πολιτείᾳ πολεμεῖ οὐδ' ἐπιβουλεύει, καὶ σκοπεῖ μᾶλλον οὐδὲ ἓν τῶν πάντων ἢ ὅπως ταύτην καταλύσει. καὶ τοῦτ' εἰκότως τρόπον τινὰ πράττει· οἶδε γὰρ ἀκριβῶς ὅτι οὐδ' ἂν πάντων τῶν ἄλλων γένηται κύριος, οὐδὲν ἔστ' αὐτῷ βεβαίως ἔχειν, ἕως ἂν ὑμεῖς δημοκρατῆσθε, ἀλλ' ἐάν ποτε συμβῇ τι πταῖσμα, ἃ πολλὰ γένοιτ' ἂν ἀνθρώπῳ ἥξει πάντα τὰ νῦν συμβεβιασμένα καὶ καταφεύξεται πρὸς ὑμᾶς. ἐστὲ γὰρ ὑμεῖς οὐκ αὐτοὶ πλεονεκτῆσαι καὶ κατασχεῖν ἀρχὴν εὖ πεφυκότες, ἀλλ' ἕτερον λαβεῖν κωλῦσαι καὶ ἔχοντ' ἀφελέσθαι δεινοί, καὶ ὅλως ἐνοχλῆσαι τοῖς ἄρχειν βουλομένοις καὶ πάντας ἀνθρώπους εἰς ἐλευθερίαν ἐξαφελέσθαι ἕτοιμοι. οὔκουν βούλεται τοῖς ἑαυτοῦ καιροῖς τὴν παρ' ὑμῶν ἐλευθερίαν ἐφεδρεύειν, οὐδὲ πολλοῦ δεῖ, οὐ κακῶς οὐδ' ἀργῶς ταῦτα λογιζόμενος.

Δημοσθηνους περι των ευ Χερρουησῳ.

SECTION I.

THE HOLY ALLIANCE.

THE HOLY ALLIANCE.

WITHIN the four score years of the life of man two powers have grown from insignificance to be the arbiters of the world.

They occupy opposite continents. They are actuated by hostile principles. They are organized on antagonist theories of political power. In each is the principle of its existence absolute, pervading every department of government, infused into every element of society, and controlling the administration of affairs. There is no formally organized opposition to the existing order of things. There is no serious division of feeling or of opinion among the citizens. The people are equally devoted to the form and to the substance of their respective constitutions. The foundations of both governments firmly rest on the express or implied assent of the people—who are ready to signalize their devotion on the field of battle.

Each is the incarnation of one of the two great spirits, pure, absolute, unchecked, uncontrolled, unlimited, which have always striven and now still strive on the theatre of nations for the mastery of mankind.

Those two spirits are Liberty and Despotism—the Ormuzd and Ahriman of the political world. Their purest incarnations are—The Republic of America and The Empire of Russia.

There are other free States beside those of America. There are other despotisms beside that of Russia. But there are none of either class so purely and simply the impersonations of the antagonist spirits. England is a free government: but the doctrine of popular sovereignty is limited by aristocratic privileges, and the field is cumbered still by the ruins of the progressing conflict. The dormant power of the people is denied by some, opposed by others, and struggles to retain while it strives to extend its confessed domain. France is a republic in form, in principle, and by the feeling of the vast majority of her people; but sinister influences mis-direct her power, conflicting pretences paralyze her activity—she is yet the theatre of conflict of contending principles, not the great domain of any confessed and conceded power. The Bourbon, the Orleanist, the Bonapartist still lift their aspiring heads in contentious emulation against the majesty of the Republic.

Austria and Prussia are despotic military monarchies:—but their thrones are not beds of roses. The people of both are alive with hostile hopes and fermenting with pent up energies and fiery wrath. They restlessly heave beneath the military weight which oppresses them. Their sighs and their groans testify to their discontent, while they confess the power of a despotism they cannot throw off.

It is only in the Republic of America that the people, imbued with the spirit of liberty, are the recognized, uncontrolled, unquestioned sovereign power.

It is only in Russia that the Emperor is met by the cheerful, unquestioning, submissive and affectionate devotion of the people. They worship in his person the embodied sovereignty of the nation; and in the tempest of an insurrection his simple words to his children—have sufficed to calm them.

On the spirit and character of the government the discontent and restlessness of the Polish provinces in the one case exert no more disturbing influence, than the millions of slaves in the Southern States do in the other. The despotism and the republicanism respectively are quite as absolutely pure and free with, as they would be without those elements of discontent. They are both sources of possible danger and of certain weakness: neither of them affects the character or the spirit of the government: neither is so powerful as to make either government pause in its career or vary from its course.

The progress of each of these powers has been equally rapid and equally illustrative of the spirit and principles which animate their policy. The one has thriven amid the arts of peace and industry. The other has gorged its greatness by the spoils of war and the fruits of intrigue.

At the date of our Revolution, Russia was just entering on her career as an European power: and her fit introduction was a deed of blood and shame. At the opening of the eighteenth century the Muscovite was confined in his northern home—barred off from civilized Europe by the colossal republic of Poland which pressed him behind the Dwina and the Dnieper, and excluded from the Baltic and the Euxine by the Swede and the Turk.

Thus for centuries pent up in the desolate north, the Dukes of Moscow had consolidated their power on the ruins of the Empire of the Mongol. They nourished the lust of conquest by ceaseless aggression on their neighbors, and trained their people to the habitudes of war while expanding the sphere of their power. But their quarrels and their conquests were alike almost unknown and uninteresting to civilized Europe till the triumph at Pultowa securely seated Peter the Great on the Baltic. The provinces of Livonia, Esthonia, Ingria and Karelia, the spoil of that day, in 1710 brought him into direct connection with the maritime nations of Europe. His genius and his ambition inspired the hope and provided the means of playing a high part on this new theatre; and from that day to this, the eyes of Peter and of his successors, whether in the ship yards of Saardam and Deptford or in the palaces of St. Petersburg, have turned with longing eagerness to the West, till their arts and their arms and their hereditary and unscrupulous ambition have consolidated a colossal Empire extending to the very heart of Europe and now—*the arbiter of its destinies.*

Poland and the Ottoman Empire were at once the chief obstacles and the most alluring objects of Russia's far-seeing ambition.

For eighty years she waged a war alternately of arms and of intrigues against the Turk—now advancing with rapid flight on the wings of fortune, now pausing in her career to secure her conquest, or with feigned moderation concealing defeat by voluntary restorations of parts of her prey—till time and opportunity should give the signal of advance. The flood of her conquest has risen and rolled onward over neighboring nations—like the tides of the ocean—each wave rolling high on the shore and sinking back to the sea with alternate advance and retreat—yet each higher than the former and steadily gaining in the midst of apparent fluctuations.

Her pretexts have been as Protean as her purpose has been single. Religion, humanity, liberty, national independence, national institutions, social order, have, each in turn, been under the disguise of protection the pretexts of aggression, and finally, the victims of her infernal devices.

Peter not only made Russia an European power: he set the example of stretching its roots towards the soil of the East. He seized Azoff and overran the Crimea: but was compelled to relinquish them. Ann followed his example and met his fortune: she again grasped at, but was obliged to abandon their possession; and to content herself with confirming her dominion over the territory of the Zaporagua Cossacks.

Catharine renewed the contest: and conquered the Crimea, Moldavia and Wallachia: but she was able to hold only Azoff and the coveted access to the Euxine. Yet true to the instincts of her Empire, what she relinquished she did not restore. She declared the Crimea, Kuban and Budjek *independent of Turkey*, and so effectually secured the future dominion of Russia.

For awhile she contented herself with setting up and pulling down Kahns of the Cossacks, till they sought refuge from her caprice in rebellion. The vengeance of the enraged Semiramis was slaked in the blood of thirty thousand people; and the Turks paid the penalty of their intermeddling by securing to Russia the sovereignty of Kuban and the unlimited right to navigate all the Turkish seas. The Euxine ceased to be a *Turkish mare clausum.*

These humiliating terms goaded the Turks into a renewal of the unequal conflict: and Catharine retired at the peace of Jassy in 1792 with a confirmation of her former conquests augmented by the territory of Oczakow and the shores of the Euxine—which the combined power of England and Prussia failed to tear from her iron hand.

She could not at a blow prostrate an empire so wide at the foundation, so lofty in its battlements as the Ottoman; but besides the fragments rent away, great crevices and cracks shewed the power of the assault and facilitated the success of the next. Russia could not hold Moldavia and Wallachia: she therefore stipulated *for their national rights under her protection:* and so loosened their allegiance on Turkey and linked their sympathies to her arms.

While all Europe was immersed in the struggle with Napoleon, Alexander pushed his conquest on the south; and at the peace of Buckarest in 1812 he secured the province of Bessarabia and the mouths and line of the Pruth.

The Greek revolution excited by Russian intrigues gave the occasion of renewed hostilities: and the treaty of Adrianople dictated within a day's march of Constantinople and only submitted to because English ships lay at the Dardanelles—transferred to Russia the delta and mouth of the Danube, cut off by a quarantine the principalities of the Danube from Constantinople, secured a perpetual right of administrative interference, and laid Turkey at the mercy of the Czar—whenever the great powers of Europe should happen to be lukewarm or engaged or unable to protect her.

Thus has Russia pressed downward from her boundaries in the time of Peter into the Turkish territory five hundred miles, swept round three-fourths of the Euxine sea, crossed the isthmus between that and the Caspian sea, and eaten deep into Armenia and the Persian territory. A few years more and *the Euxine will be a Russian lake.*

Her westward march over prostrate kingdoms and slaughtered nations—has been not less terrific, nor less rapid, but vastly more menacing to the seats of civilization and the home of freedom.

The miserable dissensions of the Polish aristocracy gave access to her intrigues; and pretexts for her interventions. She fomented factions that she might be called on to quell the disturbances. She set up and pulled down candidates for the tottering throne: and from the centre of Poland organized her deadly conspiracy against its existence.

The same victory of Pultowa which opened the way of Russia to the Baltic, secured the influence of the Czar on the throne of Poland in the person of Augustus III. On his death, Catharine II. secured by an armed intervention one of her paramours Stanislaus Poniatowski the electoral vote; and sincerely devoted to the integrity of national constitutions, she volunteered her guarantee of that vile constitution on which she founded her hopes for the future. The Romish Church displayed its persecuting propensities by way of complicating the puzzling drama; patriotism drove noble-minded Poles to defend the acts of their national church; and the Russian Catharine, the friend of scoffers and infidels, the mother of superstitious millions, the earnest supporter of the mummeries and follies and slavish submission of the Greek Church, defiled by every personal and sensual vice, and stained all over with the blood of murdered innocence,—*she*, assumed the office of an angel of light, and benevolently bent on a mission of mercy covered with her motherly bayonets the *persecuted Dissenters and Protestants.* She considerately removed to Siberia, the hardened prelates who were deaf to her entreaties, and coerced from the terrified and dismembered diet a treaty securing the dissenters' rights under *her supervision.*

That men should become impatient under such intolerant tolerance was but natural. Their restiveness caused their volunteer governess continual anxieties. They even stirred up the Turk to the audacity of aggression. That weak assault was easily overthrown. But there was little policy and much trouble in thus governing by intrigue and arms so intractable a nation. The laborer is worthy of his hire, and so devout a Princess could not fail to perceive the sanction of Providence for her just designs. She conspired with her two fellow tyrants, Joseph of Austria and Frederick of Prussia, to divide with her the burthens and the benefits of governing a stiff-necked and rebellious generation, who could not or would not govern themselves. The infamous partition of Poland in 1772—just about the period of our Revolution—deprived that Republic of her most valuable provinces and brought Russia into direct contact, on a long line of frontier, with two of the leading powers of Europe. Similar pretexts, devised from similar motives, and instigated by the sharpened appetite of Muscovite rapacity, renewed the disgraceful scenes in 1792 and 1793, and reduced the nationality of Poland to a shadow, and her territory to a speck. It was reserved for the darkest period of the storm of the French Revolution, when Austria, Prussia and Russia were clamorous at its aggressive spirit and propagandist principles, and coalitions for national defence against French arms and French disorganization were the order of the day; when those powers were the preachers of moderation, the champions of justice, and the Quixotic defenders of the weak—it was this time and with these professions on their lips, ere the echo of their howl over the death of Louis XVI. had ceased to ring in the ears of Europe, that these powers chose to complete the work so auspiciously begun, and obliterate the last shadow of Poland from the face of the earth.

It was a fit sequel to these iniquities that the spoilers should begin to prey on each other—and visit on their accomplices the retribution of their rapacity. A greater than either of them arose and dealt with them as they had dealt with their unoffending victim.—The Gaul shattered their brittle and patched up Empires—and flung a piece of Prussian Poland to the greedy Muscovite—who did not hesitate to snap at the offal. Two years later that same Gaul tore off and flung down before the same Muscovite a piece of Austrian Poland, and he greedily devoured the gracious morsel.

Similar acts, equal iniquities, less stubborn resistance, less civilized foes, have augmented the Empire of the Czars to the East and to the South—over the steppes of Tartary, and the snows of Siberia, the crags of the Caucasus, and the barriers of Persia.—The blackness of its shadow casts a gloom over Asia and Europe. It lowers on the confines of China, chills the genial warmth of Hindostan, and eclipses the crescent on the dome of St. Sophia. Naked liberty shivers and cowers at the utmost ends of Europe beneath its numbing power.

These are the triumphs of despotic ambition, wielding absolute power with a miserly devotion to accumulation of territory and power—pitilessly exacting the utmost interest in every investment in human life unterrified by the flow of blood— with a singleness of purpose and a consistency of pursuit, savoring of supernatural impulse, or satanic possession.

Thus has this semi-barbarous Empire thriven on blood and rapine; but the fragments torn from its victims by arms, have been carefully cemented by the arts of peace and industry. The area of the Empire now is a fourth greater than that of Peter. It fills the vast expanse between the White and the Caspian seas, and stretches from the confines of China, deep into the heart of Europe—where it is the neighbor of all Germany, the terror of Prussia and the master of Austria. Its population has grown from fifteen to sixty millions. Its ordinary revenue, flowing chiefly from customs, is about eighty millions of dollars. Its exports for 1843 amounted to eighty-two millions of rubles of silver. Its agriculture covers three hundred millions of acres, and yields a hundred and fifty millions of quarters of wheat and rye, of which more than nine and a half millions are exported. The vast rivers which flow from the centre to the four seas are united by canals which connect the navigation of the White, the Black, the Caspian and the Baltic seas. The vast plains stretching from sea to sea—unbroken by a mountain range—are being intersected by railways for whose construction the genius of the world is laid under contribution.

This population and these resources are devoted to the support of a military and naval power of the first magnitude. Peter laid the foundation of a navy, which sedulous culture, and lavish expense, and the absoluteness of despotism have raised to a rate second in nominal greatness to that of England only; but its automaton sailors are no match for the sea-bred tars of Albion, and freedom has still her home upon the waves. On land this Empire supports an army whose complement approaches a million of men. This stupendous force is so disposed as to be significant of the designs and direction of Russian ambition. For while 16,000 men watch the great prison house of Siberia, and a like number guard the Finland frontier, and 64,000 from Orenburg repress the predatory Tartars—the great moveable *European army of operation* consists of 465,720 men, though seldom actually numbering over 360,000; with 1250 pieces of cannon, and the European army of reserve numbers 202,480 men, with 470 pieces of artillery—besides the clouds of irregular cavalry which a wave of the imperial arm can call up from the Asiatic confines of the Empire. This power is no half-formed, ill-trained, disorganized horde of barbarians. It is well-trained, rigidly disciplined, implicitly devoted to its Emperor, and pliant to the slightest word of its officers. It is not led by a Tamerlane or an Alaric; but generals versed in all the science of modern war marshal this gigantic force in the field of action with the same familiar ease that they do a regiment on parade. The names of Suwarrow, Paskevitch and Debitch are graven in characters of indelible mould on the broken fragments of the Empire of the Turk, on the ruined walls of desolated Poland, on the shattered temple of Hungarian Freedom. Past success casts its brightness on the future. These men of iron stand now no longer on the borders of Europe and Asia, in the distant and frozen north, but in the very midst of civilized Europe, in battle array, with lighted matches and fiery zeal—and nothing between them and the Rhine but the labors of the march.

That the master of this power is ambitious by nature, by inheritance, by ancient policy consecrated by unbroken success—all history teaches. But it is the *principle* which animates him, it is the *foe* he would humble which makes his ambition worthy of our notice.

In this age of the world two principles of government divide mankind. Only in reflective minds are they stated with logical consistency and pushed to their legitimate bases; but the minds of all men are on fire with the contest, and devoted to the one or the other cause.

The one theory—rejecting with contempt the shallow fiction of the social contract, and with indignation the impious arrogance of the "right divine"—traces the fundamental principles of civil society in the nature and wants of man, written there by the finger of God, and surrounded by feelings, tendencies and capacities which in their natural development assume the shape and attributes of national existence under formal governments. The relations of civil society, those of citizen and subject, of ruler and ruled, rest on the same foundation and have the same origin with the relations of the family and of the church. Men surround themselves with families, not from any consciousness of the blessings that flow from them, nor from obedience to any divine command, but at this instigation of a divine impulse operating as a law, pointing to the family as its object, and executing itself unconsciously. Reflection develops its origin and explains its reasons, purposes and limits only after the fact. It assumes various forms, and confers various rights, whether of person or of property, according to the different views and necessities of the nation or the individual by whom they are applied. The forms and the rights of family relationship vary with the nation, the age, the religion; but all are equally forms in which the original tendency to family associations develope themselves.

It is so with civil society and the rights of government. The nature of man drives him into social organizations, varying in complexity and completeness with the state of his advance from the patriarchal family, through the Indian tribe with its chief, to the elaborate organization of the American Republic. The purposes of civil society can only be attained by the instrumentality of government, reducing to the forms of law the will of the nation, and coercing submission from its individual members. The right to prescribe these laws and direct their execution is sovereignty. That power in the state which holds that right in the last resort, is the sovereign power. The persons who actually apply and execute those laws, are the officers and delegates of that sovereign power. Wherever that sovereignty resides, it must be absolute, uncontrollable, and arbitrary. It can be subjected to no constraints rightfully. It should govern according to the rules of justice; but it must remain the only judge of those rules; and it can recognize and provide for no possible case of its own coercion or its own restraint.

The controversy of the age disputes the residence of this ultimate sovereignty.

We maintain that it resides in the mass of every nation. A majority has no inherent rights: it is an artificial creation: it holds only a delegated power: it is only the instrument provided by the previously declared will of the nation for ascertaining its decision under given circumstances. Its power is as much a delegated power as is that of any, the most subordinate officer. It may be the best or the worst mode of vesting the power: there may be decisive reasons why it should always or never be declared the criterion of government: but still it is never rightfully anything but a form prescribed, allowed, or acquiesced in, from its convenience or its expediency, by the nation. It is the nation only which is sovereign—whose mere will is the final law of all the people—from which there is no appeal—and against which there is no remedy—within the limits of civil society. The inalienable rights of self-defence, beyond, before, and paramount to all the rights and obligations of civil society, may survive in abeyance, till some irremediable and cruel outrage wakes them into activity: but they form no part of the apparatus or of the powers of civil society.

The mass of the nation is necessarily somewhat indefinite: but each case must be adjusted as it rises. One man could not be allowed to impede the will of all the rest: nor would a majority of one be any ground—except for the provisions of positive law—for the control of the other half of society. It is the duty of the mere fragments of the nation to yield their opposition to the general will: and habits of civil and political action, or the sword, will variously settle the point of submission.

This mass of the nation has the absolute power to form its constitution of government. It may be by tacit acquiescence, by historical development, by formal enactment; but however it may be, it is the will of the nation, express or implied, which gives it legitimacy. Absolute power in the King may be as legitimate as direct legislation by the people, if the nation so will it. There are stages of society when such is the best, the only possible form of government. It is so over the greater part of the Russian Empire. But this form of government may be abrogated by the same will which established it. That will is sovereign, and the absolute King is only its delegate, wielding the absolute powers of the nation against the individuals of the nation, whom it has subjected to his will. The King, however absolute his power, has no rights against the nation, and to assert them is a gross usurpation. This sovereignty has been asserted and exercised by every nation. The Czars of Russia have felt its influence while denying its right, and tacitly concede its power by carefully avoiding any outrage on the national prejudices or the national religion. England has exercised it; and her Queen now holds her crown by that title and no other. France has claimed it; and waded knee-deep in blood to maintain it. It is the fact of all history—denied by all despots. It is the acknowledged basis of the American Republic.

The despots of Europe have devised a different theory—and made it effectual by arms. In the attributes of the sovereign power they agree with us. But they deny any participation in those attributes to the nation: they arrogate them all absolutely to the crown. Kings are the plenipotentiaries of God—who imparts to them the absolute powers of his sovereignty. In his name they rule with absolute sway his subjects: they are responsible—not to the people, not to the nation—but to God, the source and giver of their power. Their outrages he may punish: but to the people they are visitations of providence, inflicted by his ministers, to be regarded as judgments on human iniquity, to be submitted to with patience, and to be made fruitful of repentance. Famine and pestilence are sent to wring contrition from the stubborn heart of man. The scourge of a merciless ruler should clothe the nation—not in arms and rebellion—but in the sackcloth and ashes of penitent submission. His power may be exercised wisely or unwisely: but that is the fortune or misfortune of the nation. It has no right to demand a change or insist on a security.

The logical consequences of this theory are no idle play of words. They have passed from theory into fact, and on bloody fields have been debated in arms, and the decisions of victory enforced by the scaffold and the chain. Such logical deductions are worthy of consideration.

If monarchs be the plenipotentiaries of God the only sovereign, they must be vested solely with all the attributes of sovereign power—a will absolute, free, irresponsible, and uncontrollable; and the nation can have no part of it. The nation is only a *subject*, bound by their will as each citizen of our Republic is by the will of the whole. Their will is that of God: it cannot therefore be bound by any promises to the people; and any security for good government is an outrage on his sovereignty. No charter, treaty or constitution can bind them: for it is only a *law*, and *that* the sovereign power may change at will—as our people, their constitution. They are likewise absurd: for their purpose is to control irresponsible power; and by the theory *that* is the very idea of their rightful power. The constitution is illegal because it assumes a right to bind them. To revoke it is no breach of faith—but a legal right. The people have no rightful claim to participate in the sovereignty: their demand of a constitution is merely an impertinence. No wrong can be done them, for the will of the prince inflicting it is *ipso facto* the law: rebellion therefore is pure treason. Time gives no sanctity to charters, prescription gives no validity: they are only old laws which the prince would change. Resistance to their abrogation is an illegal restraint on the sovereign's will—to be removed by the intervention of his fellow plenipotentiaries.

Against this system the people of this nineteenth century have perversely protested in the name of Liberty. The Liberty for which they fight is the sovereign power of the nation—the liberty of every nation, irrespective of its rulers, to declare by its will the forms of its government and the rights and duties of its rulers. Against this presumptuous claim the despots of Europe for thirty years have waged internecine war at home and abroad—inspired by the example, supported by the arms, and following the lead of the Russian Czar.

Other despots have tormented their subjects with a more cruel tyranny. Other powers, in the pursuit of empire, over a theatre as vast, and in a spirit as merciless, have wielded the scourge of almighty wrath. Not a few have displayed as relentless a hatred of civil liberty when it lifted his head within their dominions. The Czar of all the Russias, first among mankind, in this age of the world—has chosen the Spirit of Liberty, as the special object of his hate—and wages ceaseless and universal war against the freedom of mankind. It is no idle fancy, no passing caprice, no gust of passion. It is elevated to the dignity and pursued with the consistency of a principle of policy. It is sustained by the instinct of self-preservation, and covered with the holy words of God and religion. It is called the cause of peace and order against the restless and destructive spirit of revolution. He knows no distinction of time, but the propitious hour of assault. He knows no distinction of place but the reach of a decisive blow. Twenty years ago he gave the final stab to Polish freedom. Three years ago he stretched bleeding Hungary at the feet of the beardless Nero of Austria. He bides the time, with the instinct of eternity—when his deadly folds may encircle the terrible Albion, and the sting of his tail be fixed in the quivering corpse of American liberty.

This is a new thing in the world—it is one of the wonders of this age. Its origin and history are rich with warning, exhortation and example to the people of this Republic.

Our revolution was the morning gun of freedom.

Its echo waked the slumbering millions of France; and ere its smoke had melted into air, their arms in battle array glittered in her rising sun.

The Kings of the earth crowded to the rescue of their fellow, and buried their rivalries in the grave of their common terror. The friends of freedom and of the rights of men trembled for her naked youth in the shock of battle; and the breath came freer when Dumouriez hurled the Austrian across the frontier and vindicated the right of France to rule herself. But then—

France got drunk with blood to vomit crime—
And fatal hath her saturnalia been
To freedom's cause in every age and clime.

That she assailed the partitioners of Poland in the midst of their work, with her armed ideas, that her propagandist legions flung the flaming torch of freedom into the combustible structure of antique despotism, is scarcely matter of reproach on *this* side the Atlantic. It is fair to fight the Devil with fire; and the champions of the rights of Kings may surely be met with the adverse and imprescriptible rights of man. But the atrocities of her hour of madness, the blood that stained her youthful days combined with the rapid flight of her eagles, to confound the principles with the deeds of France. The eternal and spiritual truth was weighed down to earth by the burthen of her iniquities; and men fled from her rapacious triumph as from pestilence and desolation. They who struck at her liberties seemed justified by her tyrannical encroachments—though they only failed to imitate her excesses without her provocation for lack of her power.

Then one arose who knew how to control the whirlwind and to ride the storm. He turned their fury into the ministers of his ambition; and the blast of their breath shook or shattered the battlements of all the governments of Europe. It was only when he gathered their fragments in his mighty grasp and hurled them against the despot of the north, that the scale of his destiny was hung out on high and the hour of his fate was marked on the face of the heavens.

His colossal power crumbled before the finger of God. Puny men who had cringed before his frown, and been emulous of his favors, boasted themselves his conquerors, and sat down to divide the spoils.

The first coalitions made war on a principle whose ethereal essence penetrated their ranks and disarmed their hosts—as the wheels of Pharaoh's chariots were taken off so that they drave heavily—and they were overwhelmed by the flood they sought to control. But when the stupendous genius of Napoleon converted the power of the revolution into the instrument of his aggrandizement, and his Empire threatened Europe with universal subjection, the latter coalitions took up arms in the name and for the defence of national independence. The war was waged in the name of the rights of nations—the real issue between the Allies and Napoleon was, which should have the uncontrolled right to violate them. They exemplified and profited by the right of learning from an enemy; and with the aid of a little previous practice they distanced Napoleon in his depredations on the integrity of nations. The interests of the partitioners controlled the partition—freed from every consideration of the interests, the rights, the wishes or sympathies, the national history or social position of the people to be divided. Their territory and themselves were disposed of on mathematical and dynamical principles. The categories of number, extension, position, and power alone entered into the calculation. So many million souls, so many square miles of plain or mountain, were assigned to each as he could be *safely* trusted with, or from his service in the common fight he was *justly* entitled to, or from their position would serve as a stumbling block to *French* ambition. The suspicion was even secretly harbored that his moderate majesty of all the Russias might wake up and find himself hungry, and dispositions were *covertly* and *delicately* arranged to protect his accomplices from his voracity. But all progressed by arrangements between the people's masters and at their expense. Saxony was dismembered to satiate Prussia. Genoa lost the freedom of a thousand years to strengthen Sardinia. Sweden was robbed of Finland to round the Russian territory, and Denmark was deprived of Norway to indemnify Sweden. Belgium and Holland were forced into an unnatural union for the benefit of the house of Orange; and Italy was parceled out as a residuary fund, for equality of partition among the spoilers. The whole was effected on the novel principle of law—that the constables who catch and confine a thief are entitled to divide the stolen goods.

But there is little satisfaction in governing people who are so restless as not to stand still to be governed. Twenty-five years of anarchy and blood had exemplified the dangers of democratic ambition; and the minds of Kings were impressed with the necessity of ruling well if they would rule at all. They had been at their wit's ends—nearly overwhelmed by the waves, their hearts failing them for fear; and in the hour of their helpless need God and their people had mercifully rescued them. Men who escaped shipwreck in heathen times hung up votive offerings in the temples; and the church appoints prayers and thanksgiving for such deliverance. It was natural, it was only in accordance with their royal exaltation, akin to divine excellence, that these rulers of men should acknowledge their indebtedness to God and their people. They had probably prayed with lusty devotion to the former, as it is certain they had promised largely to the latter. They had learned at Jena and Austerlitz the indifference of their people to the sentiment of loyalty to masters who were indifferent to every thing but the right to rule them. They could recover their crowns only by the aid, the devotion, the affection of their people. The world had gone beyond the day when it was a coveted honor to die for one's prince. Men now preferred to live for themselves; and if they must die, they chose it should happen on some more important point than a choice of masters.

These rulers had seen the resistless power of free principles in the hands of him whose mission it was to plague the Pharaohs of the earth: and they caused their wise men with their rods to emulate his wonders.

They repented them of their misdeeds, and brought forth fruit meet for repentance. They alleviated the burthens and bettered the social condition of their people. They lightened the weight and removed the barriers of aristocratic privilege. They proclaimed liberty to the captive and bid the serf go free. They seized the terrible pen and freely invoked its magic art in the cause of Kings. They preached the rights of men and nations. They anticipated and outstript the longings of their subjects for a voice in their own affairs: and solemnly, with the earnestness of men in deep agony, with reiterated oaths, in the presence of the Most High, they promised to their people representative assemblies and the freedom of speech and of the press.

The royal word—strange to say—was once not a polite circumlocution for a lie. It was a recognized coin, of loyal stamp and ready circulation, but cheaply made—and which frequent adulterations and not infrequent bankruptcy has sadly depreciated. Even the addition of a royal oath does not now avail to restore its credit. But *then* it was not so. Kings had been subjected to the trials of other mortals. Vicissitudes of fate or fortune had pulled them down and put them up with a variable caprice richly instructive. They had felt the scourge of a power above them—before whose presence they had fled amain. They had learned to appreciate the sympathies, to value the love, to long for the devotion of the people; and they had half learned that people were more interested in themselves than even in the persons of their divinely appointed rulers.

The devotion to princes and to venerable authority had been swept away by the tornado of French conquest. This generation had grown up under other auspices, and felt the instincts of freemen. They listened to the appeal of patriotism against the stranger and believed the solemn promises of their rulers: and with the enthusiasm of the early French republic, they met and overthrew the later French despotism.

The Kings held the fruits of their promises. It remained to perform them. They redeemed their pledge on the 26th of September, 1815, by—the Treaty of the Holy Alliance. Its language is obscure and of doubtful import: but read by the light of history it was—*a scandalous conspiracy against the liberties of mankind.* It is not the only case where religious mysticism has blended with the suggestions of ambition to cover with the veil of piety deeds, which, naked, would shock the conscience and meet the execration of mankind.

It would seem from the account of Alexander, that the defeats of Lutzen, Dresden and Bautzen, impressed on the minds of the sovereigns their impotency before the terrible Emperor of the French: and drove them with new fervor to seek aid at the throne of grace. With their faces to the east—and their backs to the French—they vowed—as better men have done—to ascribe any success which might be vouchsafed to them, to God as its author. Then followed the victories of Kulm, Hotzbach and Leipsic—the fruits of their pious vow. They remembered at Paris the promises of their weakness; and how could they offer a sacrifice more pleasing to the God of Peace, than to consecrate to its preservation the power he had bestowed on them. "The Redeemer," says Alexander, "inspired every thought comprised in the alliance—all the principles it announces. It is not our work—it is God's."

It was not unnatural that those on whom the divine rights of sovereignty had been poured should be illumined by light from above on their limits, nature, and purpose. It was quite natural that Princes so recently terrified by the stupendous armaments of Napoleon, should unite in deprecating their revival, and blessing the peace which smiled in their absence. Nor is it at all surprising that the grateful pacificators of the world should feel especial horror at those breaches of the peace which involved the guilt of rebellion against the vicegerents of the God who had given them the victory. Against such disturbers of the peace of the world, it was their peculiar duty to protest, and if necessary, to arm. They could never for a moment harbor the thought of oppression emanating from themselves: and in the absence of oppression, rebellion was in their eyes, the unpardonable sin. Patience was the only virtue which the supposition of injustice could be allowed to cultivate. Rights in their subjects to participate in the sovereignty of the state were presumptuous thoughts not to be entertained—unfounded in any principle—and incompatible with the "conservative principle of social order." To assert them therefore was the grossest compound of treason and sacrilege. To attempt to wrest them from the rulers by force—was the worst violation of the peace of God they were commissioned to restore. They intended to govern well and wisely: and that was all which reasonable people could expect. They looked gratefully to heaven in the day of their triumph, and from the fulness of their hearts they poured out the divine oracle which assumed the form of the Holy Treaty. The whole circle of royal duties was comprised in the symbolical trinity which composed the treaty—the high duties of ruling according to the Christian religion—of preserving the brotherhood among sovereigns—and of confessing themselves the plenipotentiaries only of God in their exalted functions. If they were the plenipotentiaries of God, his religion was properly their rule of governing his people—and brotherhood was of all the most imperative duty. Surely none but a stiff-necked and turbulent people would lift the hand in defiance of such rule, by such rulers; and whoever did so—was only fit to be cut in pieces!!

Their sacred majesties therefore renewed the broken chain from heaven to the throne: and as if half conscious of the frailty of royal resolutions for good, they surrounded themselves with the sanctions of that famous treaty. Men were glad to learn by its first article, that they "had formed the unchangeable resolution to take the precepts of the Christian religion as their sole rule of action as well in the government of their several states as in their foreign relations."

This resolution was matter of great interest to those destined to taste the blessings of their rule: for they hoped so solemn a recognition and pledge would dispel from the future the distressing doubts which obscured the conformity of their previous conduct to those holy precepts; and that was felt to be the more important, since, if Christian principles were to be the *only* rules of government, it was felt that *constitutional restraints* were necessarily excluded.

The three Princes further promised—"in accordance with the words of Holy Writ which requires that all men should look on each other as brethren—to *remain* united by the bonds of a true and indissoluble brotherhood and as brethren *to afford help and countenance on every occasion.*" Sweeping as is this provision, guaranteeing all that the former and latter contain, the most skeptical of the faith of Kings cannot fail to confess its honorable fulfilment.

And lastly they engaged "that the states over which they ruled, Russia, Austria and Prussia, should in future form only three branches of one and the same Christian kingdom—which recognize *no other* ruler than the Most High to whom all might belongs, *as whose plenipotentiaries the allied monarchs regarded themselves.*"

This clause is the formal announcement of the divine right of Kings. It is the most emphatic exclusion of the rights of the people. It is the assertion of infinite and absolute power in the monarch,—guaranteed by more than a million bayonets!!

This singular treaty contains the history of the last thirty-five years of the contracting parties. It reveals the foundations of their political system at home and abroad. We are not at liberty with Lord Castlereagh to treat it as a harmless joke. The men who made it were in no merry mood. They had no idle time on their hands. They had put in motion and led to victory the mightiest armament the world had ever seen. They were men of practical views: and professed to be protecting themselves for the future from the evils of the past. These evils were the assertion of the sovereign rights of the nation against the sovereign right claimed for the King. The latter was designated the cause of order—and was that of the allies. The former was the cause of the revolution, which they had armed to overthrow, and now were forming a treaty to suppress. That treaty may mean more than it says—but it cannot mean less. It has been fertile of great events, and powerful in marshaling great armies to do deadly work: and history has confirmed its most pregnant interpretation.

Its first clause may express the resolution of its authors to observe in their internal and external relations the precepts of Christianity: but it expressly says they are the *only rule they will observe.* They alone are to guide their conduct. Under that principle they may rule mildly and justly and wisely; but they must rule absolutely, free from all control of human constitutions. It defines the *law* of their conduct; and they proclaim it the only law by which they will be controlled, whether in their internal or their external affairs.

It is unfortunate that the precepts of Christianity have been declared the common law of monarchs of the absolute school with a unanimity as singular as the variety of deeds they have been made to sanction. The great Armada sailed upon a Christian mission; and Alva was on Christian duty in the Netherlands. The repeal of the edict of Nantes was Christian legislation; and the Church still celebrates the day of St. Bartholomew. The Holy Office of the Inquisition was the authorized administrator of Christian justice; and the Society of Jesus has combined with its secular duties distinguished success in the cultivation of Christian morals. On which of these models the Holy Allies meant to mould their conduct it would not have been fair or easy to divine beforehand: but any or all of them were in the line of safe precedents; and the conservative motto of their chancery is *stare decisis.* Subsequent events seem to establish obedience to rulers as the only precept they very stringently enforced; and who only were rulers within the meaning of the treaty, the last clause distinctly defines.

Their political catechism has borrowed the pregnant brevity of their neighbor the Turk. "God is the only God—and Allah is his prophet" is the sum of the rights and duties of the Turk; and the Christian King recognizes for his dominions no other ruler than the Most High—whose ambassador he is on earth.

This is the most precise announcement of the right divine and exclusive, I remember to have seen. It seats the sovereignty not in the people, not in the nation, whether with or without the King. They have no relation to it save that of subordination and obedience. The King is alone *supreme.* The responsibility of the ambassador is to *his* sovereign. The only right of the subject is prayer to God for relief or for vengeance or for patience.

But this pregnant principle has been evolved into the most logical system. All concede that the sovereign power cannot bind its own discretion. Parliament cannot pass an irrepealable act. We think the people cannot bind themselves not to change their constitution. We may adopt a monarchy to-day, a republic to-morrow; and no one can impeach our caprice or our discretion.

If the King be *sovereign,* he is equally uncontrollable. He can make no bargain with his people—for the idea of sovereignty is the right to bind and speak for the people. They are not a party capable of contracting with the sovereign power—for its very definition is, the power of binding them—and its first and most inherent and inseparable attribute is freedom of will absolute and uncontrollable.

When therefore the Holy Alliance affirms its authors to be the plenipotentiaries of the Most High, the only sovereign—they mean to divest themselves of the possibility of burdening themselves by any concession, by any constitution, by any charter of privileges. Any that they may grant must be at their will, during their pleasure, of grace and not of right.

6

Its violation is the legal repeal of its provisions. Its abrogation is only the withdrawal of a favor. The oath of conformity is only a mental vow. The treaty is the simple, absolute, comprehensive announcement of the very principle which the revolution had assailed—formally laid down as the foundation of the public law of Europe and of the world. To charge a King with perjury to his people, is senseless. To cut off the head of Charles I. because they could not tie his hands was a gross iniquity in his people. To take up arms against an oppressor, is to impeach the wisdom and fly in the face of the sovereignty of God. To force on a monarch the adoption or the observance of a Constitution against his free will—is a clear rebellion—of dangerous example—and fit to be repressed by military intervention. These consequences are not the taunts of a foe nor the extravagances of an enthusiast. They are the fruits of a calm logic, applied to the plain words of the treaty. The history of the acts of these sovereigns for thirty-five years is one continued confirmation of these views. They have been embodied in a catechism of political philosophy for the instruction of the youthful mind in the dominions of a satellite of the Czar, and are elevated to a place beside the articles of the Christian belief.

The first clause of the treaty declares the rule of government; the last, the person and tenure of the ruler. The middle one contains the promise of *perpetual brotherhood between the Allies, and of help and countenance on every occasion.* This is the formal and mutual guaranty of each and the perpetual alliance of all, for the maintenance of the right of Kings to rule according to the precepts of Christianity. Their brotherhood is to be *perpetual,* the duty to help and countenance is *universal,* and the three Empires are thenceforth to be, for those purposes, only *branches of one.* Such were the formal stipulations of the treaty.

The King is to the nation what God is to the world. To him belongs might, majesty and dominion. To them pertain patience, gratitude and submission. Whatsoever is more than this cometh of evil: and its suppression is guaranteed by the treaty. This was the theory of the allies.

With this treaty in our hand let us open the history of Europe.

In the distribution of soil and souls, the Congress of Vienna was not forgetful of the cause of their trouble. The ghost of the revolution still stood before them, and they tremble at the apparition. They set a guard over maniac France; and distrustful of the competency of its keeper as well as of the completeness of the cure, they stipulated in their treaty an alliance to suppress the first manifestation of returning madness, whether apparent in symptoms of external mischief or internal aberration.

The Austrian Empire of agglomerated nationalities was at best a crazy structure, rife with the elements of ruin, and difficult to maintain even in calm and peaceful times. The whirlwind of revolutionary violence would instantly prostrate it. The fire of popular passion would involve in ruinous conflagration its dry and lifeless branches. The inspirations of modern reform, the allurements of popular sovereignty must bring the necessity and reveal the impossibility of uniting under one rule its various and adverse nations languages and laws. The very condition of its existence was repose. Its only unity was in its Imperial head. The instinct of his ambition made him the foe of freedom: and his policy not less than his principles deprecated the contagion of popular ideas—with which he was not in a condition to deal successfully or safely. His Russian brother's unimprovable people were safe neighbors on one side. The unchangeable unity of the Papal principles secured him from danger through the States of the Church on an other. But he anxiously guarded his Italian provinces from the dangerous example of freedom by solemn but secret treaties with Sardinia and Naples to repress all constitutional advance among their people—till he should be ready to take up the march of improvement. Against the perverse liberalism of Prussia, on the side of Germany, he was forced to rely on his own dead weight in her affairs; and he trusted to the unerring instinct and sympathies of despotic princes, to annul the ambiguous stipulations of the Federation.

The jealousy of Western Europe, unable to wrest Poland from the Czar, strove to prevent the consolidation of its provinces with his empire. They demanded, and Alexander accorded with seeming alacrity, a constitution providing a national administration and a separate army; and the shadow of Polish nationality was preserved by a separate coronation as King of Poland.

Alexander reciprocated the favor, and joined Prussia in forcing on the reluctant Austria some ambiguous provisions for free institutions for Germany. A substantial provision for representative assemblies was frittered away, by the perverse opposition of petty princes, and the lukewarm support of its proposers, into the illusory declaration, "That Assemblies of States will find place in all the countries of the Federation." The freedom of the press—whose alliance they had eagerly sought to arouse the great enthusiasm of the war of liberation,—was committed to the tender regard of a Diet of Princes against whom only it needed protection, with no better shield than the provision that, "at its first meeting the Diet will occupy itself with uniform legislation concerning the freedom of the press."

All these provisions stipulations and arrangements formed integral parts of the general settlement. The violation of any entitled all the powers to interfere.

The labor of the sovereigns was finished; and each returned to his several home to put in operation the complex machine.

The Holy Allies, a few years after—in 1818, met at Aix la Chapelle to consider the propriety of loosing France from her straight-jacket. Her sanity was pronounced sufficiently restored, at least under the guardianship of a legitimate King; and she was at once relieved of the restraint of their armies, and admitted to the alliance which dictated laws to the world. On this accession to their number, and at this solemn conclusion of the first act in the drama, they wisely resolved to renew the declaration of the principles and to reduce to some certainty the objects of the association. It was therefore solemnly declared by Russia, Austria, England, Prussia and France, that they as well in their reciprocal relations as in those with the other European powers, were resolved never to depart from the principles of unity which had hitherto guarded them and which through the Christian brotherhood of sovereigns among each other would be indissoluble; that this union had no other object than to preserve the common peace, which depends on the conscientious observance of treaty stipulations and the rights flowing from them; that France *reconciled to the other powers by the restoration of legitimate constitutional monarchy* bound herself to contribute to the maintenance and consolidation of the system which had given peace to Europe, and was its only guarantee; and that the parties to the act, so far as they might find future conferences between the sovereigns or their plenipotentiaries for the attainment of their expressed purposes, bound themselves by diplomatic arrangements to settle the time and place of meeting; and formally to solicit the presence of any state whose concerns were to be the subjects of consideration.

The castigation of France had brought forth the peaceful fruits of repentance. But the joy over her conversion was clouded by the sullen temper and restless spirit of Germany. Three years had taught the Princes the meaning and the people the value of the lavish promises of popular assemblies, of freedom of the press, of liberal reforms, by which they had been lured into the war of liberation.

It was the idea of liberty, of the participation of the people in the high attributes of government, which was invoked by the Princes as alone powerful for their rescue. In its power they conquered; and the people fought under the illusion that their victory was their own. The promises of the Princes were interpreted in that sense; and in that sense was their performance exacted.

About the language of the promises there could not well be much dispute. The difficulty was in the consequences they were found to involve. The monarchs had said they knew not what; when their eyes were opened they drew back with terror from the gulf which yawned before them.

The Congress of Vienna began and ended with the affirmation of the divine right of Kings. The abandonment of absolute power by the monarch was never for a moment dreamed of. Yet the King of Prussia, and the Russian autocrat, and a crowd of minor Princes, professed their willingness, and even their anxiety to secure to their people such popular privileges, such liberal reforms, such freedom of speech and participation in domestic legislation as might be suitable to their various degrees of intelligence and civilization. It never for a moment occurred to *them*, though it did to their more practical and logical advisers—that such things were in fact and in principle absolutely inconsistent with despotic and unlimited power; that the two could not dwell together in unity or in peace.

The Kings and Autocrats reasoned with the ordinary strength of royal minds—like children pursuing their fancies as facts of history.

Freedom of speech should be granted in their Arcadian groves:—but it must always behave itself modestly. Philosophy should flourish and the press be free; but it was never contemplated that their licentiousness should freely canvass the policy, dispute the pretensions, criticise the acts, impeach the faith or hasten the performance of the promises of the Princes. They contemplated a press which should signalize its freedom in defence of their policy, in adoration of their power, in proclaiming the right divine, in adulation, in obsequiousness, in dutiful submission.

Representative assemblies were to find a place in their Utopia; but it was never contemplated that they should fill a large place. They were to be vested with powers which they were not to wield. They were to sit at the feet of the throne—mild, docile, submissive—ready sources of taxation, and faithfully representing the popular submission to the royal will. That they could ever presume to intermeddle in the control of affairs against his will, much less to assert or assume any part in the powers of sovereignty was never for a moment dreamed of. Representative assemblies in the royal contemplation were to be quiet and meek aids in the conduct of the government—faithful supports of the Prince. For them to oppose his measures, deny him money, demand in the name of the nation,—his sovereign and theirs—the redress of grievances—would annul their exclusive pretensions and reduce to a shadow the right divine of the Lord's anointed. It was the inspiration of the revolutionary devil playing his infernal devices for the overthrow of social order; and such an assembly could be dealt with only as one possessed with unclean spirits which ought to be cast out.

It cost four years of experience to convince them of their folly; and for thirty years they have consistently repented of it. They learned that participation in the forms of government inspired the idea of popular sovereignty: that every concession was a restriction of their own power, and only renewed demands whose refusal roused discontent into passion and threatened to blow the smouldering elements into open conflagration. They learned that there could be no union between despotism and freedom, that each excluded the other; and that the acknowledgment of any right, of any freedom of thought, of speech, or of the press, involved the demand and compelled the concession of everything. There was no middle ground between the absolute power of the King and the full participation of the people in the attributes of sovereignty. The latter they never meant to grant and were resolved not to yield.—They felt that safety and consistency were inseparable. Every popular right, all freedom of spirit must be denied or else they must submit to the *restraints* of constitutional governments. They therefore like consistent men made their election: and set to work to circumscribe or to destroy that freedom of speech and of the press, and those assemblies of the states whose only use was to urge an issue they were anxious to avoid, to wring concessions they were resolved not to grant. What they had supposed a temporary madness of revolutionary France was now found to be the essential attribute of popular sovereignty. It was the very plague spot of the revolution, and justified the delegates of God in waging war by force or guile for his power against the mind of man.

It was the fortune of Germany to develope this truth and the purpose of the Congress of Laybach to act on it. The treaty of Vienna—which declared that "the States of Germany should be independent and united by a federal league"—made her a miniature of Europe. Two military monarchies occupied the extremes of her territory: and controlled through a Diet of all the Princes, the affairs of the crowd of intermediate States, whose insignificant size did not prevent their being dangerous neighbors to States of common language, feelings and history, despotic in form, yet struggling to be free. The Diet was to Germany what the Holy Alliance was to Europe.

The sovereigns dispersed from Vienna and went on their way rejoicing in the prospect of a golden age of patriarchal rule and child-like submission, which they had introduced. The iniquities before the flood were obliterated. The arch-fiend was bound and banished. They fondly hoped the troubled waters would subside into repose.

But the breath of liberty had stirred the stagnant waters of every land. The Princes of Germany themselves had been the propagandists. They had evoked a power which they had used but could not get rid of. They had called up a spirit which they could not lay.

Men's minds did not sink to sleep with the return of peace. They had acquired independence. They had been promised freedom. They turned to their Princes for the performance of their promises. But the storm had passed, the sky was clear, they stood erect and lofty, surrounded with glittering armies and secure of their devotion. The humbled spirit rose to its former pride. One of their cousins of ancient date and wide dominion had bewailed the evanescence of royal vows wrung forth in distress; and his successors lived to prove the truth of his bitter exclamation—

> "How soon
> Would highth recall high thoughts—how soon unsay
> What feigned submission swore—ease would recant
> Vows made in pain as violent and void!"

They set themselves diligently to work under pretext of performance, to revoke, annul and evade them—as the dangers of the concessions became apparent.

The King of Prussia, besides many valuable administrative improvements—even during the war convoked a provisional assembly to adjust his taxes and aid his reforms. But despotic power is unsociable, and popular presumption is impracticable: and the assembly was dissolved without the regrets of King or People. In 1816, the provincial assemblies were charged with the election of delegates to a general parliament, and a commission was created for the construction of a constitution. But unexpected difficulties beset the union of the provinces. The King seemed to weary of his task or repent him of his promise. The commission was adjourned for further inquiry; and ere it could meet again a change had come over the spirit of the King. The people presumed to claim as a right what was intended as a favor. The tone of public discussion had assumed an unpalatable independence. The King became impressed with the incompatibility of despotic power with guarantees against its exercise—and shrank from his promises at such a cost. He was fertile in postponements. His ministers were always prosecuting with endless labor an impossible work. Some of his people ventured to present an urgent remonstrance after the delay had extended to 1818. It provoked the royal anger that his people should dare to anticipate the time which he should hold fit for the concession of a constitution: and they were admonished that to remind a King of his promises implied a doubt of his royal word. He repelled the imputation—by proving its truth. The assembly of States failed to find a place in the dominions of the liberal King of Prussia—and at the conferences of Carlsbad his ministers were still prosecuting their Penelopean labors!!—These delays are the type of them all. In some of the States the issue was different—but only after long struggles. Baden in 1817, and Bavaria in 1818, obtained satisfactory assemblies and constitutions; but in the former they were wrung from the reluctant Duke by the hostile claims of Bavaria which drove him to seek refuge in the affections of his people; and the same necessity for cordial support induced the despot of Bavaria to nerve the heart of his people for his depredation on Baden. Both the King of Wurtemburg and the Grand Duke of Baden—trembling for the integrity of their mosaic dominions at the hands of the Congress, sought to buy the affections of their subjects by the tender of constitutions; but the niggardly offer filled them with disgust. Bickerings and higglings consumed the time till the danger was passed; and with it fled the only inducements to conciliation. A renewal of difficulty in one case, a change of sovereign in the other, finally brought about the wished for agreement. In Saxony, in Brunswick, and in many other States the assemblies never found a place. In Hesse Darmstadt they were conceded after a five years conflict. In Saxe Weimar alone,—the home of Goethe, whose Grand Duke was the protector of Schiller, Wieland and Herder—did constitutional freedom find a welcome home, and the spirit of man a free press. These liberal concessions followed swiftly on the peace, and they were fully and honestly maintained by their author. But he and they had fallen on evil days. Freedom is of bad example to neighboring despotisms: and the constitution and free press of Saxe Weimar attracted the attention, roused the fears, and finally called down the anathemas of Austria and Prussia, as inimical to the existing order.

This state of deferred expectation, of delayed promise, of earnest entreaty and cold refusal or illusory performance, would in ordinary times have tried the patience of the quietest people. But these were not ordinary times, nor this a quiet people. The minds of men were on fire and royal propagandists had blown the flame into fury. They made Germany too hot for Napoleon and they could not cool it for themselves. The spirit of the restless people broke out in the Universities, in the Gymnasia, in public celebrations, in the public press—wherever it could find a tongue. The patriotic ferment of the war of liberation worked in the minds of the people. The impetus then given to free ideas had not spent but augmented itself. It was fast verging towards a popular demand for a full share of the sovereignty—with all the inherent vigor, and the irrepressible strength of the idea of liberty. It was apparent that no subordinate place at the foot of the throne would satisfy its aspirations. Every day developed the absolute, direct, and irreconcilable hostility between the sovereignty of the monarch and of the people. The two spirits which had stood in battle array for twenty years were again face to face: and the monarchs were driven to suppress a clamor they would not gratify and could not quiet. The eloquent appeals of Görres in Westphalia against the French were continued after their expulsion, in behalf of national rights, liberal laws, and free and powerful assemblies for the people. But there was a vast difference between a free press for the King's cause, and a free press exacting popular rights at his hands. This latter was dangerous to the "existing order:" and the Rhenish Mercury was first subjected to the gag of a censor in July, 1815—and because it would still mutter between its teeth, a few months later, it was suppressed.

After the humiliating day of Jena and the treaty of Tilsit, even women united in the effort to rouse and reform the nerveless people. Queen Louise and Von Stein were among the founders of the Tugendbund. It united the first, most liberal, most able and learned men of Germany in the glorious cause of waking the national spirit and reforming the abuses which paralyzed its power. Schleiermacher, Niebuhr, Humboldt, Jahn and other illustrious men strove in its ranks and inspired its deeds. By its influence, at its popular appeal, under its promises, the nation arose and became strong. Their exertions in the national cause continued only the same exhortations after the peace as before. It was scarcely to be anticipated that success should cool their patriotism, or that after having won a title to free institutions they should sit down quietly under the refusal of them: still less can we blame their impatience at the hostility of the authors and founders of their association to the persecution of their cause. The national regeneration progressed in every department with free and rapid strides and not without the usual concomitants of exaggerated sentiment and exorbitant demands. Jahn had sought to free the nation from foreign ideas and imitation, by infusing into the youth through the influence of his gymnasia, simple habits, earnest ideas, national feelings. The holy ideas of liberty were nourished by the solemnization of the days of victory of the war of liberation—when the eye was lifted beyond the confines of a single state to the majesty of united Germany. The spirit of reform, the contagion of liberal ideas seized on the Universities, especially that of Jena. The Burschenschaften were formed to promote the revolution of national education and habits: and free ideas were their natural allies. Religion mingled with the rolling current and the advocates of one reformation looked back with kindred feelings to the days of another—the pioneer in the paths of modern improvement. The students of Jena celebrated on the Wartburg the anniversary of the reformation, and breathed the very spirit of Luther on the scene of his residence. Patriotic speeches full of enthusiasm for home and country rang over the land: and the tones woke a responsive echo in many a longing heart. But to speak of freedom in the hearing of a master is an impeachment of his rights. The celebration was reported as a reappearance of the devil on the Wartburg. Solemn statesmen had been ridiculed; and they felt sore at the jokes on their incompetency. It was treated as a formal conspiracy. Diplomatic notes were interchanged. The Duke of Saxe Weimar met the urgent remonstrances of Prussia and Austria. Their ambassadors visited the spot to investigate the events and to track the conspiracy. Unfortunately Kotzebue resided there; his reports to his imperial master Alexander were suspected as those of a spy. One was intercepted, published, commented on with bitterness. He sought protection of his master; audacity of the press and the enthusiasm of the students were condemned as dangerous: and the menacing tone of the Duke's despotic neighbors compelled in 1818 the silencing of the press.

These events excited the fear of the sovereigns then united at Aix la Chapelle; a communication was addressed to Alexander commenting on the pertinacious striving after new constitutions, by which the legitimate authority of Kings, the gift of God, was brought to naught, and pointing to the free ideas afloat at the Universities, and the audacious freedom of the press as the sources of the difficulty.

This address made a deep impression on his Imperial Majesty. Secret negotiations passed on the subject, and their fruits were apparent the following year at Carlsbad.

In the midst of this ferment of minds a half mad enthusiast—impressed with the idea that Kotzebue was a spy and a foe to his fatherland—sought him out and murdered him. The deed was condemned; but the sentiment which prompted it met the sympathy of thousands. The perpetrator was wept as a hero and a martyr. The excitement was doubled by a similar attempt on the life of Ibell. The populace caught the passion and exhausted their fury on the unoffending and defenceless Jews from one end of Germany to the other. The crisis of a revolution was fast approaching. The time was at hand when free institutions, free assemblies, freedom of speech and of the press must be granted, or the voice of clamor must be silenced by the sword. To yield to those demands—to permit the freedom of discussion on the borders of Austria and Prussia necessarily involved *them* in the concessions; or the refusal left them only the alternative of civil war. *Neither* was content to yield constitutions. Both felt their incompatibility with the unity of either Empire, with the integrity of the royal authority, with the divine idea of the King, with the existence of the precepts of Christianity as the only rule of conduct. Metternich and the Prussian minister sympathized in these views. They concurred in devising a scheme to protect themselves by the suppression of freedom in the neighboring states—equally free and independent as their own: and the chief powers of Germany were invited to a conference at Carlsbad to settle and sanction the details.

The interest of all the Princes of Germany was alike. All feared the further progress of free principles. All professed to believe in an impending rebellion, an unreasonable discontent, a disorganizing spirit—the offspring of some deep and hidden conspiracy. Its traces could never be found, but every symptom of discontent, every expression of ardent devotion to free institutions, every disorder of any sort, was arbitrarily ascribed to such a conspiracy. All the Princes were interested in having an external guarantee against their subjects, and were willing to buy the benefit at the expense of the freedom of their governments. The restraint was only on their people; and they eagerly submitted to it. They felt the advance of the rising flood and earnestly joined in erecting the requisite barrier against its ravages.

The Conference of Carlsbad was thus a conspiracy among the crowned heads of Germany, led on and instigated by Prussia and Austria, each to suppress free institutions and free discussion in the dominions of his neighbors for the security of his own. It was the first trial, among the States of Germany, of the principles devised by the Allies for the subjugation of Europe.

The results of the conferences were announced in the address of Buol-Schauenstein, President of the Austrian delegation, on the 20th September, 1819, to the Diet at Frankfort. The scheme devised was to explain away the liberal provisions of the articles of federation: and by construction to expand and strengthen the powers of the Diet so as to vest that body with a right of interference in the private and internal affairs of every State, in spite of its constitutional independence. To these arrangements the assent of the respective rulers was to be obtained in consideration of the security each derived for his despotic power against the clamors of his people; and the Diet was asked to invest them with the sanctions and the forms of law.

The address of the Austrian delegate is the resolution of the Carlsbad Conference. From it we learn that the disquiet of men's minds flowed from the indefiniteness of the article of confederation relative to the Assemblies of States; that under that term nothing more was to be understood than the old Estates which had always existed in Germany; that no one dreamt of founding any such thing as a popular participation in the sovereignty, which was inconsistent with the existence of monarchy; and that further steps in that direction should be arrested till the Diet could define the meaning of the article. In other words, the monarchs had discovered that their power was indivisible; a surrender of *any* involved danger to *all.*

The next suggestion revealed the device to control the development of each State by the power of the whole. It consisted in claiming for the Diet the right by construction to guarantee not only the outward independence and integrity of the several States but also the maintenance of the legally existing order within.

The licentious spirit of the press was accused of having shaken the faith of men in things established by its malignant or seductive coloring; to it was ascribed the prevailing conspiracy for the overthrow of social order—which like a disembodied spirit pervaded the air but could never be fixed in a place or a person; and the address with far-sighted policy struck at the root of the evil by denouncing the liberal notions infused into the minds of youth by the professors as fallacious dreams exciting to madness and ending in ruin.

These views were followed up by appropriate acts or decrees, adopted unanimously and without opposition or discussion—bartering away the rights of nations for the security of their Princes.

The confederation obtained—under the forms of an interpretation—the right to coerce any State or the people of any State to perform their *federal duties.* Commissioners were appointed to watch over the spirit of the instructions administered to the students at the Universities, and to remove professors of dangerous principles. The press was bound hand and foot: no paper of less than twenty pages could appear anywhere unless specially authorized: and on complaint of any State the commissioners could suppress any licensed publication which tended to disturb the safety, peace and quiet of any German State. Sweeping powers were given for the suppression of conspiracies, under pretext of the necessity of the impending crisis.

These were *all* blows aimed at the internal development of the independent States, for the preservation of despotic authority in Germany, and chiefly for the benefit of Prussia and Austria.

Prince Metternich had not yet attained his object. He summoned the chief powers of Germany to Vienna in the latter part of the same year. In January, 1820, they dispersed, having ratified all that was formerly done, and added numerous articles to the Acts of Confederation. The nature of the Confederation was entirely changed. The 57th Article reiterates with the formality of legal language the doctrine of the Holy Alliance:—That since the States of Germany consisted of sovereign Princes, *the whole power of the State must remain united in the Chief Head of the State:* and the Prince can only be required to admit the Assembly to the exercise of *certain specified rights:* but even that cannot extend to prevent the Prince from performing *his federal duties.*

The meaning of these provisions is—that no Assembly shall in any manner control the monarch by demanding reforms as the condition of supplies; and that, the whole and indivisible sovereignty of the state remaining in the head, any constitution, any Assembly of States exists only by his license, at his mercy, and during his will.

Here we behold the full success of the doctrines of the Allied Powers applied with eminent skill to stifle the voice of liberty, demanding the performance of royal promises. We see the practical development in this miniature of Europe of the principles which did not wait long a wider theatre and more daring application.

The Allies were at last fully aware of the utter and absolute incompatibility, as well in logic as in fact, of free institutions with unrestricted power in the sovereign. They had learned that what the people demanded was—securities for good government; and that securities meant *fetters on their power* of doing ill. They had learned that the yearning for free institutions was not a temporary madness, but the temper of the times deeply seated in the nature of man—a spirit of potent influence, of many lives, of daring character, of contagious example, and poisonous to the very fountains of despotic authority.

They henceforth repudiate and renounce all liberal ideas, repress every aspiration after liberty as rebellion in disguise; and, wherever it breaks out in fact, they regard it as the cause of God and of his vicegerent promptly to march against it and mercilessly to trample out its last sparks of life.

While the Princes of Germany were assembled at Carlsbad, they were startled by the revolutionary conflagration of Naples, which threatened to throw all Italy into flames; and that was the offspring of the explosion in Spain.

I turn to these great events, and I earnestly invoke attention to these *commentaries on the Holy Alliance*—

the first in the series of armed interventions for the purpose—not merely, as in 1792, of sustaining a *constitutional monarchy* against an aggressive and propagandist *republic* but—of extinguishing *peaceful constitutional monarchies* FREELY ACCEPTED BY THE MONARCHS!!

SECTION II.

THE CONSPIRACY

OF

LAYBACH AND VERONA.

THE CONSPIRACY

OF

LAYBACH AND VERONA.

The crash of thrones in Spain and Italy fell on the ears of the conspiring despots of Germany like thunder from a cloudless sky. The subterranean fire they had just stifled under their feet, seemed to roll on underground till it broke out, like the shock of an earthquake, in the two extreme peninsulas of Europe.

That Spain and Italy, the chosen seats of despotism, and its sworn ally, superstition, should thus confess the power of the revolutionary mania, was of startling import to the sovereigns. It seemed to betoken the universal and ineradicable nature of the plague. It was like blows received in the house of a friend.

Spain had in three centuries sunk from the freest to the most despotic country in Europe. The thunder of the French revolution failed to rouse it. It did not wake till Napoleon's assault stirred its blood and woke its ire, and the insults of a foreign despotism kindled anew the fire in the trampled and besotted spirit of its children. From 1808 till 1813 the war for independence raged with a fury elsewhere unknown. The spirit of patriotism evoked the spirit of liberty, and the sons of Spain, while they fought the battles of their captive King, wisely provided for the security of themselves and their posterity the protection of a free constitution. In 1812, the Cortes which had organized the national strength and roused its spirit, proposed a free and liberal constitution of the mixed monarchical style, based on a liberal suffrage of the people, and sweeping away many of the oppressive institutions which Spain inherited from her Priests and her Kings.

Under this constitution the war of liberation was waged; with the Cortes which it created as the representatives of the Spanish nation, the Allied Sovereigns concluded a solemn league against France; and the Emperor of Russia formally acknowledged its entire legitimacy.

In 1813, when Napoleon felt the ground slipping beneath his feet, he strove to strengthen his rear by restoring Ferdinand VII. to his throne, on condition of obtaining his support. The Cortes, in full possession of the sovereignty of the nation, refused to admit the King to the exercise of his functions till he had sworn to the constitution. The King crossed the frontier, passed the popularly inclined provinces of Arragon and Catalonia in artful silence, and first at Valencia, in the midst of Elio's troops, dropped the mask. On the 4th of May, 1814, his proclamation—promising a few administrative reforms—*annulled the constitution.* The Cortes, unwilling to take extreme measures, sent a remonstrance—instead of an army—to meet the King. In sullen and disdainful silence he marched on Madrid. On the 11th of May, his forces occupied the capital and consigned the members of the Government, the heads of the Cortes, and the general of their army, snatched from their dwellings, to the darkness of a dungeon. The moment for resistance had passed. Too much delicacy, too little distrust, had cost the nation its liberties. The Cortes had not learned that bayonets are the only arguments that weigh with Kings. They illustrated the confiding moderation of popular bodies, so often and so easily the dupe or the victim of audacious treason covered by a crown. They did not believe in the perpetration of so enormous an iniquity; and they paid for their faith with years of confiscation, torture, and blood.

The enthroned tyrant had learned nothing from misfortune. The prison of Napoleon was not a fruitful political school. He hastened to undo the work of the Cortes. The press was fettered by a stringent censorship. The Inquisition darkened the land by its frown; its familiars swarmed through the provinces, and its prisons groaned with the victims of priestly vengeance. A political inquisition was instituted. Banishment or death was denounced against the adherents of the French. The adherents of the Cortes, the men who freed their country and secured his crown, Calvo de Rosas the hero of Saragossa, Alava the friend of Wellington, the moderate Martinez de la Rosa, the poets Quintana and Gallego, the ornaments and defence of that land of glory were consigned to the galleys or immured in the African prisons. The first year saw fifty thousand freemen languishing in confinement for their political opinions. The restored monks swarmed through the land pronouncing anathemas on the constitution as the work of the devil; and the intercession of the Bishop of Mechoacan for the restoration of the banished adherents of freedom was considered as madness by the astonished King and branded as heresy by the doctors of the Inquisition. The blackness of darkness in a form which might be felt had settled over the doomed land—which nothing could dispel but the lurid fires of revolution. They flashed up at short intervals, in rapid succession, like signals of distress in the night storm at sea—but only to be extinguished in blood, till the day of wrath was fully come.

The first effort of the King was to wreak his vengeance on his revolted colonies. From the midst of his troops assembled at Cadiz for embarkation, the smothered fire broke out in September, 1814. Its suppression was followed by an explosion in Navarre in 1815. The noble Lascy paid with his blood for his failure at Madrid in 1817. Again in 1818 the forces destined for America were the focus of a conspiracy which cost Vidal his life. The measure of suffering was now full. The spirit of man had been pressed to its last retreat; the pent up power exploded all over the land with such fury that the cowardly despot feared to measure arms with the foe he had scorned and oppressed.

Riego before his regiment, at the solemnity of the mass, in the church of San Juan on the 1st of January, 1820, proclaimed the constitution of 1812.

He had miscalculated his strength and his forces were scattered in flight—when at the other end of the kingdom the garrison of Corunna summoned its officers to swear to the constitution. A junta for the guidance of affairs was created, headed by Don Pedro Agar. The cities of the province gave in their adhesion by acclamation. The whole north coast was in flames, and the commotion seemed to rise from the earth close by the very residence of the monarch. He trembled like Felix before the coming day of reckoning, and sought to propitiate his people by offering them the *ancient Cortes*,—once a powerful body, but now effete and antiquated, its very soul trodden out by his despotic predecessors. His people mocked at his weakness and saw through his trick. He was compelled, not by any threatened personal danger, not by any present military force, not by any decisive victory, but by the universal simultaneous overwhelming manifestations of his people's will, by the majesty of a nation's resolution, which he could not control and feared to disregard, to restore the constitution he had rent and abrogated.

The scenes that follow are damning to the character of Kings. Their wickedness is half redeemed when it is backed by courage. But that quality seems to have fled from thrones in these latter days. For Kings to be cowardly is as much of course as to be false and treacherous.

The courage of the King gave way before the clamor of the people; and on the 7th of March, 1820, he promised the constitution of 1812. On the 8th, a provisional ministry or junta was created, before whom the King swore to the constitution. A proclamation from the King announced that, as a tender-hearted father he had granted what his children thought essential to their happiness; and that he enjoyed the hope of contributing to the public good, in the midst of their delegates,—whom he had so lovingly imprisoned. He besought his people to confide in their King, who spoke to them in uprightness and with the deepest feeling of obligation which Providence had vouchsafed him.

The Cortes met—the people returned nearly the same men whom the King had dispersed six years before. The King opened their solemn sitting on the 9th of July, 1820,—with a lie in his right hand and a perjury in his heart. The lip curls with involuntary scorn as we retrace the humiliating scene. The King, who came from captivity to a throne won for him and without his aid by the heroism of the people he was swift to oppress, now prepares to betray them by the soft words of affection. "So soon," he assured the Cortes, "as the excess of undeserved suffering brought the long suppressed wishes of the people to a distinct expression, I hastened to pursue the course they indicated, and professed the oath of fidelity to the constitution of the Cortes of 1812. From this moment the King and the people entered on their *legitimate rights*. *My resolution was free and voluntary:* it accorded with my interest as well as with the good of the Spanish people. It lies with the Cortes to found the public well-being on wise and righteous laws—protecting religion and the rights of the citizen and the sovereign. To the royal power it pertains to watch over the execution of the laws, and especially over the observance of the fundamental law, the centre of the wishes of every Spaniard, and the surest rock of his hopes. This will be my constant and most grateful duty. To the maintaining and confirming the Constitution I will dedicate the power which it places in the hands of the King. I wish no other power. This suffices for my happiness and my fame." The solemn mockery of an oath attested the sincerity of the royal liar.

This act inaugurated the restored Constitution. That restoration was not wrung from the King by personal violence nor by the threat of it. It was not obtained by the surprise of a sudden outbreak, at the instance of an insubordinate Pretorian guard. Full notice had been given by many an effort—so fruitless that the King was incredulous of an opposition beyond his power to suppress. The outbreak was long announced; it came from a distant quarter of the realm; it was long in spreading to the capital. The means of flight were at hand. A powerful body of troops was collected in Cadiz not so infected by discontent but that they would have obeyed the word of command. If there were any portion of the army reliable, there was ample time to reach it—ample means to concentrate it. If there were any Province of the realm devoted to the King or willing to fight for his menaced authority, there was opportunity to display there the royal standard and rally the faithful round the royal person. If the friends of loyalty were dispersed all over Spain, there was ample time to call them to action by the zealous priests, the swarming monks, the devoted prelates.

Yet it is certain that the King yielded to the cry of the people, and accepted the Constitution, without any one stricken field, without two armies meeting in battle array, without any large body of troops on either side concentrating on any point, the largest force resting all the time quietly at Cadiz subject to its officer's orders.

One of two things therefore is certain. If no body would fight for the King and his authority, then it was a plain case of the distinct and formal expression of the whole body of the nation that they would no longer have an *absolute King* to rule over them. The objection was not to the *person* but to the *power* of the King—for the effort was not to *dethrone* him, but only to *restrain* him, by the fetters of law and not by fetters of iron. The event would have justified fetters of iron and a rod of iron, and the failure to use either is a serious impeachment of the wisdom and resolution of the Cortes. But they did not either use or threaten to use them.

Or, if the mass of the nation were in favor of the King and would have fought at his bidding, if the forces at Cadiz were faithful and available, and their aid was not invoked, after full information of the extent of the outbreak, and with ample time to convene them at Madrid, or to fall back on them at Cadiz, *then* the King freely and voluntarily, of his own will and pleasure,—as he swore he did,—granted the Constitution to the importunities and for the benefit of his subjects who were faithful, peaceful, and submissive.

Which ever hypothesis we adopt, the inauguration of the Constitution assumes the highest form of validity, and stands guaranteed by the most solemn and irrevocable sanctions which it is possible to conceive.

If a nation can have rights against the monarch, then Spain had them.

It is only then on the theory of the Holy Alliance, *the absolute concentration of all sovereignty in the person of the sovereign,* that Ferdinand could release himself from the obligations of the Constitution.

A spark blew from Spain to Italy, and in an instant an explosion ensued. The minds of men were ripe for change and weary of the caprices of despotic power.

Ferdinand IV. of Naples, had been driven by the French to Sicily, where the English maintained him on the throne, which, for once in the whole course of the revolutionary struggle, they caused to be surrounded with popular institutions, embodied in a Parliament modeled on their own. The King accepted, swore to, and acted under it.

The folly of Murat gave the wishes of the allies a pretext for their gratification, and his forfeited crown was replaced on the head of Ferdinand in 1815, by the Congress of Vienna.

His return to Naples was the signal for the abrogation of the Parliamentary Constitution of Sicily, and the reversal of all the reforms of the French in Naples. Justice became venal, the Inquisition lifted its head and put forth its bloodstained arms, the Jesuits swarmed amid the demoralized population, the army was not a match for the robbers on the highway. Freedom of thought and of the press expired under the stringent censorship, which suppressed domestic and excluded foreign books. Free opinions were crimes and the only crimes which could not escape punishment.

With this state of things men were not satisfied. The association of the Carbonari, originally aimed at the expulsion of the French, subsequently expanded its views and its organization, and aspired to comprehend all Italy in one constitutional monarchy. The strength and proximity of Austria, and the diversity of local interests and narrow ambition postponed and impeded the attempt, till the revolution in Spain struck the chord which vibrated in all hearts. About the 1st of July, 1820, shortly after the proclamation of the Constitution by Riego at the head of his troops in Spain, and upon the receipt of that intelligence, an inspiration seized Morelli, a subaltern officer at Nola, to imitate his example, and he found the temper of his troops in accordance with his own. He announced the result to his superior officer at Avellino; and he brought the militia of the province to a similar declaration. The infection spread all over the country. The troops sent from Naples could not be relied on to oppose the constitutionalists or actually joined them, and the crowds in the capital, under the eyes of the King and Court, were decorated with the tri-color of the Carbonari and clamorous for the constitution. Finally, so distinct and emphatic was the expression of the desire of all classes for the constitution that the King felt himself obliged to declare that in eight days he would proclaim the principles of the constitution. The people were not content with so causeless a delay. The tyrant was at once fool and coward. So he slunk from public view and consigned to his son the duties of government with the title of Regent. He proclaimed the constitution of 1812 of Spain as that of Naples,—subject to alterations required by the differences of the two countries. The Carbonari well instructed in the wiles of despotism and the cunning of kingcraft declined to accept this delegated title; and the King was compelled to issue a proclamation under his own hand, confirming the act of the Regent and promising to maintain the constitution. On the 13th of July the King and the Princes took the oath of allegiance to that instrument, and on the 1st of October the Constitutional Parliament of the Two Sicilies was formally and peacefully opened by the Regent. How quiet were the Neapolitan people since the adoption of the constitution, how universal was the satisfaction of all classes, can be shewn in no stronger manner than by the fact, that promptly on the change, the government was in a condition to strip itself of large masses of its scanty army for the purpose of prosecuting to a successful result the suppression of the Sicilian revolt.

By this time the Holy Allies were stirring.

At the Congress of Aix la Chapelle, a further reunion of the associated Sovereigns had been arranged to take place at Troppau, and Metternich cunningly screened his designs under the pretext of pursuing this resolution.

The Neapolitan Government anticipated difficulty from the Austrian treaty, and anxiously sought by repeated but fruitless embassies to make its peace by assurances of its quiet disposition. Metternich knew they could not control the spread of the fire; and he was resolved to extinguish it—by arms if necessary. They sought the mediation of Alexander, who excused himself by reason of his strict alliance with his exalted confederates, from taking alone and without consulting them, any step in a matter so closely affecting their safety. Thus rebuffed they renewed the negotiations with the master and leader of the plot. Cimitele's interview with Metternich is radiant with light on the views and policy of the allies. He sarcastically confessed his confidence in the peaceful intent of the Neapolitan government, whose weakness left little to be feared from hostilities, but for *their* interest he refused to recognize the revolutionary movement. The maintenance of the old constitution against the assaults of innovation was her only safety. She was not an enemy, but a patient; not a reconciliation, but a remedy was needed. All well disposed persons should petition the King to annul the transactions since July, and to punish the rash empirics who had brought their country to the brink of ruin. If difficulties arose, his master would remove them if necessary with eighty or a hundred thousand men. In sorrow the Neapolitan minister replied, if that be the ultimatum blood must flow:—and the conference closed.

The clear head of Metternich was free from the fumes of driveling mysticism which clouded the eyes of Alexander and Francis. He could not be seduced by specious reasoning, to favor a liberalism which he saw to be incompatible with the continuance of absolute monarchy; and he was the first to point out to his imperial masters the blunder they had been guilty of. He was equally conscious of the puerility of the Holy Treaty—the mutual pledge of royal brotherhood, the idle invocation of the truths of Christianity as the basis and principle of a political system, and the Utopian dream of perpetual peace under the guardianship of three military and despotic monarchies. But because it was idle and nugatory for the purposes and views of its dreamy authors, it was not therefore useless in the hand of a statesman whose rigid mind drew stern and practical consequences from the mystical symbols and pious effusions of his illustrious but not very bright masters.

Bewildered with delight at their deliverance, the pious monarchs had covenanted to follow the precepts of Christianity as their only rule; Metternich deduced the consequence, that as rebellion was sinful and obedience commanded, it was the duty of the allies to suppress the one and enforce the other. Since they were to remain united and to afford each other help and countenance on every occasion; he found it not difficult to persuade them that the revolts in Naples and Spain were the very cases contemplated by the treaty; and what had passed as vague generality, he interpreted into a perpetual political league for all purposes of common interest. Since they were there declared to be the plenipotentiaries of God—a war against his plenipotentiary was war against him; and they were called on by their gratitude for their deliverance to punish the daring violators of his majesty in the person of his delegates.

The effusions of gratitude, the pious resolutions, the penitent promises, the mystical fooleries of the sovereign imbecils became in the skillful hands of their great minister the plastic instruments of deep and far-sighted policy. He imbued the empty phrases with pregnant meaning. He worked on the royal fears and gratitude and piety, and the lofty notions of their heaven-descended power, and the high mission of training the insubordinate spirit of man to the submissiveness of Christian meekness—into which they interpreted their triumph over Napoleon,—till from these unpromising materials he formed and founded a great pervading enduring system for the government of Europe. He turned their enthusiastic ejaculations into the charter of a new Amphyctionic Council of which the royal and imperial trinity was the head—whose mission was the enforcement of the principles of religion as matter of government, and, under its cover, the suppression of the fierce intractable insubordinate and untamable spirit of liberty, to be exorcised as an infernal possession, and to be fled from as a deadly contagion.

However the Holy Alliance may be viewed in its origin—whatever may have been the impulses from which it emanated—it soon assumed the shape and functions of an alliance of despots for the government of Europe—of a conspiracy to persecute and exterminate every spirit that lifted its head in audacious rivalry against the absolute power of the Ambassadors of God.

The Emperors of Russia and Austria and the representatives of Prussia and England, in October, 1820, met at Troppau to consult for the cure of Europe. The dreamy and unpractical mind of Alexander was with difficulty brought to a practical resolution. A bloody revolt at St. Petersburg in the adroit hands of Metternich threw new lights on the matter, brought the question home to the Autocrat, and served as a text pregnant with instruction as to the meaning and use of the Holy Treaty. Its resuscitation, its execution he pressed as the only safety against the restless heavings of the revolutionary spirit; and at his instance a formal protocol embodied the principle, that the allies were entitled to intervene with arms for the purpose of maintaining not only the territorial arrangements but also the internal forms of government which the treaties of 1815 had recognized as legitimate in the European States. Those treaties read by the light of the Holy Treaty were converted into a final and immovable settlement of the territory and the governments of Europe; and for their perpetuity the allies were guarantors. The great principle of Metternich's policy was—the *maintenance of the existing order of things;* his instrument was—*the alliance of the three despotic powers of the north.*

The new protocol was announced only when it was completed: and England had the poor privilege of delivering a powerless and disregarded protest.

The treaty of Aix la Chapelle required notice to be given to the sovereign whose affairs were the subject of a royal congress. The King of Naples had not been summoned; and the executors of the law were scrupulously legal in their iniquity. A circular was therefore addressed to the chief courts stating the solicitude excited by the overthrow of established governments in Naples and Spain; invoking the principles of the alliance against Napoleon for the suppression of this new outbreak of the revolution; and inviting them to a conference at Laybach.

In January, 1821, a crowd of crowned heads and liveried slaves blinded the village of Laybach with unusual glitter. They plotted in gay mood against the liberties of mankind; but no resolution was promulgated till the advent of their cousin of Naples.

Ferdinand in the depths of his palace trembled like a child at the asserted power of the nation. He had known only the cringe of slaves: he quailed before the resolute air and attitude of freemen. No act was too low, no lie too bold, no treachery too false and foul which could contribute to his release, not from imprisonment, but from the restraint of honest government.

He patriotically volunteered to encounter with his aged frame the rigor of the season, the dangers of the voyage, the labors of the journey to Laybach, that he might avert the scourge of war from his beloved land. He earnestly promised his devoted efforts to confirm to her people their free constitution; but he intimated an intention to submit the provisions of the constitution which he indicated to the assembled sovereigns. The Parliament refused its consent to any journey of the King which had for its design the *improving* on the Spanish constitution he had sworn to observe. They repeated their refusal even when only *such slight alterations* were suggested as might satisfy the moderate demands of Russia and Austria. It was only when the King pledged his worthless royal word that the only object of his mission was the *maintenance of the Spanish constitution* in its integrity, that the Parliament were so simple as to believe his assurance and permit his departure. He flew on the wings of the wind to his trusty friends. His presence satisfied all the formal scruples of the sovereigns, who without his presence were quite resolved on their course of action. Metternich, Hardenberg and Capo d'Istria had arranged the results in private interviews. They dealt like men of business with practical matters. The halting protest of England was taken at its true value. Her declaration that her distance from the disturbance stripped *her* of any right of interference, but that the proximity of Austria to the infected district might admit of very different measures, was only a diplomatic way of neutralizing her denial of the right of intervention. The three despotic Powers embodied the result of their conferences in a circular, announcing that the great majority of the Neapolitan Kingdom were devoted to their King, and would know nothing of this rough and boisterous freedom—only another name for slavery; that the troops of Austria would be welcomed by them as deliverers; but that resistance from the reckless faction which controlled affairs would be suppressed by force. The legions of Russia hung like a cloud in the back-ground, to impress by their terror the hopelessness of defence.

Ferdinand came to Laybach the sworn constitutional monarch of Naples, pledged to protect the Spanish constitution. He naturally found its best security in Austrian arms, and joyfully anticipated their departure on their mission.

The home administration, not entirely satisfied of his constitutional devotion, commissioned the Duke de Gallo to defend their work against the royalist conspiracy. Remonstrance and debate, however, were justly considered out of place where resolutions were settled and the mode of execution alone was open; and the Austrian Government politely relieved the Congress from the only croaking voice of dissent likely to disturb its harmonious sitting, by arresting the Duke at Görz during its consultations. At the conclusion he was bidden to attend his master—who communicated the joyful intelligence with undisguised delight, that, in spite of his remonstrances, the Congress had resolved that affairs in Naples must revert to their condition under the treaties of 1815, or an Austrian army would put them back; and he was dispatched to bear the intelligence—with a lying letter to the Regent from the King veiling his treachery to his people under regrets for his fruitless intercessions.

The Austrian army followed swiftly on the feet of the messenger. The Parliament and people met the danger as one man. They flung back the proposal of surrender with indignation. Men volunteered for their country by thousands. Their words breathed the loftiest enthusiasm. But their measures disclosed that want of practical statesmanship, which always so fatally enervates the arm of the people in despotic states. Idle debates on municipal concerns had wasted the precious hours which should have been sacred to preparation. Money, arms, discipline, military skill—all but devotion, were wanting. Half-armed crowds of militia find enthusiasm a frail defence before the deadly missiles of war. It is a feeble substitute for discipline and skill; and it soon cools beneath the influence of the sharp lessons of defeat and flight. Inexorable time crowded the work of years into days—but could not add the might of giants to the strength of men. The Austrian was in battle array ere the Neapolitans had time to assemble their men. The powers of despotism were ever ready to strike at naked liberty. They hastened to anticipate the hour of preparation: and rushing on the enthusiastic but ill-prepared youth of Naples, scattered their hastily assembled forces—and marched to the occupation of the city.

The heroic King rested—as Kings now usually do—at a distance from the scene of conflict—till his people had been dragooned into submission—the hateful Parliament dispersed—the sworn constitution abrogated; and then at leisurely stages he approached his capital, and resumed his throne amid the clamor of the lazaroni and the military salute of the Austrians.

The usual results followed in swift succession. The schools were closed lest light should illumine the people. The Jesuits were recalled, to bewilder their consciences. The press was fettered, that no free word might disturb the stillness of despotism. The people were relieved of their useless weapons;

and the secret possession of them punished with death. The prisons were crowded with the most illustrious friends of freedom, and military tribunals dealt from the drum-head quick destruction on the adherents of the vanquished cause of the country. The bloody and reckless wrath of the tyrant could only be controlled by the terrors of desertion by his allies; and the horrors of his rule may be estimated when Austrian pity interposed to shield the victims of his undistinguishing madness. The condition of his kingdom *then*, is best learned from Mr. Gladstone's pamphlet painting that of his successor *now*.

With these excesses we have nothing to do. They are too common to justify description. We deal with the *political fact*, that the three despotic powers assumed and acted on the principles of the Holy Alliance as above defined. They found a constitution in full and peaceful play—sanctioned by the royal oath—safe in the affections of the people—strong enough to put down domestic sedition—able to meet and discharge all the duties of international neighborhood—stained by no blood—and free from aggression on its neighbors. They left in its place the stillness of despotism—broken only by the groans of the prisoner.

They did this, because the example of the peaceful working of a free constitution was dangerous to the quiet of their states. They secured by treaty with the King the right to control his people—just as at Carlsbad they conspired with the Princes of Germany to suppress the development of political life. In the very act they declared war against every free government—against the very life and being of freedom. The question of its suppression was only one of time, policy and power.

Had Naples been left to herself, all Italy would have been a free and united Kingdom, strong in liberty, free from Austrian despotism—a support and a comfort to the cause of mankind. She is, what despots only can make mankind, the image of themselves—cruel, cowardly and debased. The destruction of the Neapolitan constitution dragged after it the suppression of the promising efforts for constitutional rights in Sardinia. There too the King had fled—Charles Albert was at the head of affairs but trembled before the outbreak he had himself fostered; and his vacillating character left the energies of the friends of freedom to waste themselves in fruitless and disconnected revolts. The partisans of the French and of the Spanish constitution divided in hostile bands; the decisive sword of Austria was freely offered to the former to crush the latter: and that was followed by the necessary submission of their allies. Italy again lay at the feet of her masters.

This was a grand step for despotism. The example of the American revolution and our peaceful republic shook all the despotisms of Europe. The example of free, peaceful and united Italy would have been deadly poison to the absolute power of Austria. Her dominions would have been curtailed of their Italian provinces. She would have been driven to legal, moderate, constitutional government.

Russia would have been deprived of her faithful ally and servant, and confined in the frozen North till the fires of liberty should reach her. Germany, free and popular, would have been released from Austrian dictation; and now she would have been a glorious Empire of confederated states on the plan of our magnificent union, quietly reposing on her conscious strength, defying assault from abroad, and maintaining by the even operation of equal laws the peace and quiet of her citizens—a barrier against Russian aggression—an example to restless and uneasy France—a model of constitutional liberty.

The children of despotism are wiser in their generation than the children of light; they saw the dilemma, and manfully threw away their liberal professions in the face of a despotic necessity.

The proximity of Naples to the Italian provinces of Austria, excited her solicitude and demanded her first attention. The facility of her success gave the leisure and confirmed the resolution of repeating the experiment in Spain. The congress of Aix la Chapelle had admitted France to the confederation of monarchs. It was fit that having kissed the hand of her masters, she should be eager to show her devotion by some work of repentance. The arms of Austria had been stained by her onslaught on Italian liberty. The legitimist monarch of France aspired to equal honors, at the expense of Spain. The example of her constitutional government was of damning example by the side of the retrogressive monarchy of France. Her free constitution won by the swords which had expelled the invader was a standing libel on the fraudulent charter of the French—the emanation of the grace of a Prince who won his crown by foreign bayonets, and reigned by the right divine and Russian permission. Impelled by the Furies who urged to that madness which precedes ruin, that shade of a monarch urged the intervention of the Allies, that his might be the glory of the execution.

The Congress of Laybach had adjourned late in 1821 with the resolution of meeting at Verona, within a year—when the results of the operations in Italy could be known and the extent of the inflammation estimated,—to determine on the treatment of Spain: and in October, 1822, Verona swarmed with princes, priests, diplomatists and pilgrims on the holy crusade against the political miscreants who defiled the soil of Spain, sacred for centuries to despotism and superstition.

Let us, ere we recount their deeds, estimate the weight and character of the monster whose life they sought.

The constitution was sworn to on the 7th of March, 1820. On the 9th July, 1820, the first Cortes were opened by the King—in that speech whose promises were all perjuries in advance. His feeble mind longed for his absolute power—so soon as the ebullitions of the revolution sunk to quiet under the constitution. His spirit was unchanged—it had only yielded to the commanding voice of the nation. If that voice could be changed, if its power could be curbed, if foreign aid might supply the deficiencies of internal strength, and silence the clamors or suppress the movements of the people, no fear of perjury stood in his way—for absolution was ready beforehand—no promise was an obstacle—for he was the sovereign and his will could not be bound. His was the cause of God and of his order—and any means were holy in such a cause. On this system he acted: and the constitutionalists were simple enough to permit it.

The King hastened in the fall of 1820, even before the dissolution of the Cortes, to hide his chagrin at the Escurial; and instantly on its dissolution, without consulting his ministry and in violation of the very words of the constitution, he changed the military command of the province of Madrid from the trusty hands of Gen. Vigodet—an avowed and honest but moderate constitutionalist, to those of Carvajal its secret foe. This was the first step in the counter revolution to which the undivided and unscrupulous efforts of the King were directed. The discontent excited by this act, in connection with the discovery of a plot against the constitution, having its seat in the very neighborhood of the Escurial and implicating the King's confessor, roused the people to violent demonstrations, which were appeased only by his return to Madrid.

This salutary indication that the public temper would not be trifled with led to a substitution of Baldes, a vigorous liberal, in the place of Amarillas, as minister of war: he at once recalled Riego to the command in Arragon: and Arco Aguero, Lopez Bannos, Mina and Velasco, reliable men of the constitution, were placed in command of Estremadura,

Navarre, Galicia and Seville. In their hands the country was safer than the King cared it should remain.

A collision between the guards and the people—brought on by the former resenting the cheers of the latter to the "Constitutional King"—compelled the ministry, in the spring of 1821, to disband the guards for the sake of order. The King retaliated by dismissing the ministry,—whose place was filled by men of constitutional opinions but of little energy.

Under their guidance the Cortes, which met in extraordinary session on the 1st of March, 1821, exerted itself to found an adequate military force to suppress internal disturbances which seemed to have their fountain near the throne. Summary tribunals and prompt proceedings, and martial law when the civil arm was overmatched and defied, preserved the cause of order: yet so moderate was their course, that their punishments were ascribed to treasonable leniency, and provoked the mob in one case to a summary execution of a priestly conspirator condemned to the galleys. The incompetent ministry failed to punish the outrage: and the King seized the moment of public terror and revulsion to relieve himself of Villalba as military commander of Madrid, and to substitute in his place Murillo, a man of distinguished firmness but of sinister views as to the constitution, and devoted at once to the King and to the essential modification, if not to the abrogation of the constitution. Thus the King had Carvajal for the province and Murillo for the city—men not devoted to the constitution they were appointed to defend. The appointment of Murillo, though distasteful to the Cortes and the liberals, was permitted to pass without objection, in consideration of the disorder he was appointed to suppress.—The Cortes might have shewn equal moderation in a different manner, with more safety to the country and the constitution.

Thus strengthened, the King strangled by his veto not only the law against political associations; but fastened on the people the iron fetters of the feudal system which the Cortes in the true spirit of free government strove to break. England had passed such a law in the time of Charles II: France had torn up the system by the roots: and Prussia made a similar radical reform the first boon she offered her people to incite them to the war of liberation. Ferdinand knew the connection between feudal rights and despotic power: and with his eyes on the restoration of the former, refused the abrogation of the latter. That excitement should boil up in the public mind on such events is not surprising. The wonder is that it did not break out in deeds of violence. The feeling of security fled with the session of the Cortes to whose conservative liberalism all men looked for protection against the adverse machinations of the Court and the Clubs: but the policy of the King was to justify the royalist by the popular disturbances: and he therefore postponed, against the urgent solicitations of the people, the meeting of the Cortes till October. The event justified the adverse fears and hopes. An accident occasioned in August a collision between the guards and the people. The people clamored for Murillo's removal; but the King not only refused to dismiss him but discharged the Minister of War for accepting even his resignation—replaced him by an incompetent dotard of royalist sympathies—and followed up his advantage by striking Riego from the command of Arragon, where his faith and energy and heroic spirit would have bid defiance to the French deliverers. The false and slanderous pretext was, that against all his known constitutional tendencies he had proclaimed the Republic in his province. It was worth a lie and a libel to be relieved from the terror of such a name. The ministry of war was successively offered to Contador, and Rodriguez, whose incompetency would destroy its efficiency: and on their refusal the King provided in the person of Salvador an opponent of the constitution to conduct its defence—who answered his master's expectations by treasonably betraying it in its last retreat. The fortunate results of the assault on Naples and Sardinia had raised the hopes of a like rescue: and the King was thoughtfully intent on giving his friends as little difficulty as might consist with his safety till their arrival. The people could not be both blind and dumb while their friends were stricken down, and they themselves delivered defenceless to their foes. These outrages of the King called forth counter manifestations from the people. In Madrid, in Seville, Malaga and Carthagena, processions and assemblies bespoke the deep feelings of the people for freedom insulted in the person of Riego; and the throne was assailed with petitions for his restoration, or the reasons of his removal. The country was excited to the strongest manifestations of discontent:

but they did not break out into revolutionary violence.

These events introduced the session of the Cortes which opened on the 28th of September, 1821. Thus far, the people, though threatened by foreign war and domestic treachery, however violent in language, had been on the whole moderate in their deeds. The Cortes followed their too tame example, and without holding the Government to a strict accountability for these significant acts, proceeded to the consideration of matters of ordinary import, when the state of the country threatened them with a royalist revolt and the King was smoothing the road for foreign invasion. Encouraged by their apparent indifference, he took another step in the same direction. He recalled from the most important military posts the friends of the Constitution, Jauregui from Cadiz, Empecinado from Zamora, Velasco from Seville, and the heroic and unconquerable Mina from Galicia, and supplied their places by men lukewarm or hostile to the Constitution, who would infuse no energy into the defence of the country, and would not be likely to mistake the King's friends for the foes they were to oppose.

Venegas the bitterest opponent of the revolution, the last to give in his adhesion to the triumphant constitution, was sent to command the stronghold of Cadiz. The city rose in indignant outcry against such treachery and refused him admission. Madrid joined in the remonstrance. All the large cities of Andalusia demanded the dismissal of a minister who could consent to such an appointment. The excitement raged in the clubs, and fierce words, such as Danton or Marat had spoken and acted out, were muttered in no doubtful tones. Venegas shrank from the storm. Andilla, his successor, equally objectionable, met with an equally abrupt opposition. Daviz, intended as Velasco's substitute, was unceremoniously driven from Seville; and Mina was forced to resume his post in Galicia by the indignant people. They met and foiled artful villany with blunt honesty. They were justly little scrupulous as to the mode of dealing with it. The ministry bent before the blast,—but the King found them too useful tools to be willing to part with them.

The Cortes disapproved of all the illegal violence yet failed to remonstrate with the King on its causes—till seeing the country on the verge of civil war, they spoke in manly and moderate tone the truth to the King, laid to his ministry's charge the popular discontent, and besought their removal from his councils. He delayed as long as he dared, and it was not till January, 1822, when the cloud was black all over Spain, the south in arms, and Catalonia ready to defy his authority, that he surrendered his advisers.

Instantly the angry waves subsided. It was no revolutionary rage, but manly resolution to do what our English ancestors and our American fathers did, a readiness to snuff despotism in the tainted breeze, and defy it while yet distant. The removal of the danger quieted the fear, and the first step of the Cortes was to signalize their revolutionary madness by passing a law to suppress the violence of the press,—in spite of the furious clamor of the clubs! But still the military power and most important posts were not in the hands of the friends of the constitution.

The members of the new Cortes were elected in the midst of the excitement, and were the devoted friends of the constitution. Immediately on their meeting, in February, 1822, a new ministry, with Martinez de la Rosa at its head, took the reins of government—men signalized for their mild and moderate constitutional views, admirable advisers for quiet times, but not gifted with the rough energy of pilots for such a storm. For now it was apparent that domestic violence conspiring with foreign force threatened the constitution.

As the ferment subsided among the liberals, the intrigues of the court and the priests stirred up the adherents of despotism to deeds of violence infinitely surpassing those of their opponents. Strange compounds of the priest, the renegade, and the robber, united themselves in bands of defenders of the faith, and swarmed through old Castile and Navarre, and infested the mountains of Catalonia; while weaker troops ranged over the southern provinces, drove the trade of loyal robbery, at the bidding of monks, in the cause of the King. In Valencia, the tyrannical conduct of one of his officers brought the people and the soldiery into bloody collision, and threatened to spread the flames of war throughout the land. These things were done with the knowledge, by the partizans, and for the benefit of the King, who quietly watched and secretly instigated disturbances which threatened to dissolve the bands of social order. They drew their origin and support from the fanatical wrath of priests and monks, and the countenance of the King and Court; while the French army lined the borders, instigating and aiding the outbreaks, and waiting to complete what they might leave undone.

The Cortes had long watched with solicitude the course of events, dissatisfied with the ministry—which sought to avert danger by conciliating the King, and leaving in their places the dangerous officers he had appointed—yet unwilling, against the remonstrances of Rosa, to break in on his policy. But now the impending danger of civil and foreign war was so great that while preparing an army and contracting loans, they besought the King to quiet the minds of men and give energy to the administration of the law, by appointing men who possessed and were entitled to the confidence of the country. Nothing could have been more distasteful to the King. He feigned illness as an excuse for delay, and watched the gathering cloud, till finally, on the 30th of August, 1822, he felt himself strong enough to venture to present himself before his people at Aranjuez. Shouts of "long live the absolute King," pleased his ear, and but for the timely advent of the National Guard of Toledo, the loyal mob, joined by the guard, would have swollen to a royal army. On the same day in Valencia, part of the garrison in like manner began the revolt, but were quelled, after sharp fighting, by their colleagues. The patience of the Cortes was exhausted. They demanded the return of the King to Madrid; but he evaded compliance, till on the 30th of June he came to close the Cortes. The excited rabble, as the procession passed, shouted huzzas for Riego. The guard and the people stood face to face. An officer, a decided liberal, in staying the collision, was shot by one of his own men. The guards, it was known, had been tampered with by the Court; and this deed was ascribed to that source. Thousands of the people and troops surrounded the Palace, where the guards entrenched themselves.

After thus standing in hostile attitude for a night and a day, four battalions renounced their obedience, encamped out of the city, and refused to return, in spite of Murillo's assurances of the safety of the King. The latter openly took the part of the revolted guards. He detained the ministry in the Palace so that no orders could be given; and Riego and Ballesteros were driven to assume authority to concentrate an adequate force to repel the expected assault of the guards. The King laid before his ministers a rambling paper assuming that the existing disturbances had broken and abrogated the constitution and remitted him to his unrestricted power; and he spoke of rewarding the guard whom the liberals had excited, and denounced bitterly Riego's conduct. They replied he had no powers but under the constitution, and that the guard should be punished and not rewarded. Still he would not yield, nor strike a decided blow; but waited in the hope of something turning up from the seething whirlpool. The guards in the Palace were prepared by drink and money and caresses to join the revolt.

In this condition of affairs the four battalions made a formal assault on the city, gained the interior by treachery, were foiled in an attempt to seize the arsenal and occupy the open place before the palace, into which they were forced to throw themselves. The troops true to the Constitution crowded to the scene, and stood ranged in battle array before the palace; and the King, and the guard were at their mercy. Yet after every provocation, in the moment of easy victory they were guilty of no excess, of no violence, of no threats against the guilty King, but contented themselves with demanding the disbanding of the guards. This was agreed to. The two battalions which had not taken active part in the disturbances, marched out to their cantonments. The other four marched out in battle array, but as if about to stack their arms—till when close upon the constitutionalists, without a word or a provocation, they poured a volley into their very faces. Fury, rage, madness, and death in an instant ruled the hour; and a general massacre of the guards righteously rewarded their blood-thirsty treachery. The victorious troops of the national guard at once occupied the Palace, and the King with supple and cowardly hypocrisy hastened to return them his eager thanks in the name of the country for their faith and patience!! Verily they deserved them—for letting him continue to live!!

These are the scenes which the Emperor of Russia alludes to when, concluding his climax of the horrors of the Spanish revolution, he says—"On the 7th of July, 1822, blood was seen to flow in the Palace of the King and a civil war raged throughout the Peninsula!!"

It is true—blood did flow in the Palace of the King: but it was the blood of constitutionalists, shed by the rebellious partisans of the King, in treacherous and cowardly violation of the terms of a merciful capitulation. A civil war did rage in the Peninsula; but it was the offspring of the machinations of the King, and his priests, and foreign Allies—a revolt not by, but against the constitutional government of the country!! So much for Muscovite history!

But that civil war was soon as effectually hushed by the vigor of the Cortes and the new ministry—as the revolt of the guards was put down by the national guard.

The ministry were promptly dismissed; devoted but inexperienced friends of the constitution succeeded them: commands were conferred on reliable men; Mina promptly dispersed and drove from the country the Royalist Junta of d'Urgel, who assumed the powers of government in the name of a captive King. Other revolts shared the same fate. The constitution was triumphant over all its domestic foes, unstained with blood or cruelty—strong for all the purposes of maintaining internal peace and order, too strong to rest its power on violence or the threat of it, and free from the slightest imputation of propagating revolutionary principles beyond its borders, content with mild and moderate rule and rich in all the promised fruits of a blessed freedom. Such was the conduct of the Spanish Government, so moderate, so mild, so equitable, so considerate, so pure in its high office, that fiends could find no cause against it.

There was no attempt to propagate their principles in any neighboring land. There was no revolutionary violence which was not discountenanced and punished by the ministry and the Cortes.

The Cortes, elected by the free suffrages of the people, and therefore embodying the spirit of the revolution, were moderate, sedate, respectful to the King and the constitution, and finally sacrificed their cause and themselves in a vain effort to ward off an attack rather than adopt the measures of energy requisite to repel it. They left the conduct of the war and the appointment of officers in the hands of the King, who was the centre of the internal insurrections and of the external assault: he encouraged the one by the priests and monks, always on the side of the power of darkness; he facilitated the advance and ensured the success of the foreign enemy, by opposing to them, on the most important points, men indifferent and cold towards the Constitution, or its secret enemies, who betrayed it on the first opportunity. And while the Cortes strove energetically to suppress and punish insurrections against the King—provoked and justified by his treacherous conduct and scandalous appointments; he encouraged those against the Cortes even to the last moment.

While these events were transpiring, the allied despots were conspiring at Verona how to find in them a pretext for destroying the liberty of Spain. The Congress met in October, 1822.

There appeared the Emperors of Russia and Austria and the King of Prussia with their ministers, breathing the spirit of Metternich, who on the journey had dispelled the doubts of Alexander, and turned his eye from the dangerous attractions of the Grecian struggle by lofty suggestions of his mission for the restoration of monarchical order in Europe. England and France were there—the youngest converts to the infernal conspiracy—the former already tired of the burthens and disgusted with the dishonors of the association; and struggling under the lead of Canning to free herself from its influence. The latter, the instigator of the crusade against the liberties of Spain—which she felt to be a dangerous example from their complete success. And honorably seated amid the potentates of Europe were the delegates of the revolutionary junta of d'Urgel—a band of rebels against the government but for the King of Spain, crowded into one corner of the kingdom and crushed ere the Congress ceased its deliberations: and *they* sat at the board of Kings who assumed to be the apostles of *order*, as the representatives and in the name of the nation by whose laws they were denounced and punished. In the name of France, Montmorency pressed on the Congress the impossibility of tolerating on her borders revolutionary disorders of such dangerous example; and demanded their countenance and support in the event of hostilities. He spoke to no cold and indifferent listeners. They were zealous for the cause of Kings, and the Emperor of Russia promptly tendered the aid of forty thousand troops on whatever frontier of Spain

France might need them. The Duke of Wellington spoke a somewhat different language from that of Castlereagh at Laybach. The scope of the intervention looked beyond Spain to her American Colonies. England declined to be a party to any armed intervention in the affairs of Spain; but distinctly asserted her right and intention to recognize the independence of the colonies, in case of an attempt by the allies to reduce them; and abruptly withdrew from the conferences. But England did not do for *freedom*, what its foes were doing for *despotism*. It was her first step in the right direction; and we must pardon its faltering tread.—The Congress resolved on stringent remonstrances with the constitutional government of Spain concerning the ruinous course of political affairs in the peninsula, and on the withdrawal of their representatives upon their failure to effect a change. In this event it was left to France to take such steps as her safety might require. They vainly but slily hoped that French intrigues and influences, the threat of her impending force and the encouragement of domestic dissension and royalist revolts, would do the work of the friends of order without the needless scandal of a public execution.

At the dissolution of the Congress the "Three Powers" renewed their assurances to the other Courts of Europe, that the Holy Allies adhered with unshaken resolution to their principles; that the Allied Monarchs were resolved to war *upon revolutionary movements, wherever and in whatever form they might appear:* that they had rejected the prayers of the Greeks and ordered the recall of their ministers from Spain; but that the earnest concurrence of all governments was essential to the attainment of the object they proposed to themselves—*the support and maintenance of social order*; and should they lend an ear to other counsels, they were robbing themselves of their only means of guarding their subjects from the ruin which threatened them.

A change of ministry in France modified the spirit but not the objects of her policy; delays indicated a shrinking from the last resort; but still the object was pursued of wringing from Spanish fear a change in the constitution. Even England joined in the effort to subdue the courage of the constitutional government, and violated her own principles by advising concessions to a foreign demand for a change in the constitution, and tried to shake their resolution by painting the disastrous results of an unequal conflict. One and all were repelled by the spirit of independence which scorned advice supported by a menace.

The remonstrances of the three Northern Powers were presented simultaneously with that of France. Equal in insolence, impertinence and insult, in audacious arrogance and despotic pride, their very tone closed the door to conciliation, even had their object been any thing itself, if couched in the most courtly phrase, but a wanton and daring outrage on the independence of nations. They all in dolorous strain bewailed the unhappy condition of Spain, ascribed her misfortunes to the blind fury of the revolutionary spirit, and saw no remedy for the evil so long as their enlightened and liberal monarch, Ferdinand VII. was stripped of his uncontrolled and despotic power.

The canting hypocrisy, the insolent criticisms, the ignorance and falsification of plain historical facts, the libelous blackening of the character of the Spanish liberals, with which these memorials abound, poorly supply the place of reason—and only illustrate the usual course of deliberate villany, which always blackens the character of the victim to extenuate the crime. The liberal King of Prussia was aghast at a constitution "which confounding all elements and all power and assuming only the single principle of a permanent and legal opposition against the government, necessarily destroyed that central and tutelary authority which constitutes the essence of the monarchical system." It would seem therefore that the opposition in England—which is now grown to be a somewhat chronic disease—in monarchical eyes is only secured from criticism because the jest might prove too serious!!

He considered a sufficient condemnation of the Spanish Government, "that it was at once powerless and paralyzed. All its powers were found concentrated, accumulated, and confounded, in one single assembly; this assembly presented only a conflict of opinions and views of interests and passions, in the midst of which propositions and resolutions of the most heterogeneous kind were constantly produced, resisted or neutralized." The concentration of all powers in *one man* would have been quite unobjectionable: and the latter clause not unaptly describes an American Congress or an English Parliament.

He complains that the "ascendency of the fatal doctrines of a disorganizing philosophy," augmented "the general delusion"—till "every notion of sound policy was abandoned for vain theories."

He expressed some disappointment that such a despotic faction did not fall to pieces; but he found the conservative principle of its existence in the "delusive declamations of the tribunes and ferocious outcries of the clubs;" and it was asserted as the chief of the grievances laid to the charge of Spain that "doctrines subversive of all social order are openly preached and protected. Insults, directed against the principal sovereigns of Europe fill with impunity the public journals. The revolutionists of Spain disperse their emissaries, in order to associate with themselves in their pernicious labors, whatever conspirators may be found in foreign countries against public order and legitimate authority."

I do not know of which of these crimes this Republic is not thrice guilty.

Prince Metternich assured the Spaniards that "conformably to eternal decrees good can never arise to states any more than to individuals from a disregard of the first duties imposed upon man in social order; the amelioration of the condition of subjects should not be commenced by criminal illusions, by perverting opinion and by misleading the conscience; and military revolt can never form the basis of a happy and durable government."

How miserable and insecure then is the condition of the people of this Republic.

Prince Metternich states with logical precision the principle of his policy, and lays bare what is the object of his fears and his hate. He would have felt "a just repugnance to intermeddle with the internal affairs of an independent nation," "if the evil operated by her revolution *was concentrated or could be concentrated* within her territorial limits. *But this is not the case:* this revolution even before it arrived at maturity, had been the cause of great disasters in other states; it was this revolution which, *by the contagion of its principles and of its example,* and by the intrigues of its principal partisans, created the revolutions of Naples and Piedmont; it was this revolution *which would have excited* insurrections throughout Italy, *menaced* France and *compromised* Germany, *but for the intervention of the powers which preserved Europe from this new conflagration.* Every where the destructive means employed in Spain to prepare and consummate the revolution, *have served as a model* to those who flattered themselves that they were paving the way to new conquests. Every where the *Spanish constitution has become the rallying point, and the war-whoop of a faction,* combined alike against the security of thrones and the repose of subjects;" in consequence of these things "her relations with the greatest portion of Europe are deranged or suspended," and they could be restored only by revesting the King with the power "of restoring order and peace in his kingdom, of surrounding himself with men equally worthy of his confidence by their principles and talents, and finally of substituting an order of things in which the rights of the monarch shall be happily blended with the *real* interests and *legitimate* views of *all* classes of the nation."

The Emperor of all the Russias, learned in constitutional lore—but oblivious of scenes in which he had been a conspicuous actor—vilifies the Spanish revolution as the act of "perjured soldiers," who "turned their arms against their sovereign and their country, to impose on Spain laws which the public reason of Europe, enlightened by the experience of all ages, stamped with its highest disapprobation." He might have recollected that a perjured King had annulled those very laws which he had sworn to maintain, and which the people sought only to restore. He could scarcely have forgotten that he himself had formally recognized as legitimate those very laws and that very government, which he now insolently asserts the public reason of Europe stamps with its highest disapprobation!

He painted "the evils that are inseparable from a state of things where the conservative principle of social order had been forgotten," and among the grievances to be redressed by foreign arms, we are startled to find enumerated "ruinous loans and contributions unceasingly renewed—religion despoiled of her patrimony—the throne of popular respect—authority transferred to assemblies where the blind passions of the multitude seized upon the reins of government:" and lastly, the climax of horrors is capped by the impudent assertion that, "on the 7th of July blood was seen to flow in the palace of the King, and a civil war raged throughout the Peninsula."

The English debt, and her despoiled monasteries may yet provoke the reforming hand of the Czar!

The throne of France has been despoiled of respect sufficiently to require his restoring zeal! He may find on this side the Atlantic many cases of authority transferred to assemblies where the blind passions of the multitude have seized the reins of government; but he will have his hands full if he undertakes to wrest them away! It was not unnatural that the successor of the murdered Paul should be somewhat sensitive to the flow of blood in royal palaces; but the example hardly strengthens his case!

These insolent pretences were met and repelled with manly bluntness by the ministry. They looked war calmly in the face, while they tendered the ministers of the allies their passports. With laconic point they assured the minister of France that his master's solicitude for the welfare of Spain would be best displayed and relieved by withdrawing his army of agitation from her borders. The Austrian minister they dismissed with the cool reply, that his Catholic majesty was indifferent whether he maintained relations or not with the court of Vienna. To the Russian, the minister of foreign affairs applied words of just and indignant severity—*You have shamefully abused (perhaps through ignorance) the law of nations,* which is always respectable in the eyes of the Spanish Government. I transmit by order of his Majesty the passports you desire, *hoping your excellency will be pleased to leave this capital with as little delay as possible.*

Still the irrevocable step was delayed, till Alexander, impatient at doubts he could not comprehend, urged France to act in the spirit of her negotiations;

and Austria and Prussia promised aid in case the Spanish war should kindle domestic disturbances in the rear. Ministerial doubts yielded to such suggestions. Louis XVIII. in January, 1823, in opening the Chambers, defined the purposes of the intervention to be to secure the *safety* of his own people, and Spain from *extreme misfortune;* at the call of the God of St. Louis, to maintain a *descendant of Henry IV. on the throne of Spain;* to obtain for Ferdinand VII. the *freedom* to bestow on his people *those institutions* which they could only obtain *through him,* and which alone could assure their quiet, and dispel the solicitudes of France.

On the fifteenth of March, the Duc d' Angouleme, to whom the conduct of the expedition was fitly confided, left Paris for the Army, and immediately the French legions passed the Bidassoa, on their disgraceful crusade.

For Spain, the conflict was hopelessly unequal. Nothing but miracles of valor and skill, devotion and unity, could save her. She was deficient in all. Her treasury was empty—her taxes unproductive—her army weak, scattered and undisciplined. In a contest for life and death, the conduct of the war was in the hands of a traitor, who stirred up the sedition he had sworn to suppress, and eagerly hoped for the arrival of the foes of his country, as his deliverers. He seized the moment of the adjournment of the Cortes in February, when the French were ready to cross the frontier, to dissolve the constitutional ministry, and strip the northern army of its only reliable commanders, Mina and Ballesteros; and their restoration at the clamor of a mob, left small hope of energetic and concurrent action. The King had systematically filled every important post, so far as possible, with men doubtful in their politics, indifferent to the cause of the constitution, and ready at any convenient moment to betray it. The ministry, with ruinous moderation, had deferred the evil day of decisive action, under the vain hope that they could soften the hate of the allies by conciliatory conduct. They were in the midst of a crisis, when desperate remedies were the only wisdom,—and they acted as men who hoped for peace, if they gave no cause for war. They forgot that the *existence* of the constitution was the cause of the war—that the more quiet and peaceful and satisfactory was their rule, the more damning was their example, the more ruinous their influence, the more worthy of extermination. They therefore were obliged to meet the enemy, not only with forces utterly inadequate to a contest in the field; but, of the four divisions of their army, *three* were commanded by persons lukewarm in the cause, or secretly hostile to it, or despairing of its success; all of whom hastened its doom by treachery and treason. Abisbal, who commanded the capital, opened negotiations with the enemy on his first advance, divided and disheartened the troops, and was removed from the command by his officers. Morillo, at a critical period of the contest, abandoned the cause, and carried his troops over to the enemy; and Ballesteros, disheartened by the defection of Abisbal, conducted the war not as a desperate revolutionary struggle, but with a view to good terms at its close;

and finished, after a few indecisive skirmishes, by surrendering upon good terms for himself and his followers. Mina in Catalonia, and Villafranca in the south, alone conducted the war in the desperate spirit which the occasion required. In the same false hope of conciliating, the Cortes neglected to appeal to the revolutionary spirit to which they owed the constitution, in its defence, and left themselves destitute of the only energy which could supply the deficiencies of money and of men. They relied on the guerrilla warfare, yet feared to employ its leaders. The enthusiastic devotees of the constitution they left in obscurity; and only called the heroic Riego to command, when nothing could be done but sacrifice his life to the cause. They paralyzed the whole conduct of the war, by leaving it to a perjured King, whose hopes were blasted by victory, to whom defeat gave despotic power, and in whose name swarms of priests and monks roused the lower rabble to revolt, and preached sedition in the cause of order.

Such a cause, so defended, was lost from the first.

Before the advancing foe, as treachery, and lukewarmness, and the weakness of despair relaxed the energies of their defenders, and their armies melted into nothing, the Cortes, carrying with them the reluctant King, eagerly covetous of captivity at the hands of the French, adjourned from Madrid to Seville. They scarcely drew breath, before they were compelled to seek safety in Cadiz. Even there, treachery had anticipated them, and prepared in their last retreat defenceless and dismantled fortifications—untenable even by Spanish valor. There, in the last ditch, surrounded by her faithful children, the liberty and the constitution of Spain fell before the murderous assault, after a defence such as only the sons of liberty know how to exhibit.

With their fall closed the second battle of light and darkness in the nineteenth century; and the cheering dawn was turned into night.

Stripped of the pretences which thinly veiled the dark purposes of the despots, their act assumes the form of a high crime against the liberty, laws, and independence of free nations. It has a meaning, which it becomes us deeply to ponder, under the light of recent revelations.

The safety of France was not implicated in the Spanish Revolution, save by the bare example of a free government established in spite of the opposition of the King. Social order was not disturbed by the constitutional authorities. They were devoting their best energies successfully to maintain it against the partisans of the King, the intrigues of his priests and courtiers, and the countenance and support of the menacing army of France.

The blood that flowed in the Palace was shed by the King's guards, at his instigation, in a revolt against the established government, to re-instate him in his unlimited and despotic power; and he hypocritically thanked those who suppressed the insurrection.

The ruinous loans and exhausting taxes, which were insolently put forward as grounds of interference by a foreign nation, were chiefly occasioned by the impending war which the accusers were bringing on the country; and the terms of raising them were rendered more oppressive by the insecurity their threats and the King's intrigues threw over the "existing order."

There was no propagation of the revolution abroad, or danger to the life of the King at home, by the very confession of Morillo, during the insurrection of July. The government earnestly and energetically suppressed every symptom of insurrectionary violence, controlled the clubs, restrained by salutary laws the excesses of the press, and so carefully and delicately dealt with the King's inclinations, so anxiously avoided even the appearance of restraint on his person or of opposition to his wishes, that against the opinion and remonstrances of the Cortes, they continued the opponents of the constitution appointed by the King in the most important military posts, till their moderation was their ruin. They fell victims of a vile conspiracy, because they too much shrank from being what they were charged with being. What England would have been, if Parliament had continued Charles at the head of government—what France would have been, had Louis conducted the defence of the country against the European coalition—that Spain became, because her moderation stopped short of their examples. Europe combined against France because she did, and crushed Spain because she did not depose and fetter her crowned and anointed traitor.

There remains then, *nothing* as the cause of the war, but the single fact, that Spain had freely established a constitution, moderate in principle, conservative in its administration, resting on the popular will, yet leaving ample prerogatives in the hands of the King for the due administration of the laws and his own protection; only controlled by the responsibility of the ministry, and the restraints of every free constitution. Against *this* the war was waged. It was waged to destroy the *example* of a free and peaceful government, which despots called revolutionary. It was undertaken, because it was at last fully felt and seen, with all the clearness of the logic of history, that free ideas were dangerous playthings. They soon grew from pets to masters. They were inconsistent with the existence of neighboring despotism. They were a living light that would shine into the adjacent darkness, not because carried there, but because it is the nature of light to diffuse itself. It will dispel darkness—and this, to despotic power, was ruin. They therefore resolved to *extinguish* what they could not *hide* nor *escape*. To *be free* was the sin. The only atonement was death. With this, there is no reasoning but the sword. There is no law for it, none against it—but the law of self-defence. The Holy Allies would yield none of their power, and held fast to the central principle of their policy—the absolute, uncontrolled, and uncontrollable sovereignty of the King;—and against whatever was inconsistent with this, they consistently waged a war of hate and extermination, under the name of revolutionary madness.

We are equally settled in maintaining the sovereignty of the people—their absolute and unlimited right to change their institutions at their pleasure—

and this is absolutely incompatible with the principle of the Holy Alliance. We *must* therefore be ready, not to *argue*, but to *fight*. These principles go to the foundation of civil society—they are the criteria of the rights of Kings and of men—there is no arbitrament but the *sword*. The allies had become conscious of *this*, and acted with rigid and unflinching consistency. The Spanish ministry were deceived in supposing the *pretexts* to be the *cause* of the war, and they sacrificed their country by their blunder.

With the blood and torture which signalized the triumph of Ferdinand, we have nothing to do. It is all included in the historical meaning of despotic power. We leave Spain weltering in her blood, for another field of agony, which rushes red upon the sight.

SECTION III.

THE REVOLT OF

FRANCE AND POLAND

AGAINST

THE HOLY CONSPIRATORS.

THE REVOLT OF

FRANCE AND POLAND

AGAINST

THE HOLY CONSPIRATORS.

From 1824 to 1830, the people of Europe sunk panting and exhausted from the fruitless conflict into restless repose, haunted by ghastly dreams, and oppressed by the nightmare of despotic power.

While they slumbered, the eyes of all the Courts were fixed on the earthquake which shook the soil of the Turkish Empire, where Greek rebellion and Russian ambition threatened to shatter its decayed and tottering fabric. These events are not within the precise line of the contest between freedom and despotism, but they bear on and illustrate them. The preservation of order in Europe was only a means to an end with the Emperor of Russia. He wished repose in Western Europe, that he might without disquiet at home prosecute his schemes in the East. The death of Alexander in 1825 changed the person, not the policy of the Emperor; and what was lost by the removal of one endeared to his brother despots by relations of long personal friendship and the memory of common dangers and common triumphs, was more than compensated by the more vigorous and consistent politics of the Emperor Nicholas, his more clear appreciation of the necessities of the times, and his greater ability to meet them. He seized the moment when Turkey was left defenceless by the annihilation of the Janizaries, to wrest from her helplessness the treaty of Ackerman in 1826. Alexander had rejected the prayer of the Greeks for aid; Nicholas eagerly caught at the opportunity to weaken the Turk: and England and France, anxious to maintain the integrity of the Ottoman Empire, were forced to appear on the side of Russia, dictating terms to the Porte for the purpose of setting bounds to the aggressions of the Czar. The famous intervention of England, France, and Russia, for the Greeks, sprang from no sympathy for their heroic cause, their barbarous sufferings, their historic renown, nor from any consideration of the debt of gratitude to their classic ancestors. While the people of Europe swayed to and fro with the varying fate of the war, and breathed earnest aspirations for the victory of the oppressed, the Governments of Europe were in the field, the battle of Navarino was fought, the French army swept the Peloponnesus—not to defend the Greeks, not in the cause of liberty, but—for the protection of the Ottoman Empire against the aggressions of the Russians, and its too great enfeeblement from the success of the Greeks. Russia was there, in spite of her horror of revolutionary violence, because Turkey was to be weakened through the success of the Greeks: England and France were there to see that Greece by the aid of Russia did not succeed too far. They preferred the maintenance of a shadow of the Ottoman Empire, to the creation of a strong vigorous Christian Kingdom covering ancient Greece and Macedonia, and capable of maintaining all the relations of peace and war—for fear that Russia might augment her power. Yet by their usual temporizing policy they lost all the fruits of their intervention—and only postponed the inevitable day. They rested on their arms when they should have dared the utmost. Honest aid to the Greeks would have at once driven the Turks across the Bosphorus, placed the political power in the hands of the Christian population, and raised a vigorous and firm power to bar the progress of Russia. They temporized till the battle of Shumla had left the road to Constantinople without a defender: and then, under the mediation of Prussia, permitted the treaty of Adrianople to sever the Danubian provinces from the Turkish Empire, under the paternal guardianship of Russia, to strip one bank of the Danube of its fortresses, to exempt Russian subjects from Turkish jurisdiction, to burthen the Sultan with the overwhelming expenses of a war for his religion, his empire and his life. They only postponed the final consummation of the ambitious hopes of Russia for a few years in the life of nations.

Such was the spirit of the famous, the lauded, the popular, intervention of France and England and Russia on behalf of Greece—a despicable political squabble between the Courts for political power.

The treaty of Adrianople was concluded in 1829, under the impending threat of an English fleet in the Dardanelles, and of an Austrian army on the borders of Hungary. The Czar paused before such a combination, and postponed for a future day the realization of his dreams.

He was on the threshold of 1830. Events were on the wing which would soon give employment to his sword in the holy cause of social order.

Emboldened by the impunity which attended the outrage on Spain, the Bourbons of France struck for the absolute power of their ancestors. God hardened the heart of Charles—as formerly of Pharaoh—that he might draw down on him resistless wrath. The restored exile had learned no wisdom: and he tried beyond the point of submission the patience of his people. The charter was itself a fraud on the nation. It professed to emanate from the grace of the sovereign, who reigned by the grace of God. It gave the semblance rather than the reality of freedom. Yet the spirit of even its niggardly concessions had always been the plaything of the royal caprice. Its words had become elastic in the hands of his ministers: till emboldened by past impunity, he violated its very letter, and abrogated by the decrees of July, the most essential rights of speech and of the press. This was the fatal spark. The mine exploded in the revolution of the three days of July.

All Europe trembled in sympathy—as if an earthquake rolled by.

Germany ever oppressed and patient, uttered a groan and turned uneasily beneath her burthen.

Belgium, forced into unnatural and ruinous union with Holland, summoned the energies of long discontent for a final blow; asserted her independence: and, in September 1830, drove their King beyond the borders.

Poland, wearied with the oppressions and outrages of Russian insolence, sprang to her feet, as the thunder of the western revolutions seemed to sound the fatal hour. In November 1830, she expelled from her capital the tools of her perjured tyrant—and, with arms in her hands, summoned her children to consult for her welfare.

The revolution of July was the precise case contemplated by the treaty of Aix la Chapelle. The Bourbons, for whose restoration all Europe had been in arms, had been again expelled by revolutionary violence. They were parties to the Holy Alliance, they had shed the blood of liberty in its cause, and now were victims of their devotion to its principles. They did not appeal in vain to their confederates.

Nicholas, promptly on the news of the revolution, took measures for its suppression. The Polish army was put on the war footing. On the 18th of August, orders were transmitted to Warsaw for the requisite funds. Masses of Russian troops were crowding to the Polish frontiers. General Diebitsch had been sent to Berlin; and the campaign was concerted to commence on *the Rhine*—which of course involved the alliance of Prussia. The news of the breaking out of the conflagration in Belgium was an additional admonition of the danger of delaying to extinguish the flames before they spread. The obsequiously cringing letter of Louis Philippe of the 19th of August was written after war was resolved on: and the scornfully evasive reply of Nicholas would, by any other prince, have been treated as its declaration. Louis Philippe trembled on his throne, feared to appeal to his people, and continued by hesitation to compromise his dignity, till Poland lifted her majestic arm against the foe he feared.

She was scarcely the shadow of her former self. Her spirit burned brightly—but her arms were drained of their life-blood. She stood alone surrounded by the waste of despotism—a withered leafless lifeless trunk, reft of her fairest boughs, stretching her bare arms to heaven in vain invocation of its mercy—drawing down on her thrice devoted head the lightnings of Russian wrath, which the Czar had gathered to hurl against the newborn liberties of France.

At the council board of the Congress of Vienna one place was vacant. It was a void which might be felt. It could not be forgotten that Poland was not there. Her ghost still hovered before the memories of her murderers searing their eyeballs, and would not down at their bidding—till due reverence had been done to her manes.

Such was the power of her name, the importance of her enslaved children, the agony of Europe as remorse pointed to the folly which sacrificed her—that the first article of the final Treaty of Vienna is dedicated to her re-instatement among the powers of Europe.

That article stipulated for the erection of the Grand Duchy of Warsaw into the Kingdom of Poland—whose crown should rest on the head of the Czar. To him it was declared bound by *its constitution*: and it was solemnly stipulated that the Poles within the three Empires of Russia, Austria, and Prussia, should obtain a representation and national institutions, to be regulated according to the political principles which the Government to which they belonged should judge useful and convenient.

This solemn stipulation, introducing the long train of adjustments on which the peace and independence of Europe were made to depend, was not intended to be mere verbiage. It had a political import, an international significance, indicated by its prominent position. It is perfectly well known to have been the result of long negotiations, of conflicting claims, of reciprocal distrusts quieted by mutual concessions; and that in this article pretensions found their solution which threatened to re-open the wars of Europe, and had actually led to secret re-unions against the exclusive voracity of Russia.

The parties to the treaty therefore meant—what their language imports, and what is well known in the history of Europe—not to incorporate Poland into the body of the Russian Empire, but—to preserve its nationality, while they united its crown with that of Russia on the head of the Czar. They meant to create a separate and independent political body—united by the head of the common Emperor. The relations of Scotland or Hanover to England, of Hungary to the Imperial Crown of Austria, were the models. The object was—to raise a barrier however feeble against the western ambition of the Czar—to stay at its lowest point the augmentation of his power which must flow from the possession of Poland. The plan was—to preserve intact and fresh the national feeling, the historic memory, the traditional spirit of the Pole by means of national institutions and constitutional guarantees.

So Alexander understood the treaty, and in its spirit was the constitutional charter framed, which he promulgated on the 27th of November 1815. It declared the Kingdom of Poland united by its constitution to Russia: in conformity with it alone the sovereign authority should be exercised: the solemnities of a coronation at Warsaw and of an oath to observe the charter were the slender bonds on the royal conscience: but the substance of a free government was embodied in the perpetual representation consisting of the King and the two chambers of the Diet, wherein resided the power of taxation and legislation: and the national army of Poland decorated with national military orders, and severed from the Russian service, was at once the emblem and the support of her perpetual and living sovereignty.

Such a constitution was sufficient any where but beneath the Upas shadow of Russian despotism.

With soft words and fair promises Alexander opened in 1818 the Polish Diet. He held out the hope of the re-union of the great provinces which formed the Poland of history, as the reward of good conduct. He complimented the independence which rejected a proposal of the government: and adjourned the Diet with bright hopes for the future. But a cloud came over the sky. Italy had been shaken by revolutionary violence, and the absolute sceptre had been wrested from the hand of Ferdinand. Alexander had disregarded the limitations of constitutional power, and he sought to control the restless discontent of the Poles by a more efficient or more subservient judiciary armed with a more summary code. The Diet of 1820, in the spirit of the English Barons, refused to exchange the open procedure and jury trial of the French for the secret and prompt proceedings of the Imperial code. The smile of favor was darkened by the frown of discontent. His Majesty took it ill that the freedom he had conferred should venture to thwart him. He closed the Diet in the utmost indignation at their presumption: and admonished them of the serious consequences which might follow the spread of so unseemly a disposition.

The more his Majesty saw of free government the less he liked it. He got tired of playing at free government when his people refused to consider it a plaything. He had dreamed of complacent Diets, docile judges, a complimentary press. He had looked with patriarchal eyes on an obedient people—whose freedom would find its best reward in conformity to his will, and who in case of unhappy differences would exemplify their grateful acknowledgments by cheerful self-denial. He had painted the constitution in his fancy as the best support of the burthen of an absolute crown—not limiting its illimitable and heaven-derived powers, but a subordinate aid in their administration. To oppose his will, thwart his views, criticise his policy, reject his proposals—these things were not freedom, but its seditious excesses not far removed from revolutionary violence. The Poles in his view were like the Roman freedman—liable for ingratitude to be again reduced to bondage: and not to do his bidding was the height of ingratitude. He did not see—he had to learn from experience, from Metternich's sinister commentaries, and his logical pursuit of principles to their results—that two sovereign powers in one State are as contradictory as two Gods in Heaven. If the King be absolute the people must be nothing. If the people are associated in the exercise of sovereignty, its attributes must follow it and fall on the heads of its possessors. These lessons he learned—and never forgot. He loved freedom—but he hated its exercise. He was the friend of liberty while it was complacent; but when oppression and misrule had stung it to madness, he turned in fury on his pet, and died frowning hate upon the work of his own hands.

Ere Alexander's death in 1825, the oppressions of his tools had driven Poland to the verge of rebellion. Nicholas saw the political blunder of the constitution, and reluctantly swore at his coronation to observe and maintain it—only because perjury was less dangerous than civil commotion prematurely provoked, and its refusal might be met by armed resistance. But injuries and outrages had sunk too deep in the minds of the Poles, in ten years of misrule, to be obliterated by an additional perjury.

From the grant to the revocation of the constitution, its existence was only a name. Its most solemn provisions were perpetually set at naught—as if they did not exist. The first act of Alexander was the appointment of the Grand Duke Constantine commander in chief of the national army of Poland—in the very teeth of the constitution; and with that illegal post he conferred an undefined and despotic power to which no legal limit could be assigned, and for which no authority of law existed. Nominally above him, in reality his tool, was placed Zajaczek as Viceroy of Poland—a feeble irresolute old man, a fit veil for the arbitrary and illegal administration of Constantine and his assistant in iniquity Nowosilzow. This *national* administration bent all its energies to the annihilation of Polish nationality; and the means were indifferent, so that the end were reached. Every manifestation of national feeling, of manly freedom, or restlessness under illegal oppression was the excuse and the occasion for more stringent measures. The Grand Duke was a member of the first Diet, when the freedom of the press, the abolition of the police and the spies, the removal of high officers stained by high crimes, were the topics of vigorous debate shocking to despotic ears; and the Diet was ordered to conform to the opinion of the Duke. Armed men surrounded their sittings—to exemplify the freedom of debate. The voice of remonstrance died away in their hall—or fell on the ears of laughing minions to whom alone the police gave tickets of admission. The presumption of the press was punished by a stringent and stifling censorship. The members of the Diet who dared to complain of their wrongs were denounced as turbulent, and excluded by violence from the sittings. The publicity of their deliberations was arbitrarily taken away. Indignities led to conspiracies; and conspiracies to spies—who swarmed through the land noting every chance word, and denouncing the best and noblest of the nation: and close on their heels trode the police with arbitrary searches, illegal arrests, unexplained and indefinite imprisonments, secret and summary executions. The constitution was a word, a name, a mockery, to the tools of despotism—who gnashed at the legal restraint on their outrages, denounced the constitution as an impediment to the administration of government and the course of justice, and elevated to the dignity of principle of their policy the maxim—that "the Grand Duke is the best constitution."

The countrymen of Kosciusko thought war better than that peace—death better than that life. A wide spread rebellion was disconcerted by the sudden death of Alexander. The elevation of Nicholas doubled the necessity for one. The revolt at St. Petersburg was extinguished in some of the best blood of Russia and of Poland. But the blood of the martyrs was the seed of liberty. New men and new plans filled the places of the departed. The time for the final blow was fixed by the approaching war against France and the consequent removal of the Polish army. A temporary excitement hastened the outbreak which, appointed for December the 10th, occurred on the 29th of November.

On that night Constantine was expelled from the capital of Poland.

Chlopicki was by acclamation named dictator. He sought safety in negotiation, in delay, in deputations, in conditions. Two precious months fled unimproved. He refused to rouse the great Polish Provinces—till masses of Russian troops were encamped in their midst. He suppressed by force the popular violence which broke out on the reception of the Imperial proclamation: and even then refused to abandon his temporizing policy. He feared by energy to get beyond the reach of reconciliation: and did not venture to hope for success. He finally was compelled to renounce the dictatorship; and Prince Czartoriski and Radzevil divided between them the civil and military departments.

While Chlopicki negotiated, Nicholas armed. The delegates returned with the peremptory demand of submission. The Diet considered this the close of the door of reconciliation. Energetic measures for defense were taken. The proposal was made to depose the house of Romanoff: but men shrank from that irrevocable step. One of the deputies, Jesierski, repeated the insolent words of Nicholas, scratched on the margin of their memorial: "Je suis roi de Pologne, *je la roulerai.* Le premier coup de canon tiré par les Polonais anéantira la Pologne." That dispelled every doubt; they flung away the deadly hope of conciliation; declared the deposition of the Czar, and grasped with vigorous hand the sword as their only safety.

The temporizing policy of Chlopicki inspired Nicholas with hopes of easy success. His tone was lofty and dictatorial while Poland deliberated. He turned pale before her final resolution. He had supposed her troubles could only impede his march to the theatre of western war, postpone for a month the opening of the campaign, and transfer the scene of operations from the Rhine to the Elbe. Such was Diebitsch's boastful menace to the Polish deputies. But the stern face of her patriot armies boded more than a military brush. Discipline, and arms, and devotion, are dangerous elements to encounter. Success however certain must be bought dearly, with blood, and treasure, and time—and triumph would leave deep scars on the Empire and in the minds of his subjects. He would now have negotiated. He could not retreat without ruin. An energetic remonstrance, backed by military force, in the name of France or of England, could have secured all the Poles had demanded, saved the integrity of the treaty of Vienna, and preserved Poland from annihilation. Neither the spirit, nor the will, nor the policy, nor the statesman's prescience existed in either. The hearts of the people were right, and beat with fervid hope for their suffering fellows. The rulers and cabinets of England and France were blind and dull with selfish aspirations and dynastic ambition.

Nicholas had promptly recalled his ambassador from the Court of France, upon the revolution. He had scornfully repelled the cringing advances of Louis Philippe. He had prepared to war upon his throne in behalf of his rival, and in combination with Prussia. These facts were communicated to Louis Philippe in December by the Polish government, with the official correspondence of the Russian government by which they were proved. He knew that the Polish revolution was the sole impediment to an immediate attack; that its close would leave him exposed to the imminent danger of a Russian invasion. A bold policy could have saved him for the time, and seated him firmly on the throne and in the affections of the people of France. The people stormed the chambers and the King with petitions for Poland, and for armed intervention. They burned with hatred of Russian despotism and were eager to retaliate the indignities of their invasion. The Poles were destined for the vanguard of the invasion of France. They wheeled upon their sovereign, and became the vanguard of France against her deadliest foe: and, though Louis Philippe knew that their army was the sole barrier between his throne and Russian invasion, he repressed the ardor of his people by his calculating, selfish and obsequious policy. He preferred to reign by the favor of despots, rather than to dictate the law to them in the name of his people. He curried favor with Nicholas by allowing him to designate the French minister he would accept. Mortemart was charged by all means to secure the favor of the Czar. Poland was left to her fate, that Louis might reign by the leave of Nicholas; and her envoys were mocked by the fruitless sympathies and timid intercession, which Mortemart was charged to whisper with prudent reserve in the imperial ear. A cowardly wisdom threw away the hopes of Europe, and left a noble and devoted people to the tender mercies of the Tartar horde. England's heart was fat with the good things of the world, and too gross to beat in sympathy with Polish sufferings. She had commercial treaties and good understanding with the Emperor; and her mercantile views could not be seduced even where generosity was the highest policy. She did not, or would not see, that the battle of Constantinople could be fought on the plains of Poland. She contented herself with debating the reform bill, and keeping France out of Belgium—while Russia broke down the barriers of the treaty of Vienna, and grasped the power which England had at the Congress avowed her readiness to wrest from him by arms.

Deserted by mankind, this heroic people trusted in God, their sword, and their cause. With the military details of that stupendous conflict, whose varying events exalted with hope or wrung with agony the heart of Christendom for the fate of her earliest defender—I cannot now deal. I only draw the lesson which all history confirms. Poland fell—because her patriots trusted in moderation—because while free nations sympathized, despotism armed—and while they protested, despotism struck.

Unequal as were the numbers of the parties, courage and devotion more than overbalanced the disparity. Chlopicki's delays had driven Poland to the defensive, deprived her of the aid of the northern provinces, and made her soil the seat of war. Diebitsch crossed the frontier with treble numbers, fulminating boastful proclamations and furious threats, in February. Ere its close, on the plains of Grochow, the Poles with a third of his numbers scattered his army and drove him across the frontiers. Such is the power of liberty from Marathon to Sarmatia.

With reinforced power again, in March, Diebitsch renewed the struggle, with scarce better success; the confines of the Kingdom were the scene of war; and the provinces were beginning to be restless spectators of the struggle.

The stern and stubborn defense of her people raised up for Poland a strange defender—from a strange and unexpected quarter. One of the Holy Allies began to fear the fraternal hug of his northern brother. Austria had stood ready to cross the road of Russia to Constantinople. Prince Metternich saw—what England did not—that the inevitable battle had better be decided in Poland. He rejoiced at the unexpected opportunity of creating, in the Kingdom of independent Poland, a real and effectual barrier against the threatening ascendancy of Russia. He could not breathe freely within the comprehensive embraces of Russia, sweeping from Gallicia to the mouths of the Danube, in acknowledged sovereignty; and extending her control with an indefinite authority over the Danubian principalities to the passage of the river from Hungary. He shuddered beneath the chill shadow of Russian protection—more than he trembled before the fiery spirit of the revolution. Metternich saw in the battles of February and March the elements of a power equal to the brunt of a Russian onset. Russia had sacrificed her horror of revolution to her rapacity, and supported the

Greeks that she might weaken the Turk. Prince Metternich profited by the example he had opposed, and retaliated on Nicholas his insidious policy. He devised a scheme to weaken the Czar by succoring the Pole: and to relieve the Austrian Empire from the pressure of the Colossus of the north by the creation of a firm support. He acted cautiously, circumspectly—with a sharp look to a possible failure and a keen sense of the dangers of discovery. He suggested to the Polish government, that his master was not disinclined to aid in the establishment of Polish independence, under an Austrian Prince, with Gallicia to augment his territory—if France and England would concur in the proposal. Louis Philippe did not repulse, but he did not accept the Austrian overture. He declined to entertain it unless it met the favor of England. Palmerston, the liberal and the fighting minister, then guided the foreign affairs of England—but alas! in a different spirit from that of Canning. His eye could see no foe but France whose aggrandizement could threaten England. His soul was absorbed in preventing France from acquiring a part of Belgium. He was tangled in the inextricable mesh of the London conferences. He could aspire to nothing beyond elevating one of the house of Saxe Coburg to the Belgian throne.

Before so momentous an object, the cries of suffering Poland, the rights of constitutional government, the aggrandizement of Russia, the balance of power of Europe, the integrity of the treaties of Vienna—were as dust in the balance. Besides—the best understanding existed between His Majesty of

England and His Majesty of all the Russias. These tender ties he could not lacerate in any sentimental cause of human suffering or human liberty. Belgium, supposing herself safe when her King was expelled, had fallen among thieves who strove by guile to filch her freedom. A treaty of eighteen articles embodied the obnoxious conditions on which her independence would be tolerated by the London Conference. The assembly at Brussels sturdily repelled them as humiliating and insolent. But they had a fellow feeling for their suffering brethren of Poland, and were willing to sacrifice something for their success. It was intimated that a favorable consideration of the Polish case might reconcile the Brussels Assembly to the "eighteen articles;" and Palmerston refusing a formal engagement, yet dropped hints which might mislead but could not bind, that the acceptance of the "eighteen articles" would be a great service to Poland and her cause: and Talleyrand promised in that event to renew the overtures to the British Cabinet. The suggestion produced the acceptance of the articles; but the note of Talleyrand met with a refusal of polished insolence from Palmerston; and Metternich and Louis Philippe hastened to abandon a project which might call down on them the indignation of their master, if discovered. The benefit to Poland was—the delay which precipitated her overthrow.

To this day, Poland, supplying by heroism the deficiencies of numbers, had more than maintained her cause. She had foiled the advance of the enemy on the right of the Vistula, and defied his approach to the fortress of Praga. Cholera or poison had removed Diebitsch. Paskewitch was rushing to fill his place and supply his losses with the fame and the army of the Asiatic frontier. He transferred his troops to the left bank of the Vistula in July, and leisurely prepared without molestation for the final conflict. An inexplicable paralysis had seized the Polish Dictator. Skrzynecki lay on his arms for two fatal months—deaf to the cries for battle which greeted his appearance in the camp, and covered by suspicions of the most disheartening character. He failed to assail the Russian army in its dangerous and difficult movement round Modlin as a centre—when a decisive blow could have finished the contest—or wrested tolerable terms from the Czar. The right bank of the Vistula was stripped of the enemy and the road to the Provinces was open and unguarded. A simple march would have called to his standard thousands of eager recruits and doubled his efficient force. Yet he rested in vile repose, till his people's spirit rusted, till the foe advanced to the shock, and the fires of death were lighted on the last battle field of Poland.

Skrzynecki temporized till he was hemmed in by overwhelming forces, and till the peremptory order of the Diet forced him to resume operations. He was waiting the result of the negotiations in London, which Lord Palmerston's ambiguous words had taught the Polish envoy to anticipate; and which he had induced Skrzynecki to rely on. The messenger was sent with the knowledge, at the expense, and on the suggestion of the Cabinet of Louis Philippe,—to relax the energies and suspend the activity of the Poles with the vain hopes of negotiations and good terms.

Skrzynecki did not know that Cabinets are a vain trust for freedom; that desperation is the only safety for those who draw the sword against a despot; that moderation had ruined Spain and must ruin Poland; that atonement was impossible. To fight and to die—the example of Thermopylæ, and the immortality of fame—was all that was left them. The day of grace was gone. The day of victory was passed. Nemesis and despair alone ruled the hour. Dembinski's immortal retreat to the field of battle cast into the shade that of Xenophon's ten thousand; and heroes of more than human mould enacted, beneath the battlements of Warsaw, the deeds without the fortune of Marathon. Peace be with their ashes—immortality to their names!!

The third battle of light and darkness was closed. Grim despotism glared over the land. English indifference contented itself with the Czar's assurances that he would restore the constitution, preserve the nationality, and guarantee the rights of the Poles. The victory obliterated the promises from the Imperial memory. He had tested the indifference of the Cabinets of Europe. If they would not aid the Poles in arms, they would scarcely renew the war for their constitution. Louis Philippe was on his good behaviour for his crown. Palmerston confessed the outrage, but considered the matter not important enough to call for English intervention. Nicholas acted on these dispositions. In February 1832—having trampled out the last spark of resistance—his edict of abrogation appeared. He reversed the political blunder of Alexander. He reduced Poland to a province of the Empire, annulled the constitution he had so recently but so reluctantly sworn to observe, dispersed the Polish soldiers throughout the Russian army, and ploughed up the very foundations of her nationality of a thousand years, consecrated by heroic deeds in the cause of Christianity and of civilized Europe—whose Kings looked on her ruin with tearless indifference.

The axe, the gibbet, the knout, the mines, the dungeon,—the trains of fainting pilgrims toiling to Siberia—the blood and smoke of ravaged cities guilty of the sin of liberty—why mention these things in the land of "social order," beneath the paternal sway of the inexorable enemy of "revolutionary madness?"

It is difficult to estimate the enormity of this compound of cowardice, folly, and crime.

All Europe was a party to the treaty which stipulated for the constitution. No one contemplated a grant revokable at will. Even despots admit in theory the validity of a treaty with a foreign power—whatever scruples they may entertain as to the possibility of binding their sovereign freedom by charters to their people—and Russia had led the van of the crusade on liberty with the cry of the sacredness of treaties on her lips. Yet no one lifted voice or hand to prevent or to punish this gross invasion at once of the rights of nations, the obligations of a treaty, and the sanctity of an oath—though, being only a royal oath, it must be taken with many grains of allowance, and was hardly worth a war.

The balance of power of Europe was at stake. The proposition of Austria was a simple and effectual curb to the menacing aggrandizement of Russia, and recommended by every consideration of humanity and of policy. The Poles alone had more than sustained the weight of their enemy; and before the proposed intervention, Russia must have succumbed almost without a struggle. So urgent were the circumstances, that one of the leaders of the Holy Alliance made the proposal and offered to contribute a province to the Kingdom. Yet England and France—the two free powers of Europe, alone interested in the maintenance of constitutional liberty,—refused their countenance, and left their powerful natural ally to sink unaided beneath the stabs of their common enemy.

The fall of Poland settled the results of the revolutions of 1830. Belgium was severed from Holland—but passed under the surveillance of the Holy Allies stripped of the attributes of sovereignty, and only tolerated under bonds for good behaviour. Restless and feverish Italy sprang to her feet—but her despicable princes stretched out supplicating hands to Austria for help they could not afford themselves; and her bayonets prostrated the revolution ere it was erect.—Again order reigned in Europe amid the silence of the grave, unbroken save by the groan of the captive in his cell—the muttered curse of the oppressed who cast his agonizing glance to heaven for the aid mankind refused. The long and weary years dragged on till the cup of wrath was again full to overflowing.

The people of France and England were on fire to rush to the aid of Poland. But the history of the last thirty years has been that of a combination of Kings against the people; and Poland is only one of many victims of the conspiracy. Terrible indignation burst out in England at the melancholy sound of her funeral dirge. Tears, and sadness, and the silence of the plague, reigned over Paris. The theatres, the shops, the marts of commerce were deserted. The people forgot their own misery in the fall of Warsaw. They were as the people of Athens on that evening when the occupation of Elatea was announced—or when the fugitives of Choeronea entered the city. It was as if another Waterloo overwhelmed them with its agony. Yet the Kings were placid, smiling, quiet and unconcerned—the ministers parried with a joke or a sophism the interpellations of Parliament and the Chambers. England was absorbed in her merchandise. Louis Philippe was nursing his infant crown. Nicholas improved the opportunity of their indifference to rid himself of a thorn in the side, and his frontier of a dangerous quicksand. He firmly planted his foot on what before was a treacherous bog—and, in the attitude of advance, stood ready to assert by diplomacy or by arms his newly founded supremacy in Europe.

His eye was fixed on Louis Philippe—who quailed beneath its glance—and deprecated its ire. He did his best to deserve his pardon for the presumption of wearing a crown. The price for his toleration was, the bridling of the revolution. Perhaps the Autocrat was softened by his abandonment of Poland. Perhaps he thought the cost of deposing him would exceed the benefit. He admired his adroit management of the factions. For the eighteen years of Louis Philippe's inglorious reign—France ceased to be felt as a power in Europe. So disgusted were her people with his rule, that none were found to lift a hand in defense of him or his dynasty. In spite of his skillful jockeyism so insecure was his seat that he tumbled at the first jostle—like a child from a wild horse. He was pardoned because he was powerless for mischief, of a quiet and orderly disposition—took care of his family and left Nicholas to take care of the world—and withal made an excellent police constable for maniac France.

The humiliating reign of Louis Philippe was a long preparation for its violent close. The elder Bourbons were re-seated on the throne against the will of France. They signalized their triumph by a fraudulent charter which cheated the people out of the fruits of twenty years of revolution; and finding even its restraint intolerable, they drew down the national indignation by adding to perpetual disregard of its spirit the most despotic outrages againt its letter, and the rights and feelings of the nation. Louis Philippe assumed the vacant crown at the call of the leaders of the revolution of July. *The nation* was not consulted in his elevation. His rule was acquiesced in on the faith of the guarantee of names dear and venerable to the French people, and only in expectation that his government would exemplify the principles and breathe the spirit of those who had chosen him. He was regarded as the symbol of the national sovereignty—the personification of the people's right to control their own affairs. His crown was held by the tenure of conformity to this first principle of its origin.

France had reached conscious political life—when a revolution meant more than a personal preference or dislike for a ruler. It was not a mere designation of who should be her master; but of the principles which should control her executive in wielding her power. She could tolerate no king who refused to abide by this law.

There are two clearly defined states of political life—connected by a transition period of indefinite duration—and passing into one another through imperceptible shades. The one is before the nation have learned to have a will of their own on all public affairs;—their rulers are then the symbols of sovereignty; their will is that of the people; and absolute monarchy is its natural form. The other is the offspring of advancing intelligence—when the people have learned to hold definite opinions on the conduct of affairs;—this is the period of legal popular constitutional government; and none other is possible—except at the point of the bayonet. The transition period of balanced light and darkness is the equinox of the national cycle—the region of stormy revolutions, which may dissolve society into anarchy, or prostrate it at the feet of despotism.

France had reached the day of political maturity when Louis Philippe accepted the crown, forfeited by Charles for violation of the fundamental law according to which alone kingly power was possible. He held it on condition of conforming to that principle. It involved the necessity of governing by ministers, whose policy should follow the popular will as expressed by the votes of the Chambers—regardless of that of the King. This is the fundamental condition of the English monarchy, which, however it may strive to modify, never hesitates to obey the will of the people when once declared. To the existence of this system, a parliament accurately representing the will of the nation and not of a class is absolutely essential. At best, it is a sorry contrivance to reconcile with an immovable head the fluctuating tides of popular feeling. It is intended indirectly to attain the end of our elections—periodically expressing in an authentic form the will of the people on the conduct of their affairs. It was the misfortune or the sin of Louis Philippe that his reign was one unbroken violation of every condition on which his power rested.

He was the symbol of the people's sovereignty, invested with their power, to do their will, for their benefit. He wielded that power to do his own will, for the consolidation of his dynasty. His fault was, the perversion of the powers of his high trust to selfish ends. His blunder was in supposing the best means of attaining even those ends lay in a policy which, *at home*, stifled every popular feeling, refused every concession, and punished by military execution or judicial proscription the ebullitions of discontent springing from disappointment—and *abroad*, bought peace at the cost of national humiliation, by cringing before every power which presented the alternative of concession or of war. His system was peace *abroad*—and war *at home.*

The revolution of July was made by the people: yet their voice was never heard in their legislative halls. They were as powerless under the younger as under the elder Bourbons. The charter of Louis XVIII. confined the right of suffrage to persons assessed with three hundred francs in taxes. The charter of the revolution of July reduced the qualification to two hundred and forty francs. The value of the revolution to the people was sixty francs in the qualifications for voting. The revolution conferred on two hundred thousand persons alone, out of thirty-five millions, the right of electing the Chamber of Deputies, charged with expressing the legislative will of France, and forming, in the political machine, the index for the regulation of the executive conduct.

The exorbitant greediness of the upstart royalty disgusted the people. They remembered that a million and a half of francs had adequately remunerated the three consuls—whose head was the conqueror of Italy. They could not forget that the legitimate Bourbons were content with the moderate sum of four millions and a half. They cried out against the King of the barricades and of the bourgeoisie who demanded over twenty millions—which the complaisant chamber granted within a year of the revolution. They were continually scandalized by bickerings about allowances, claims for dotation, for apanage, for family establishments for the King's numerous progeny at the expense of the nation. The press spoke the popular disgust: and the King pursued the editors with all the harshness of legal prosecutions armed with government power, with domiciliary visits and arbitrary arrests and seizures, which would have roused the phlegmatic spirit of the Briton to rebellion.

That insurrections should accompany the change of dynasty was to be expected. The continuance of discontent after the acquiescence of the people accuses the faith and the competency of the government. The press teemed with fierce denunciations of the retrogressive tendencies, and the harsh and arbitrary acts of the King. He smote the accuser on the mouth, for a charge he could not deny. The sale and distribution of pamphlets through the streets were subjected to the license of the police; and Paris was stung to madness by the bloody and indiscriminate vengeance taken on a peaceable crowd assembled to procure them. The right of association is essential to liberty: and the public discontent had covered France with wide-spread organizations to maintain the rights of the people against the daily encroachments of the King. He sharpened the existing laws against them, abolished the distinction between periodical and occasional assemblies, leveled the same punishment against the leaders and the led, and transferred the cognizance of the accusation from the jury to the Court, in direct violation of the constitution. The people answered by the insurrections of 1834, which wrapped the Kingdom in flames—and which the King is accused of having fomented for the benefit of suppressing them. The brutality of the execution lends countenance to the suggestion. Irregular and ill-organized insurrections flamed up without concert, and were extinguished in detail. Lyons was the centre and the leader: her punishment left her in blood and ruins. Paris was the scene of military executions more barbarous than any which the revolutionary republic visited on its foes. The Rue Transnonain is as eternally infamous as the republican baptisms of the Loire. The occasion was eagerly seized by the King to wrest from the national guards of the disturbed districts and cities their arms—whose only danger lay in his own misrule. Arbitrary imprisonments and searches, long confinements on suspicion without examination, harsh treatment and reckless cruelties characterized the governmental proceedings under pretext of suppressing or punishing the insurrections. The iron sank deep into the soul of the French people. The assassin's hand was armed again—and furnished the pretext for the arbitrary laws of September 1835—which placed the liberty of the press and of the subject at the mercy of the King. The barriers of formality were swept away in prosecutions for rebellion, at the will of the prosecutor: only seven jurors were required to concur for conviction: and every publication against the person of the King or *the principles of the government* subjected the offender to be punished by heavy fines and severe imprisonment!!

The bloody lesson of 1834 taught the people the wisdom of patience. They waited till the accumulated grievances should press the nation into one party.

The King diligently pursued his advantages, relentlessly wielded his legalized despotism, and eked out its deficiencies by corruption or by usurpation as the case required. The Chamber of Peers, the Courts, even the Deputies were his willing supporters. The rest of his reign was a war against the press, a series of prosecutions against freedom of thought, a struggle against the ever increasing demand for legislative reform. The press denounced the outrages of the King. He replied by state prosecutions. The country got on the side of the persecuted editors; and jurors refused to find verdicts against them. The jury lists were tampered with—to secure *enlightened jurors.* Changes of venue evaded foreseen difficulties, and secured facile triumphs in well disposed districts. Obsequious Courts supplied the deficiencies of juries, and moulded the law to the exigencies of the case. They applied to prosecutions for publications against public officers the rule of private libels; and in the face of the words of the law forbad the *truth* to be pleaded in defense. The new assessments roused the passions and provoked resistance; the press associated itself in the defense. Prosecutions were repeatedly thrown out. The King and his ministers were mad against the editors. The Chamber of Peers was invoked. The attempt on the life of the Duc d'Nemours was attempted to be fastened on Dupoty, the editor of the Journal du Peuple. He was prosecuted as an accomplice—that the blow might discredit the press. The evidence failed—yet the chamber condemned him for "complicite moral." French ingenuity left the clumsy contrivance of constructive treason far in the back ground. Dupoty was condemned—not because he had known or encouraged either the *crime* or the *criminal*—but because the criminal had read his *paper*, and his paper tended to defend the crime. Such madness betokens the end of dynasties.

The same spirit presided at the suppression of the Polish anniversaries—of the reform banquets—of every outward expression of political feeling, or of national and popular memories. Petitions for electoral reform for eight years in vain poured in on the King and the Chambers. The one hundred and sixty-one officials in the Chambers, the officials swarming through the country out-numbering the voters, and the close corporation of the Chambers themselves sympathized with the fears, the hostility, the contempt of the King in regard to the people and popular government; and the petitions were scornfully rejected At last patience was exhausted—the burthens and increasing deficiencies of the revenue in time of peace exceeded the cost of the wars of Napoleon—and the disgust of the people left the King without support. Surrounded by his cherished army, and his gigantic fortifications, he was tumbled from his throne by a Parisian mob! Some people call this an accident. I call it an inevitable, long prepared, and richly deserved *fatality*.

Throughout his ignoble reign, France was the sport and mock of continental Europe; for Louis Philippe preferred his crown to his country, and he placed his safety in conciliating the contempt and quieting the fears of his legitimate neighbors.

The most signal instance of his folly and cowardice was the abandonment of Poland—to buy the favor or the toleration of Nicholas. He assisted at the tangled intrigues of the London conferences to deprive Belgium of the fruits of her revolution, and France of the influence she could have won by supporting her. He coveted the throne tendered to his son—for it lay in the line of all his aspirations; yet he hastened to renounce it before the protest of England, in favor of one of England's creatures; and France saw her own government a party to territorial arrangements which were aimed at her most cherished aspirations when about to be accomplished—without a protest or even a murmur.

The absolute powers had commended to the Pope's consideration the propriety of yielding certain reforms and concessions to gratify and quiet his people and ensure the repose of Italy. His Holiness clung to his infallibility, and refused to stultify his government by a change. His people sought redress in insurrections, and the trembling Priest besought secular aid. The people of free France were scandalized to see the minister of Louis Philippe among the first to assure His Holiness of their aid to bring his rebellious subjects to unconditional submission. Austria anticipated him by the occupation of Bologna; and Louis Philippe, in an ecstasy of jealousy, hastened to seize on the quiet and unoffending Ancona by way of innocent and safe bravado.

The throne of Spain was disputed between a constitutional Queen and a legitimate pretender. The success of the latter would be a thorn in the crown of Louis and in the side of France. He begged a subordinate place in the triple alliance of Spain, Portugal, and England, concluded behind his back, for the exclusion of the pretender. He posted an army of fifty thousand men at the Pyrenees; yet, in spite of his minister's advice, he repelled two earnest solicitations of both England and the Spanish Queen for help in the critical hour of the contest. He was ambitious of continental recognition; he dared not, for the interest of France, fire a gun against a legitimate pretender.

Switzerland—the natural ally and impregnable defense of France—was an inconvenient refuge for the persecuted victims of Austrian tyranny. Metternich instigated Louis Philippe to bully the people who protected his own exile, for extending similar hospitality to others. The Duc d'Orleans was suing for the hand of an Austrian princess; and Louis Philippe hastened to destroy the influence of France in Switzerland, by peremptorily demanding the exclusion of the political refugees, under a threat of armed intervention. When he was fully embroiled, Metternich had no hesitation in finding the match too unequal between a Prince of the July revolution and the daughter of a hundred Cæsars.

The progress of Mehemet Ali's arms threatened the Ottoman Empire on one side, as much as Russia menaced it on the other. England was interested in the control of the Isthmus of Suez; Russia, that no body else should seize Constantinople; France, that her ally, the Viceroy of Egypt, should consolidate a power over which her influence predominated.

They were all parties to negotiations in London. With that studied contempt which Louis Philippe's peaceable disposition had so often provoked, Palmerston and Nicholas announced the secret conclusion of a treaty from which France was excluded—for the purpose of imposing terms on the ambitious Pasha, to be enforced by arms if not acquiesced in. Louis Philippe was furious at the insult. He swore vengeance, and began to arm. All France rang with warlike preparation. Her people were on fire to punish English and Russian insolence, and support the cause of the Pasha. Louis Philippe seized the opportunity, to increase his army of suppression, and to incarcerate the capital of France by fortifications for the control of the populace. In the midst of his preparations, they were treated as a sham by the Allies—and Beyrout was bombarded. What all had anticipated came to pass. The French fleet was hastily withdrawn to Toulon—for fear its aid might be invoked by the Viceroy. The insult was digested. Louis contented himself with his fortifications—and acquiesced in the settlement Russia and England had agreed on.

So spiritless and powerless was his rule, that he paid the United States indemnity under the pending threat of President Jackson; and it was the vigorous and resolute rejection of the treaty for the right of search by this country, which drove him, by the storm of popular indignation, to refuse the name of France to its ratification. He concluded the long drama of selfish aggrandizement at the expense of the honor and dignity of France, by consummating the Spanish

20

marriages. He dared the risk of universal war for the advancement of his house, at the expense of France--when before, against her manifest interest and loudly expressed will, he had compromised her dignity and destroyed her influence by clinging to peace lest he might endanger his throne. Such a reign, tyrannical within and cowardly without, found a fit termination in a street fight—so destitute of friends that none was found to do battle for the dishonored crown. Europe had wondered at the firmness of his seat on a throne hitherto shaken by revolutions; and its astonishment was unspeakable at such a fall. But his repose was—the balance on the tight rope—wonderful only because it was precarious and difficult to maintain—yet such that a touch of a child could overthrow it.

The restoration of the ashes of Napoleon to the bosom of France was his only popular act; and the enthusiasm it excited was the bitterest sarcasm on a reign which studiously shunned the glories of the Empire.

Italy and Spain fell before the armed assaults of the Holy Allies of the North. The policy of the reign of Louis Philippe was the offspring of the terror they inspired. Nicholas despised the revolutionary royalty of Louis; but he met a stumbling block in the fiery Poles; and his oriental ambition attracted him to easier and more fruitful fields. But he never more than tolerated the upstart crown of the revolution of July; and he always nourished the hope of one day resuming the cross of the Holy Alliance against infidel and rebellious France—to tame her factions by the sword.

Louis Philippe trembled before his threat, was too pusillanimous to repel it by an appeal to the spirit of his nation, and bowed the haughty head of France before the Muscovite,—for leave to wear his crown, to perpetuate his dynasty, to walk about a shadowy unsubstantial semblance of a King among the real Powers of Europe. For this poor privilege, he stooped to be the jailer of his people, and chained the terrible spirit of France, before whose untrammeled might his foes would have fled.

Yet he could not hide a blush at the contrast between his position and his conduct. His wounded vanity took refuge from the humiliations of the present in the recollection of his illustrious descent: and found strange consolations for the contempt of Nicholas in the oft repeated soliloquy: "Am not I the grandson of Louis XIV?" One would have supposed his eye would have turned away from the glories of the Grand Monarque, which must have recalled the fact that he was a slave on that throne where his grandfather was the arbiter of Europe.

His faith was equal to his spirit. The King of the Barricades—the sworn monarch of a constitutional realm—spoke contemptuously of the people who honored him, and of the law he swore to observe and tried to annul. "Constitutions"—he said—"are the malady of the day. It will pass—but one must know how to treat it. The continental Kings shrink from it with terror—but as for me—I treat it after the homœpathic method, and that answers my purpose." He meant to say:—"The Kings of the continent destroy liberty with the sword—I, by the safer and surer method of slow and deadly poison." He humbly claimed for himself the subordinate character of the fox—and left the part of the lion to his masters.

His long reign of eighteen years was a painful preparation for the era of revolutions.

SECTION IV.

THE REVOLT OF EUROPE IN 1848

AGAINST THE

HOLY CONSPIRATORS.

GERMANY.

THE REVOLT OF EUROPE IN 1848

AGAINST THE

HOLY CONSPIRATORS.

GERMANY.

DURING the whole reign of Louis Philippe the fear of the Holy Allies controlled the destiny of France. Before them her proud spirit was abased—till the cup of her indignation was full against the man who wore and disgraced her crown; and then she rose and shook him off.

The boasted power of Louis Philippe vanished like the morning cloud—dissolving into thin air without a flash of lightning or a roll of thunder to announce its departure. It was not even honored with a military burial—but fled before the hoots of a mob and the terrors of an evil conscience to hide itself in a dishonorable grave.

France—relieved from the incubus—stood erect in her majesty and power—gigantic in her proportions—terrible in the glance of liberty—and hurling defiance at the powers who had dared to insult the hour of her humiliation. All Europe shook at the sound of her voice. It was the trumpet of the resurrection of imprisoned liberty. The giant lay beneath the mountain weights imposed on him at the great overthrow. From time to time weary of his constraint and panting beneath his burthen, his restlessness had moved kingdoms from their bases and shaken eldest dynasties. The time of his liberation now seemed fully come; and as he turned heavily in act to rise, the earthquake of 1848 passed along. Every monarchy in Europe shook to its foundations; and from the seven hills of Papal Rome to the city of the Great Frederick, and from the Bay of Biscay to the Vistula, not a throne was left erect. Europe was covered with the ruins of her political edifices. The prison doors were shaken open and the captives were free. Their shackles were off, and their Kings were cringing in humble supplication before the people they had despised, insulted and oppressed.

The signs of the times might have been read on the dial of the Vatican. Pius IX. the successor of Gregory, represented the progress of fifty years; and his concessions to the spirit of the age were the offspring of an urgent necessity. But like Louis XVI. he had evoked a spirit which he could not control, and whose power would not be stayed at the bounds he prescribed. Charles Albert had oscillated again to the side of freedom, and granted his subjects a fair constitution. The successor of Frederick the Great, after alternately spurring to madness and curbing to submission his patient people, had disguised his absolute power beneath the shadowy forms of constitutional rule. These things prepared the minds of the people for a step in advance; and the overthrow of Louis Philippe was the signal for the march.

The rising of the people, the agitation of mind, the looking for of great events, were every where to be seen. In France only was the revolution absolute master of the field, and securely enthroned in power. Every where else the people forbore to exact from their Princes the extreme penalty of their iniquities; and they were left at the head of affairs armed with the powers of Government, which they prostituted to the overthrow of the people who mercifully spared their hour of weakness. The conflict began in guile, was waged under artful disguises by diplomacy, and was closed by the sword. Europe was one great battle-field where strove for the mastery the tyrants and the people. The battle swayed with various fortune on many fields. It was decided by a sudden blow in a distant and obscure corner of Europe. But the result of the movement depended on the success of the people of Germany; and that was wrapped up in the cause of Hungary. Success here gave the key to the field of Europe; and failure here rendered success on other points matter of detail determining nothing. For the contest was between the People and the Kings. Without the arm of Austria, Italy could control her petty despots, and Germany could realize her longings for substantial unity. The independence of Hungary would have paralyzed the arm of Austria for purposes of mischief; and, with United Germany under a free constitution, would have opposed an impenetrable barrier to the arms and influence of Russia; while their proximity and example would have assailed her power in its citadel, by weakening the hold of despotism in the minds of her people. To overthrow Hungary was therefore the shortest and safest method of arresting the progress of the revolution. To have assailed Prussia would have armed all Germany; and a million of bayonets would in a month have bristled on the frontiers. Russia did not care to waste her powder nor to endanger her success. She therefore, under cover of the Austrian invitation, entered Hungary as the ally of a German Power. The intervention was not felt as an assault on the people of Germany; her Kings could safely close their eyes to a campaign whose success must be for their advantage; and, by their connivance and the apathy of their people, the contest was settled before they were conscious it had opened. The game was played with eminent skill; the faith of Kings, their royal oaths and right royal perjuries, the simple confidence of the people and the decisive argument of the bayonet, concessions and soft words in the hour of weakness, retractions and defiance in the hour of returning strength, are the elements of the game. Their application for the suppression of freedom is one of the most instructive as well as the saddest pages of history.

The result was ruinous to the rights of the people—and damning to the character of Kings.

The details of the simultaneous rising of the people of Germany in each of her thirty states would be only the tedious repetition of the same events varied by circumstances of place and person. From Berlin to Vienna, from Frankfort to Dresden, in every kingdom and principality, the people rose as one man, inspired by the pervading spirit of liberty, and urged by the resistless yearnings after that national union embodied in a national representative government without which all local reforms were useless. They strove in their several states for the rights which were at issue in our revolution: and as their only adequate guarantee, they were driven to contend at the same time for the great constitutional organization which we effected, in peace and quiet, ten years after the revolutionary storm had passed.

The demands of the people, spontaneously pouring from the hearts of millions scattered over the length and breadth of the land, so simultaneous as to preclude the supposition of concert, so uniform as to indicate the pervading extent and depth of the grievances to be remedied and of the conviction as to the proper remedy—were almost entirely free from the excesses of revolutionary violence or radical recklessness. They partook of the eminent moderation of the German character, and betokened a political maturity in the people which was the best assurance of their competency to wield the powers they claimed.

There were doubtless three parties. The conservative party clung tenaciously to the Metternich principle—"the existing order of things." The radicals stimulated with an unreal enthusiasm the republican spirit and blood-thirsty recklessness, without the courage and energy, or devotion and simplicity, of the school of Robespierre and Danton: but they were few, powerless, and insignificant, and always under the control of the Burgher guard—till the counter revolutionary tendencies of the governments sharpened their hostility into the madness of despair, and drove them into rebellion, which ended in disaster, and closed the scene of this memorable drama. The people of Germany,—they who demanded the rights of the nation and awed their rulers into submission,—were guilty of no such excesses. They were the great mass of the people—the sons of the men who rose in the war of liberation,—demanding the long deferred rewards of their valor. So universal was the upheaval, so lofty and threatening the wave which agitated Germany, so resistless the still might with which it lifted the thrones and dynasties of solidest mould and deepest foundation from their bases, that at once, almost without a collision of arms, certainly without more than enough to feel the weight and earnestness of the masses, Emperors, Kings, and petty Princes, at Vienna and Berlin not less than in Baden and Cassel, with one voice, but with various views, bowed their crowned heads before the majesty of the national will.

That will did not ask republican institutions, nor socialist theories, nor jacobin madness. It confined itself to the essential rights of free government, under monarchical forms, with the guaranties without which chartered concessions are only the will of the King for the moment. It demanded the freedom of the press from the shackles of the censor, and of peaceable association for the consideration of grievances—that the wishes of the people might find a voice and free consultation devise a remedy. The public administration of justice and the trial by jury were demanded—that the people might aid in administering the laws, and bring the judge before the bar of public opinion. The claim of a Burgher's guard is only the German form of the American right of the people to bear arms—the only guarantee that the right of self-government will be a reality—and to which the oath required of the army to the constitution was an essential addition. The people insisted on representative assemblies, on constitutional forms, on liberal suffrage, on religious freedom: but they never asked or imposed a condition inconsistent with the continuance of the royal power—they never denied any right fit to be held by a constitutional King. They left him a part of the Legislature, the whole of the executive power, and prerogatives more extensive than those of the Kings of England. These demands were made in a tone of firm and manly moderation: they were yielded every where—almost without hesitation—under the pressure of the universal demand.

But in addition to these essential powers and rights, every where the national aspirations after national union breathed not only fervent prayer, but spoke in tones of decided import. The people felt that no victory in the several states was safe so long as a close corporation of princes ruled the confederation, conspired against the liberties of the people, fulminated decrees inconsistent with the very shadow of constitutional government, and enforced them by the intervention of the armies of Austria. So long as the decree of 1832 interpreting and enforcing that of 1820 remained in force, constitutional government in any German State was an impossibility. Local victories were fruitless. Local concessions were powerless to limit the despotism of the prince. Those laws declared that the sovereign power must remain intact and undivided in the hands of the Prince—that the grant of taxes could not be made conditional on a redress of grievances—that the publication of legislative debates must be at the mercy of those sovereigns who governed so badly that the voice of free discussion was of ill example to their subjects. These things were dangerous to the monarchical system, and were to be suppressed by the federal power as inconsistent with the groundwork of the confederation—a Diet of Princes absolute and irresponsible. These laws had been stringently enforced to destroy the fruits of the popular victories won in Saxony, Hesse Cassel, and Hanover, under the inspiration of the French Revolution of 1830. The people felt the blow; and now sought to paralyse the arm which dealt it. They aspired to the blessings of a united popular government in lieu of the confederation of Princes. They wanted a guarantee of the rights of the people in place of the Princely conspiracy for their suppression. This demand was first and chief among the popular requisitions; and it was universally acquiesced in by the Princes.

The hopes of Germany were centred in the Frankfort Parliament and the confederated constitution it was charged to form. The success of the effort was to be decided at Berlin and Vienna. Victory or defeat followed the fate of the contest on these two decisive points. The rest of the field must follow them. The power of imperial Austria was debated on the plains of Hungary; and the vacillating resolution of the King of Prussia rose and fell as his ambitious hopes swayed to and fro in the trembling balance. The terrors of the Russian name and the weight of the Russian sword decided the fate of Germany.

The bloody day of Jena had thrown a pall over the glories of the Kingdom of Frederick and definitively shattered the hold of Prussia on the past. From that day she was nothing—but what she made herself in the war of liberation. Her power lay in her devotion to the cause of German progress, in opposition to the despotic conservatism of Austria. These two powers impersonate the spirits which for forty years contended for mastery in Germany. Both have been absolute monarchies, but Austria has boasted herself a consistent despotism. Prussia has professed liberal principles, made popular concessions, promised constitutional guaranties and cultivated her people to no small degree of political knowledge. Her King had gradually reluctantly and late added moderate political powers in the shape of Provincial Diets of very limited faculties. As if anticipating the storm, just before the outbreak of 1848, he conferred a charter and a United Diet on the people of his kingdom. The charter thinly veiled the retention of absolute power in the last resort by the King. It revealed how reluctantly Kings part with any prerogative; for the absolute power of the Prussian monarchs has always been moderated by their dependence on their people's favor, and by gratitude for their eminent sacrifices in two great national crises—the seven years war, and the war of liberation. They always claimed, yet feared to exercise otherwise than mildly, their absolute power. They weakened and undermined its influence by continual promises to abandon it, yet fretted and worried their people by continually deferred hopes. They seemed to value their power as a miser does his hoards—not for the use but for the possession, living in terror of the inevitable day of parting, yet eternally talking of his posthumous benefits and the day of distribution.

In this state the wave of revolution struck the vessel. The accomplished trifler who held the helm of Prussia, feeling himself powerless to oppose, aspired to lead the storm and convert its power into the means of his ambitious advancement. He flung overboard with free hand those weighty prerogatives it was dangerous to retain. The raging waters were covered with the glittering emblems of empire devoted to appease their voracity.

Tumultuous agitations broke out in Berlin on the 13th of March. An enormous meeting for reform was the occasion of a collision between the troops and the people. The King may have taken this mode of testing the temper of the people: but if he did the trial was satisfactory. The continued excitement and renewed collisions attested the depth and permanence of the feeling, and the King felt the import of the movement, assuaged the raging masses by ascribing the collision to accident, withdrew the obnoxious troops, bowed graceful acquiescence in the will of his faithful people, and set earnestly to work at once to gratify them—and advance himself. The imperial height sparkled in the distance, and with his eye fixed on it, constitutional concessions to his people sunk in value, and seemed cheap in exchange for future glories.

A week had satisfied his mind and nerved him to the final step: and on the 18th of March, the royal revolutionist issued his first proclamation. He lifted the censorship from the public voice. He created and armed the Burgher Guard as the protector of public order and popular liberty. The United Diet was summoned to provide for a National Assembly, commissioned to devise a constitution. "But above all," the King declared, "we demand that Germany be transformed from a confederation of states into one federal state,"—the precise change in our own condition from the confederation to the constitution, the source and security of our peace and greatness. He declared a federal constitution, based on popular representation, united by a single imperial constitutional head, defended by a national army, graced by a national flag, secured by a central tribunal of ultimate resort, and enriched by the free flow of commerce and community of citizenship—to be the indispensable condition of their power and freedom, the imperative demand of the people and of the age. He pledged himself to strive for its attainment.

It required no second sight to see that the inspiration of the King was quite as much the offspring of his ambition, as of any deference for the will or welfare of the nation. On the 21st of March, the successor of Frederick the Great, decorated with the tri-colored German flag, paraded on horseback the streets of his capital, and, pausing beneath the statue of his illustrious ancestor, inaugurated by his solemn words in the hearing of his people the restoration of the Holy Empire. While he declared the colors he wore not his own and that he would usurp nothing, he did not fail to declare his belief that the hearts of the Princes yearned toward him and the will of the nation supported him; and the royal ordinance, addressed to the German Nation, announced—that Frederick William IV. had taken the lead of the German Nation, and invoked the blessings of Providence "on our constitutional Prince, the leader of the German people, the new King of free and regenerate Germany."

If, then, the people demanded a central government, it was the King who assumed the lead in the attempt to secure it. Yet his course was a series of blunders and contradictions, of liberal acts and violent retractions, of bold steps in advance followed by humiliating retreats and pitiable weaknesses. His nerves failed him in the decisive hour, and Germany remains as she was—divided, powerless and dishonored.

The National Assembly met on the 22d of May. It was chosen under a law proposed by the King, adopted by the United Diet which he had created, and formally approved by him. It existed under a law sanctioned by all the known powers of the state. It was elected by the vast majority of the people. If this assembly did not embody, with the King, the sovereignty of the state, no assembly can be any thing more than a consultative commission, nor have any more permanent tenure than the royal pleasure.

The King greeted the assembly at its opening as one charged by the general election of the people to unite with him in making a constitution destined to create an era in Prussia and Germany; and expressed his confidence that they would strive at once to secure the people a large share in the affairs of state, and to place the rights of his family on a sure foundation. The assembly do not appear to have been induced to depart from either of these high purposes, either by the seductions of popular inclination, or the terrors of the Berlin mob,—which occasionally assumed an unruly tone, but never obtained the mastery of the assembly. They freely discussed the constitutional plan submitted by the government, and they were inclined to alter some of its provisions; but they did not deviate into jacobinical excesses, nor in any manner impair the just security of the crown; and surely it was not supposed that this formal assembly had received the sanction of the people, that they might in turn accept without discussion such law as the monarch might dictate. The conduct of the King is merely another illustration of the tenacious grasp of royal hands on despotic power. Frederick was willing to concede a constitution, but he rebelled at its logical consequences, and sought pretexts in the turbulence of the revolutionary mob to usurp his original authority. The first serious outbreak, on the 16th of June, was occasioned by the conciliatory resolution of the Assembly, that the events of March were not a revolution but a transaction between the King and the people; but that was directed against the Assembly, and was promptly suppressed by the Burghers' Guard. From this point the re-actionary tendency of the King and his councillors is sufficiently manifest. The pretext was the popular violence, not of the Assembly, but directed against it. The ministry proposed and the assembly rejected an increase of the military force. It was apparent that a spirit of hostility to them was being encouraged in the army; and they, on the 9th of August, required the Minister of War to order the officers to cultivate a spirit of conciliation and kindness towards the citizens. The minister resigned rather than execute the order, and another performed the rejected task. The King confided the command of the troops to Von Wrangel, whose harsh and dictatorial address breathed the spirit of his appointment. An occasion was sought to remove the assembly beyond the influence and the protection of the Berlin Guards. The Assembly was invaded by a promiscuous multitude late in October, when it was proposed to pledge the government to aid the Viennese patriots; but the Burgher Guard completely protected the Assembly. No pretext remained. Yet the King committed the government to Von Brandenburg, a man not merely of great resolution, but of known hostility to the popular cause: and he assumed the right to prorogue the

Assembly from Berlin to Brandenburg, where it was required to meet on the 27th. The Assembly saw the design and repelled the usurpation. Excluded from their Hall, they sought another. Again foiled, they met in a Coffee House,—and resolved that no taxes should be paid till they were allowed to resume their free sittings in Berlin. They were then forcibly dispersed. Not enough met at Brandenburg to transact business—where their voices could only echo the influence of the army and the ministry. They were again prorogued till the 7th of December, and before that day arrived, while the National Assembly was in full being, after the King had parted with his absolute powers by two distinct and solemn acts, he suddenly resumed them in their highest plenitude, dissolved the body in which was vested the sovereign legislative power of the state, and in his own name, by his own plenary authority, proclaimed on the 5th of December a full and complete constitution for the state!

So impossible is it to impress on royal minds the pervading nature and high authority of popular sovereignty—unless the lesson be enforced by the sinister memory of a banishment, a deposition, or a scaffold; or the presence of an ever armed and resolute people oppose an insurmountable barrier to royal arrogance. The absence of this experience left Frederick free to revoke powers irrevocably granted. He found the Assembly not inclined to take any such constitution as he might propose; he therefore violently usurped the powers of absolute sovereignty, and imposed on the nation such a constitution as he pleased. Of course its duration was equally dependent on his pleasure, so long as his army was more than a match for those who were willing to fight to place freedom and the *rights* of the nation above the royal grace; and the assembly it authorized swiftly followed the fate of its luckless predecessor. They met on the 26th of February, 1849, in *Berlin*—whence the former had been arbitrarily driven. The King's speech proposed for consideration a multitude of topics, but the first case of independent opinion was the signal for their dispersion.

The Frankfort Parliament had completed an admirable constitution, and the Imperial dignity was tendered to the King of Prussia. He shrunk from the responsibility and on frivolous pretexts which ill concealed his irresolute and trifling character, declined the dignity, in opposition to an earnest and manly appeal from the Assembly. The Assembly reiterated their urgent prayers, but the pusillanimous monarch who had first led the great central movement could not be coaxed or driven by his imploring people to meet the expectations he had raised. He preferred to disgust them by his refusal, rather than to gratify the mass of the German nation by giving effect to the grand constitution which had just been voted by their august Parliament.

The Assembly then voted, that the constitution of the Frankfort Parliament bound the people and states of Germany. *This* the King and his ministry construed into an impertinent usurpation in the representatives of the legislative power of the State, and this with their expression of opinion on the unconstitutionality of the state of siege of Berlin under the King's own instrument, were the occasion of their arbitrary dissolution!

The dispersion of the legislative body was promptly followed, while the constitution of the 5th December was in force, by the King's electoral law, the foundation of the whole constitutional structure!

Such trifling with constitutions, such childish vacillation, such arbitrary appeals to the sword to break the stubbornness of a popular assembly, would have been intolerable to any nation whose spirit was not weighed down by the incubus of a gigantic military power. It far surpasses the outrages on truth and faith which sedate and law-abiding Englishmen visited on their sovereign with the axe and the scaffold; and had Frederick William worn the English crown, his name would probably have graced the prayer-book of her church in company with "King Charles the Martyr." But the King felt himself secure in his army, and he chose arbitrarily to defy the opinion of the assembly whose only purpose was to limit and control his discretion—whenever it ventured to take the constitution as a reality, and in its spirit and by its authority to speak in opposition to the good pleasure of the King.

This surely gave poor promise of constitutional government in Prussia. Yet while allowance must be made for the revolutionary agitation of the times, it cannot fail to strike us that the Assembly were disapproved of and dissolved, for advancing the views with which the King himself opened the movement for a central power. That his *opinions* had changed we have no reason to suppose. That he longed for German unity and the imperial dignity we know. Why then this retreat in the face of the earnest protests and exhortations of his people and his Parliament?

It was the shrinking of a weak mind from a decisive step at the appointed hour. Frederick William had too little of the blood of Frederick the Great. He stood in awe of the powers the latter had defied and beaten off. He saw Austria across his path, and from far in the back ground the frown of Russia darkened the prospect and chilled his ambition. He feared to strike a decided blow for the people and his own glory, against his brother sovereigns;—and in less than a year he was driven to a levy of the mass of his people, to repel their aggression against his independence, and to guard his influence in the country over which he might have ruled.

The King's treachery was one of the results of the struggle in southern Germany and Hungary. Let us there seek the explanation.

The events in Vienna followed the same course with those in Berlin; but the imperial court is free from any suspicion of honest intention. Despotic rule never for a moment abandoned its throne in the hearts of the princes, and the concessions were only devices to gain time for their retraction. The ultimate aim was to defeat the renovation of Germany by the Frankfort Parliament; for that would have involved the overthrow of the conclave of petty despots through which Austria ruled Germany, and the elevation of her liberal rival to an imperial crown of real power.

The shock of revolution struck Vienna in March, 1848. Early in that month, the Hungarian Parliament addressed to the monarch an exhortation to surround his throne with institutions in accordance with the spirit of the age; and the tone of that address was caught and echoed by the Diet of Lower Austria,—one of those feeble and fading relics of the liberties of feudal times which still survive, like the ruins of old castles, the period of their grandeur. Anxious consultations occupied the court. The Emperor was a shadow; the substance of power had long been held by Metternich, who struggled against a current he felt to be irresistible. His opinion supported by that of the more despotic of the royal family prevailed, the petitions were rejected, and proclamations for the suppression of the agitation and the dispersion of the crowds were being printed—when the people infuriated by their disappointment flew to arms, the troops refused to act against them, and terror seized the hearts hardened by irresponsible power. Metternich felt that his hour was come, laid down his dignities, and fled where none pursued him save the consciousness of evil deeds. The Imperial court helpless and bewildered, after throwing out an ambiguous decree which the people scoffed at, felt itself obliged to yield to their reasonable requests. The freedom of the press, a national guard, the convocation of the deputies from the provinces to consult over the constitution which should be granted—were the rich fruits of a single day of manly resolution and moderate conduct on behalf of the citizens of Vienna. This first step, faithfully pursued, would have restored Austria to her dignity among the nations, and laid anew the foundations of the empire. But the spirit of a tortuous policy presided at the conception and execution of the plan. The concessions disguised a step towards that centralized unity which had been the day-dream of successive emperors for a century. The bitterness of defeat was assuaged by the thought of the opportunity it afforded, under cover of a general constitution which guarantied no substantial rights and was revocable at pleasure, to break down the several nationalities which hitherto had proved an inseparable obstacle to the creation of an absolutely centralized despotism.

On the 25th of April, the Emperor published his constitutional scheme for the consideration of the Diet. It had a liberal appearance; but its legislative body was only to meet when convoked by the Emperor, its consultations were confined to his propositions, and nothing indicated any limitation of the absolute powers of the monarch during its vacation. It was a convenient cover for the exercise of absolute power under constitutional forms. The Diet met at Vienna on the 22d of July, and was opened by Archduke John, in a speech of mild and earnest exhortation to moderate counsels. The Emperor who, impelled by causeless terrors, had run away from Vienna to Innspruck in May, returned on the 8th of August, and was met by the cheerful and enthusiastic greetings of the people of the capital. The Diet pledged itself to guard his constitutional throne, whose presence was the symbol and guarantee of its union with the people, and the Emperor professed himself bound to labor for the reconstruction of the monarchy on a representative basis. The Diet entered on its mission in the midst of explosions of national animosities, entangled by the complex responsibilities of daily legislation, and filled with solicitude by the arbitrary outrages of the Imperial cabinet on the rights of Hungary. The scandalous negotiations with Jellachich, the invasion of Hungary by an imperial army, under the command of a rebel, at the order of a King who was professing liberal principles and pretending to assume the restraints of constitutional government, were contradictions which destroyed all confidence in the sincerity of the court. It was plain that time and opportunity alone were expected to accomplish the restoration of arbitrary power. If the time-honored constitution of Hungary had no sanctity in the eyes of the Emperor, he could not look on the creature of his own hands with more regard. If Hungary fell, no protection remained for constitutional concessions in any part of the empire, and the Diet was deliberating only to give time for the construction of an armed force for their overthrow. The order to the Viennese regiments to march on Hungary on the 6th of October confirmed every fear, and impressed the people with the fate which awaited them. The troops refused to march, the people flew to arms, scenes of violence filled the streets. The Diet required a new ministry, the Emperor trifled, evaded, refused half their demand, and on the 7th, before day, fled from his capital to

Olmutz, leaving an intimation that he went to return with power to overwhelm them. The constitutional Emperor summoned the Ban Jellachich with his Croats and Windischgratz from Bohemia to bombard his capital into submission; and summoned the Diet, which sympathized with the outraged Hungarians, to meet at Kremsir—where they would be at the mercy of the Emperor's constitutional bayonets.

Vienna fell before the military power which the Emperor had created by treacherous bargains with the leaders of the Sclavonic insurgents, who purchased worthless promises of privileges to themselves as the price of the blood of their German and Hungarian fellow-citizens. They did their work faithfully: on the 31st of October, "order reigned in Vienna:" and with Vienna began the series of re-actionary successes, which, by a fit retribution, prostrated Sclavonic and Hungarian pride alike in the dust. The Imperial court from this triumph drew new resolution and spirit in the war for absolute power. Under its inspiration, and ere the might of liberty and Hungarian heroism had humbled the Imperial head in supplication to the Czar, the Diet of Kremsir met—and were dispersed.

Their deliberations progressed with moderation and firmness, but they laid too deep the foundations of their work. The Court felt the supports of absolute power shake, when the Diet proceeded to declare the people the source of all power; and Count Stadion peremptorily interdicted the dangerous theme.

They proceeded to discuss and adopt wise and conservative provisions, giving rich promise of a solid and enduring structure in the new constitution, when suddenly the instincts of absolute power saw how fatal would be a constitution emanating from an elective body, and guarded with statesmanlike wisdom. The constitutional Emperor forgot his mission and his pledges, dissolved and dispersed the Kremsir Diet, and himself proclaimed on the 4th of March, 1849, as the emanation of his grace, a constitution for the Empire. Sclavonians, Zechs, Bohemians, Italians, and Magyars were melted and confounded in one centralized monarchy—moulded by the Imperial omnipotence into "*the one and indivisible Empire of Austria.*" Its greatest fault was its greatest merit, in the eyes of its author. It was merely waste paper without life or power, meeting the wishes, wants and expectations of no part of the Empire, rejected by all, defended by none, a thin veil for imperial absolutism, an illusory deception convenient to divide the liberal party, yet powerless to control the royal will. It was an unreal unsubstantial piece of gossamer floating in the air, holding fast by no historical recollections, answering to no national expectation, a web of a day, to be blown away in an hour. It never assumed, even in appearance, the symbols of power. The triumph of the Hungarian arms followed swiftly on its announcement: and the Boy-Solon found his constitution in danger of being without a kingdom. From the absolute dictator of the law to his vassals, he was humbled in the dust as the vassal of Nicholas—imploring his protection against the people he had outraged.

But prior to the disasters of March and April, the court were exulting in their fancied triumph; and secure of absolute power at home, they employed all the resources of diplomacy and intrigue, to defeat the Frankfort constitution, to frighten the King of Prussia from accepting the proffered dignity, to retain Germany divided that she might be weak, and weak that they might rule her.

The evils of Germany flowed from her confederation. Her patriots wished to convert it into a blessing. Her statesmen met at Frankfort under the commission of the people and of the princes of Germany to effectuate the momentous change. The conception of a federal representative government for the whole of Germany, operating in harmonious concert with local governments for the respective states, was a sublime idea, worthy of the greatest statesman to devise, and only second to our own glorious government because following it in time. It was the only refuge for freedom against the league of princes who conspired its ruin, and converted the existing confederation into a Holy Alliance to stifle every free manifestation in each state by the combined power of all. This end had been completely attained by the supplements to the original articles in 1820 as expanded and enforced in 1832. The far-sighted men of business felt that detached victories must be fruitless; and that the power and dignity of the nation not less than the freedom and happiness of the people were sacrificed by the existing isolation of the states and combination of the princes. They therefore devoted their energies to wrest from the governments such concessions as would suffice to create a wide enduring and powerful union. Their efforts were ridiculed as enthusiastic dreams by the people, and their success deprecated by the government of England—the only free nation of Europe—as famous for tenacious conservatism and practical wisdom in their own affairs, as for an unmeasured contempt, or incapacity for the comprehension, of any system not like their own. We greeted with just pride the deference of modern Europe to the western system for combining a wide area and diverse interests beneath the protecting arm of one powerful representative government. Our revolution inspired the Frenchmen of 1789—our constitution was the classic model for the German Parliament of 1848.

The Frankfort Parliament was not the offspring of revolutionary violence—but the instrument of a peaceful and legal reform. It was not dictated by a mob behind a barricade, in the streets of a single town. It was the calm and deliberate device of statesmen and princes to avoid revolution by removing its causes, in obedience to the settled and universal will of the nation.

The pervading idea of German Unity, the symbol and instrument of national strength freedom and honor, first assumed a practical form at a meeting of fifty-one gentlemen of note, chiefly members of the Legislative Chambers of Prussia, Bavaria and other states. On the 5th of March, 1848, they met at Heidelberg, declared a Representative Assembly chosen by all the German states in proportion to their numbers, to be a measure of imperious necessity, and charged a committee with the preparation of a scheme. They convoked a preliminary Parliament to meet at Frankfort on the 30th, to provide for the election of members to the National German Parliament, to which the hopes of all looked forward.

So public and approved was this design, that the Diet of the confederation, created by the treaties of Vienna, wielding the powers of the existing confederation, composed only of the plenipotentiaries of the German sovereigns, and hitherto the fatal tool of the Holy Alliance for the department of Germany, in session at Frankfort on the 8th of March, formally invited to participate in their deliberations and join the ranks of the Diet, seventeen of the leaders in this popular movement, and among them were Von Gagern, Welcker, and others of the Heidelberg committee.

The preliminary Parliament met on the 30th of March, at Frankfort, fixed the ratio of representation for the National Assembly at seventy thousand souls, settled the mode of election by the people, and appointed May the 18th as the day for their meeting. On that day the representatives met at Frankfort. They were the direct representatives of the votes of the people of Germany, elected by *law* in every state. The Diet of the confederation—which bore the same relation to them that the Congress of the confederation did to the Grand Convention in many respects—hastened on the first days of their assembling to present them a message, expressing the desire of the Diet to act in friendly unison and co-operation with them. The legal character and high functions of the Frankfort Parliament were thus formally and promptly acknowledged by the Diet which they were to supersede. It was the solemn inauguration of the Assembly as the representative of the national sovereignty of Germany: and they at once entered on its actual and plenary exercise.

They did not confine themselves to devising a system of constitutional law, which was to be operative only when approved, whether by princes or people or both. They assumed the functions of actual government in the name of the nation; and their first debate continued till the end of June the consideration of the powers of a central executive. The result was the law of June 28th, constituting a Provisional Central Power for the administration of affairs touching the whole of Germany. It was vested with the executive power in the affairs of the nation, with the command of the armed force, and with the right to send and receive ambassadors, to make war and peace, and with the assent of the Assembly to conclude treaties. These high prerogatives were to be conferred on a Regent elected by the Assembly, himself irresponsible, but surrounded by responsible ministers, without whom he could not act. His power was limited to the period of the completion of the constitution, and he was directed to exert it, as far as compatible with his duty, in good understanding with the plenipotentiaries of the German States. The German Diet was declared to cease from the moment that the Central Power began to exercise its functions. As the Diet represented the whole executive authority of the confederation, this latter provision was essential to prevent a double and conflicting executive—if the Frankfort Parliament and their Central Power were to be any thing but shadows and names. The recognition of this law by the German Powers involved the recognition of the legal and sovereign nature of the Assembly. They elected the Archduke John of Austria, Regent under the law. The Diet of the confederation placed in the hands of the committee of the Assembly appointed to announce the election of the Archduke, a letter expressing the satisfaction of the Diet at the result, and assuring him that, pending the debate on the law, the plenipotentiaries composing their body had been instructed to declare in favor of his election. The Archduke, a subject and in the service of Austria, after consultation with the Emperor, his brother, accepted the dignity. On the 12th of July he was solemnly inaugurated as Regent of the German Empire, and in the presence of the National Assembly declared that he would obey and enforce the law under which he was appointed. He forthwith surrounded himself with a ministry, filling all the departments of a complete and elaborate government charged with the internal and external affairs of a great Empire, and entered on the active discharge of the duties of his station. His appointment and his powers were formally announced by the Prussian ministry to the Prussian Assembly; and both the person and the authority were approved, with some little hesitation at the transferring from the Diet to the

Regent of the powers of war and peace. Even that hesitation was forgotten in the alacrity with which Prussia acted in his name in the Schleswig-Holstein invasion. The Malmö armistice was not ratified at first by the Frankfort Parliament: and on its vote refusing the means of executing it, according to the custom of constitutional monarchies, the ministry which had approved it resigned. A change of circumstances induced a change of opinion: the Assembly finally resolved to adopt it, and the Regent was instructed to negotiate with Denmark on the subject. In this view of the functions and position of the Regent and the Frankfort Parliament all Germany seemed to concur. They were every where recognised as the *governing power of the confederation, and not merely treated as a convention devising a scheme of constitutional law, but having no legal and sovereign power either to make or to enforce laws binding the people and the states.*

But the recognition of their character however it must involve, did not secure the recognition of the consequences. The Austrian acquiescence was rather the time-serving consent of a helpless power, than the honest acceptance of the great change involved in the successful evolution of the scheme of the Frankfort Parliament. Her arts and intrigues were roused to deadly activity, to strangle in its infancy a power whose full grown might it would be dangerous to cope with. She entered the field without a declaration of war, herself powerless if unaided, but armed with the votes of Austrian delegates in the Assembly, with the sympathies of dependent kingdoms whose proximity subjected them to her sinister designs, and with the strength of promised Russian aid which sufficed to awe into submission the light and frivolous, the ambitious but irresolute King of Prussia. He aspired to the imperial dignity—but trembled before the difficulties which intrigues and jealousy reared in his path, and concealed beneath a simulated tenderness for the rights of his brother sovereigns the cowardice which palsied his arm in the execution of his darling plan, and the treachery to his people whose cherished hopes he sacrificed after proclaiming himself their champion.

On two points hung the results of the Frankfort Parliament—the structure of an efficient popular constitution—and the selection of a head to defend and enforce it. It was certain from the beginning that Austria would accept no constitution which was honestly based on the popular will: and that the elevation of Prussia to the Imperial supremacy would be met by armed resistance. The success of the attempt to found a German Empire on a popular basis depended upon the power of Austria to prevent it; and that depended upon the readiness of Prussia to try the question in arms rather than yield her hopes or falsify and dishonor her pledges to the world. The acceptance of the constitution depended on the acceptance of the Imperial dignity: for if it were rejected by Prussia, she would also reject a constitution which necessitated her own subjection to some other Emperor; and she was the only power which could for a moment sustain the cause of the nation against the interest of Austria and Russia to enfeeble and divide it.

If the constitution once concentrated the power of Germany, or of any considerable part of it, in the hands of a popularly elected Parliament and a liberal Emperor, from that day Russian influence would be dead, Austrian domination would cease, both powers would be assailed along their whole frontiers by the inevitable propaganda of liberal ideas and mild constitutional rule exemplified in the affairs of the confederation and of the states. They both, therefore, had a deep stake in its defeat: and the treachery and cowardice of Frederick William yielded, without a blow, all that the most successful campaign could have wrung from disaster.

The Frankfort Parliament, on the 28th of March, 1849, elected Frederick William of Prussia to the dignity of Emperor of Germany. A committee of thirty-two members announced to him his election on the 3rd of April, 1849. His answer betokened a melancholy change in the royal mind since the 18th of March, 1848. The royal hypocrite had turned his gaze to the King of Kings—whom they strangely conceive as made after their image, and in whose name their treacheries and perjuries are perpetrated. He recognized, he said, the voice of the German people, and acknowledged that their vocation gave him a title he knew how to prize; he confessed his willingness to assume the burthens and the thorns of the proffered crown, but—with many circumlocutions, with much hesitation, under thin pretexts—he declined to assume the Imperial dignity without the voluntary assent of the *crowned Princes* of Germany. *This* was equivalent to a refusal: for it was refusing to control those whom the constitution was intended to control—without their several and individual assent. If only on that condition the labors of the Frankfort Parliament were to be successful, sensible men would have staid at home—or taken the field before their royal enemies had time to organize armed resistance.

The course of events throws light on this result, so overwhelming to the popular cause. Something had obliterated from the memory the procession, the oath, the proclamation, the devotion of the 21st of March, 1848. Then the King of Prussia had addressed the *German Nation*—not his fellow-princes, who would then have been glad of his countenance and aid—announcing that *he* had taken the lead, relying on *their* political regeneration for his support as the *leader* of the German people, the new King of the free regenerated German Nation. He declared that thenceforth the name of Prussia was fused and dissolved into that of Germany. He promised a plan for the conversion of the confederation of states into a federal government, urged its prompt execution, and proposed to surround it at once with an army at its disposal. In April, his ministry had explained these acts so as to remove the impression that the King meant to anticipate the unbiassed decision of the sovereign Princes and *the people* of Germany, in the assumption of the Imperial crown before he was called to it. But this did not import that, when called by the authorized representatives of *Princes and People,* he would not accept, unless every Prince gave his individual assent. Such an interpretation was then in no one's mind. It was as little contemplated as the assent of each individual of the people. Either Prussia or Austria must represent the Imperial dignity; and neither could for a moment be expected to assent to the elevation of her rival—if her veto could defeat the election of the people. It must therefore have been contemplated, that the Frankfort Parliament, speaking as the representatives of Princes and People, should invest by their vote the object of their choice with the *right* to bear the sceptre of united Germany, and with the power to coerce the refractory by the common arms. The creation of the Provisional Central Power, a regent for the conduct of an actual government, vested with the powers of peace and war, surrounded by a ministry responsible to the Frankfort Parliament and not to the Diet of the confederation, and endowed with the capacity of voluntary independent action in the affairs of the nation without consulting the Princes or their plenipotentiaries except so far as he might consider it proper so to do, was absolutely inconsistent with the supposition of a paramount title in the Princes to control the deliberations or to counteract the policy or to defeat the enactments of the Parliament—the full representative of the national will. To await their individual assent was either a hypocritical device to defeat the constitution inspired by subsequent events, or—it covered the King of Prussia with the stain of premeditated treachery, and proved him to have betrayed his country with the kiss of Judas. His ambition stands surety for his early sincerity: his fears, his vacillation, his cowardice were the causes of his faithless abandonment of the national cause.

Since the ebullition of the royal enthusiasm for an Imperial crown in the disguise of popular and national aspirations, Austria and Russia had intimated their opinions on the contemplated innovations. For some centuries Germany had been an agglomeration of discordant and powerless states. It was seriously to impede the westward march of Russia, that its scattered members should be knit into one articulate and nervous frame, animated by one spirit, and moving with concentrated might. At the outbreak of the revolution, the Czar professed neutrality: but as the agitations shook the thrones of Germany, he illustrated the Russian idea of neutrality, by augmenting his armies and crowding them to the frontiers. They stood ready at a moment's notice to cross the imaginary line which divides Prussian and Austrian from Russian Poland.

In July, 1848, thus prepared, the Czar communicated to his agents at the German Courts his views on the National Union. It was to be a popular government, it was the result of revolutionary agitations, it was to replace weakness by strength, division by union, the conspiracy of princes by the powers of the people. No one need doubt what Nicholas would think of this. In the eyes of the head of the Holy Alliance, it would be a gross violation of the laws of good neighborhood. The mode of expressing his sentiments is peculiarly Russian. He boasted his disinterested aid in the Liberation war and his recent proffer of his deadly alliance. He complained of the imputation of intrigues, which he hardly denied: and then in a sentence of dark import he declared,

"We have never ceased to recommend and *maintain in Germany concord and unity*—not indeed that *material unity* which is now the day-dream of a democratic spirit of levelling and aggrandizement, and which if it were possible to realize it as conceived by ambitious theorists, would infallibly sooner or later plunge Germany *into war with all her neighbors*—but that *moral unity*, that sincere harmony of views and intentions in all *political* questions which the German Confederation formerly treated of. It is the maintenance of *this union*, it is the consolidation of the bonds which unite the German *governments together*, which has ever been *our sole aim*, because we desire the peace of Europe: and in our opinion the surest guarantee of this peace has ever been lodged in the intimate union of all the *Governments* which constitute the German Confederation."

Of the meaning of Russian neutrality there could be no doubt after this communication. It was equally insolent, menacing and humiliating. Nicholas formally declares that his arm has been laid on the German people to maintain concord and unity between the governments of Germany; and history explains the purposes and results of that concord to have been the suppression of freedom. He declares his sole aim to have been the maintenance of *this union*—as his predecessor Catherine had maintained anarchy in Poland by guaranteeing the "*liberum veto*." In language not to be mistaken, he denounces war against any union among the people of Germany which should create a power self-sustaining, and a union which he would not be required to sustain—as his predecessor suppressed by force of arms that wise liberal and peaceful constitution of Poland whose introduction elicited the well considered eulogy of Edmund Burke. What he opprobriously terms "that material unity" "the day-dream of a democratic spirit of levelling and aggrandizement" was the wise and liberal renovation of German nationality with which the Frankfort Parliament was charged—the creation of a popular and powerful federal government demanded by the voice of the people whose rights it was to protect, and whose arms would defend it—and sanctioned by the very princes whose union Nicholas was so anxious to maintain. The threat of hostilities was plainly spoken in the prophetic assurance, that the realization of that unity, the creation of that central and tutelary power after which all Germany yearned, *"would infallibly plunge Germany into war with all her neighbors:"* for Russia was one of those neighbors—the only one interested to defeat the efforts of the Frankfort Parliament. Russia had already denounced those internal changes which threatened to elevate Germany from insignificance to the dignity of a Power among the nations—as an aggression on her rights which required her to arm; and her hordes crowded to the frontiers in token that her words were no idle threat. Such was the position of the ally of Austria formally announced in July, 1848, when the debates on the central power, the law defining his authority, and the draft of the proposed constitution were fully known and had clearly defined the purposes of the vast majority of the Frankfort

Parliament. To these things—not to the wild theories of irresponsible enthusiasts—the words of Nicholas apply. The Parliament thenceforth deliberated under a Russian threat.

Austria sympathized with her ally. Her German provinces were represented in the Parliament, her Archduke presided over the nascent Empire—yet it was known that she was hostile to the change. She would consent to no federal union in which her supremacy was not secured. That was an impossible condition, on any probable contingency. The very purpose of the union was—the change of the confederacy into a federal state—subordinating each separate state to the will of the whole. If the Frankfort Parliament changed the relations of the states, and created a central sovereignty, embodied in a representative assembly and hereditary Imperial crown guarded by constitutional restraints, *that* would be incompatible with absolute power in the Austrian provinces. It was still more hostile to the policy of Austrian unity, whether popular or despotic. It involved the subjection of her German provinces to a foreign power. If the whole of the Austrian Empire were embraced in the confederation, it would have been folly to talk of placing the Imperial diadem out of the house of Hapsburg. But this was absolutely incompatible with the conditions of a popular representation. Such a constitution must have been a dead letter. Austria might have consented to it—safe in the assurance that it never could be enforced. But all Germany would have repelled such an union. It subjected the German to a host of alien tongues and races, it merged forever that nationality they were striving to embody into a political fabric. The only scheme at all reconcilable with that central despotism which was the sole unity of the Austrian conglomerate was the existing confederation. The Diet of Princes could find a place for Austria. Her influence could control them on matters of general interest. Her weight could deaden every stirring of political life in the individual states, with the aid of the local sovereign. The subjection of her German provinces to the Diet was only a circuitous way of governing them herself. She was free to pursue her course of consolidation untrammeled by laws for her provinces above her own control.

When the Frankfort Parliament met, the Emperor of Austria was an exile from his capital, and threatened with a struggle for his crown. His empire seemed dropping to pieces. He could not openly oppose the universal wish of Germany—procrastination was impossible—intrigue and treachery alone remained.

His provinces appeared by their representatives. Their vocation was to strangle the infant Hercules whose cradle they pretended to guard.

Every delay was a gain. It gave time to reconstruct his shattered power. He could not secure the Imperial crown—he therefore opposed its creation. He proposed a central directory of the crowned heads of Germany, whose power would be divided between Austria and Prussia—and whose divisions would paralize the power the assembly was convoked to found. The proposal was defeated.

The triumph of Prussia was imminent, unless the constitution could be made so obnoxious as to insure the rejection of the crown it created and conferred. The Austrian members voted with the radicals for universal suffrage that they might disgust the moderate masses of the nation. They supported the qualified, in place of the absolute veto, that they might humble the pride and chill the enthusiasm of a King used to absolute power, by the offensive prominence of the limits which confined him. Months wore away in this war of parliamentary tactics. The difficulties were great even were honest intentions striving for the solution. But anarchists of the two extremes were blending their forces to ward off a result equally fatal to both. The radical and the despot were equally overthrown by the establishment of a wise and liberal constitution. Between this double fire fought the patriotic representatives of the mass of the German nation—driven by this dishonest combination to concessions alternately to each of the allies, yet so strong in the power of reason and the favor of the nation, that finally they baffled their united foes. The real difficulty was the German provinces of the Austrian Empire which formed at once an integral part of the existing Confederation and of the Austrian Empire. The assembly could not include them without dividing that empire.—They could not exclude them without cutting off part of the existing Confederation. Austria voted in the assembly, was impracticable, and immovable. She would neither come in nor go out—but adhered pertinaciously to the existing arrangement, and tried every art to defeat any other. Equal difficulties seemed to beset either course—when Austria herself gave a solution.

The debate had opened on the 11th of January, 1849. On the 4th of March, the Emperor of Austria, after dispersing the Diet of Kremsir, proclaimed a constitution for his empire, melting into one its numerous provinces, vesting the absolute legislative power in the Emperor and the Diet acting on his proposition—and thus utterly cutting himself off from the German Confederation. He did for his empire with a single stroke of the pen, what he was studiously engaged in defeating for the German nation at Frankfort. This act solved the difficulty. There was no more question of the treaties of 1815—those foul shackles on the arms of Europe—for, besides a thousand former violations, Austria had formally abrogated all that related to her German provinces. There was no more question of the fitness of excluding Austria—she had pronounced the separation of herself from Germany. The Parliament had only to give her credit for sincerity, to take her at her word, adopt a constitution covering the rest of Germany, and leave the relations with Austria for future negotiation. The propitious moment seemed to have arrived: and Welcker hastened to improve it. On the 12th of March he moved a series of propositions based on the result of the constitution of Count Stadion. The contest was protracted in an animated debate worthy to decide the fate of an empire, till the 21st of March. All Germany hung with breathless suspense on the words which were to decide the fate of their fatherland. Multitudes who desponded of success, or were disgusted with the factious squabble that had more than once disfigured the symmetry of the plan, now looked up with renewed hope. The prompt adoption of the propositions would have changed the whole course of events and probably ensured the acceptance of the constitution. They were voted down by a factious conspiracy between the conservative and the revolutionist aided by the Austrians who, pending the debate, poured into the Assembly where they had not previously sat. Their number was increased from eighty to one hundred and ten; the motion was lost by a vote of two hundred and fifty-two to two hundred and eighty two—by the precise number of Austrians added to the Assembly. The result was produced by votes which ought not to have been admitted; for Austria by her constitution had severed herself from Germany; and from that day it was an outrage to mingle in her affairs and control her destiny. The defeat of this proposition probably decided the fate of the constitution. After further delays the constitution was finally adopted on the 28th of March: and Frederick William of Prussia was elected Emperor of Germany in spite of the pertinacious opposition of Austria. Yet he refused to take the crown proffered by the nation. The despotic powers were again successful.

The result of the consultation of the German Princes by the king might well be surmised beforehand. It can be regarded as nothing but a form to disguise a previous resolution. The refusal of the crown was resolved on before the consent was either asked or refused.

The *Sovereigns* of Austria, Bavaria, and Saxony declined to accept the constitution and to sanction the election of Frederick William. But no one ever dreamed of the concurrence of Austria; and the King of Bavaria was his satellite. But the whole of Germany north of the Mayn and of the Erz mountains would have supported Prussia, if her King had not been false and cowardly. Twenty of the states, with their Princes, formally accepted the constitution and the Imperial headship of the King of Prussia. Among them were the important states of Baden, Hesse-Darmstadt, Oldenburg, Mecklenburg, Brunswick, and the four powerful and wealthy Hanse towns, Frankfort, Hamburg, Lubeck, and Bremen. Their population with that of Prussia exceeded twenty millions. They alone sufficed to sustain the constitution till its silent pleading would have coerced the accession of the rest. Hanover and Saxony alone of all northern Germany interposed objections; and they spoke the mind of the King and not of the people who would soon have compelled the acceptance of the constitution. The people of Prussia through the Assembly at Berlin spoke their mind in no measured terms. They were willing to encounter the sacrifices and the burthens which their hypocritical King was too tender to ask them to assume. The upper chamber, on the news of the election of the King, anticipated the arrival of the committee by resolutions urging him not to refuse the fulfilment of the hopes of the nation. The Assembly heard with the greatest indignation the halting reply to the committee, resolved unanimously to enter on the immediate consideration of the subject, and adopted an address professing the utmost readiness to encounter the burthens and dangers involved in the acceptance of the crown and constitution which the distracted state of the country and the threatening condition of Europe so imperatively required; and concluded with praying him not to refuse the summons, but to fulfil the hopes and expectations of the German people. But his majesty had turned his gaze from the people to the princes. He placed his complacency to the latter on the false ground of reluctance to entail on the former the burthens and dangers incident to a compliance with their wishes.

It still remained to accept or reject the constitution. The ministry advised the rejection. The King was impelled by his ambition to keep the door open for his future elevation, and decided not to recognize it. The Assembly of Prussia, by the constitution of the King an integral part of the legislative power of the country, supposed themselves entitled to a voice in the acknowledgment or rejection of a constitution which was to be the supreme law of the land. They could not consent that the King should alone decide on a question of such magnitude, nor that he should arrogate the exclusive right of either subjecting the nation to another jurisdiction or excluding it from a union essential to its interests. They had no ambitious hopes to gratify: and with the good of the people whose voice they uttered before their eyes, they clung with patriotic devotion to the constitution which concentrated the hostilities of all crowned despots,—and formally recognized it as valid and binding. This was no more than expressing in words what the princes and people of United Germany had impliedly sanctioned by the creation of the Central Power and vesting it with the attributes of actual sovereignty. Yet the constitutional King treated as an insolent usurpation this claim of the Legislature to a voice and an opinion on this great paramount law of the land. He dissolved them instantly and contemptuously, without deigning to assign a reason or intimate beforehand his intention.

From the leader of the German people, Frederick William, in less than a year was become the defender of the German princes. In March, 1848, he was ready to devote his kingdom and his sword to the Union of the people: in April, 1849, he offered his sword to the princes to silence the indignation of the people at their base betrayal. That year involved a whole cycle in human affairs.

The absolute princes, in March, 1848, found themselves in a moment prostrated by a storm whose sound they heard, but whence it came or whither it went they could not tell. Their armies were not to be relied on. Their people were clamorous for constitutional rights. All society was tossed in tumultuous agitation. Its waves shook the solidest fastnesses of despotism. The noise of their people's rising was as the voice of many waters.—A year of agitation had cooled the ardor of some, disappointed the hopes of many. The delays, the intrigues, the conspiracies, the combinations of the despots had disheartened the friends of constitutional Union. The masses of the nation began to despond. They were without a leader in whom to confide, devoted to their cause, nothing without it, his all dependent on their success. They had speakers, politicians, philosophers—but no one man of action to unite the people into an organized body whose will should be law. No Hampden arose to dare the worst in the logic of freedom, and to sound the hour when concession was madness and arms the only hope. No Cromwell arose to lead to victory men who stood ready to shatter by the last argument the brittle and fragile contrivances of royal conspirators. No Washington was there to inspire with his venerated name confidence in adversity and unity in the midst of distractions. No Frederick the Great was there with the genius of a lofty ambition whose dictates stood in the place and performed the offices of the highest virtues—with an iron grasp to seize the proffered crown so that all Europe could not wrest it from his hand—with an earnest devotion to the greatness of his people which is willing to accept the conditions on which alone that greatness is possible,—and with clearness to comprehend and self-relying courage to adhere to the dictates of practical wisdom. From his day to the present, the German nation has not produced his like nor his second. The storms of the French revolution failed to awake a spirit of more than the most mediocre stature. The bureaucracy of the thirty years of peace has deadened every energy and suppressed as dangerous every independent manifestation. No field of action has been opened to train her youth to high thoughts—the essential prerequisite of high deeds. Her princes are pusillanimous, narrow-minded, incompetent for any thing higher than the routine of oppression. And on the throne of the Great Frederick, the acknowledged and only leader of the spirit of the times, sat a trembling irresolute trifler—accomplished in all the accomplishments of a literary nation, with sympathies for freedom and progress, but covetous of arbitrary power and hostile to the consequences of the liberty he admired, susceptible of lofty conceptions, but too light and frivolous to give them form and shape in practical life, and without that one essential quality of him who would do great things for himself or for mankind, the knowledge of the appointed hour, and the resolution to commit himself to the rise of the tide which bears onward to the wished-for haven—whose swell once passed will never return. He lacked the energy to do and dare. His idle vanity feared to risk his peaceful repose for greatness and his country's good.—The constitution was in some respects distasteful to one who held absolute power. Universal suffrage was represented as the revolution legalized. The suspensive veto was described as a pliant door for the invasion of democratic ambition and the overthrow of kingly rights. The acceptance of the constitution and of the crown when the princes over whom they were to rule refused their assent—once already given to the Parliament,—was described as taking the part of the revolution against his fellow princes—as reversing the traditions of thirty years—as treachery to the cause of royal conspiracy. These reasons were now armed with all the authority of obedient armies; and these relaxed the strenuous devotion which the King had expressed for constitutional rights—when their refusal might have left him without any. Von Wrangel was master of forces adequate to control any but universal and organized resistance. Austria held a position and a power not to be contemned: and her voice was decisive. The arms of Windischgratz and Jellachich had subdued Prague and Vienna. No leader appeared to concentrate the scattered might that slumbered in the peasant's arm. Discordant nationalities were cheated or defeated in detail: and the Imperial government, wielding the powers of the law, selected and combined an army which stood ready to do its bidding—while the clamors of the people for constitutional rights were silenced by the deceptive charter which Stadion in the name of the Emperor flung down before them as the apple of discord. The Hungarian war was raging—but it had not yet assumed the character of a war of independence. The advantages seemed on the side of the Emperor. His generals had won great victories. His troops though checked still stood with their face to the enemy. The question was one of internal administration which a little concession could compromise at any moment. Obstinate persistance threatened absolute overthrow—for the decisive battles which demonstrated the unity resolution and heroism of the Hungarians had not taken place. The declaration of independence was yet to come.

They might even accept the Stadion constitution. The sword of Russia was already drawn in this domestic quarrel—and seemed to render resistance futile. A shudder ran over Europe when the Russian eagle was seen in the mountains of Transylvania and announced what all had foreboded, the alliance of the two despotic powers for the suppression of revolutionary freedom. The armies of the Czar hung like a black cloud over the horizon of Germany, and the flash of the lightning from the distant quarter of Transylvania betokened the storm which might pour over Germany at the will of him who controlled it. Europe looked on in silence. No voice protested, no arm was raised to shield the oppressed from the blow. The princes of Germany could not quarrel with a volunteer ally. England and France were wrapped in secure and selfish indifference. This was a combination which might have caused a firmer heart, a more devoted spirit than that of Frederick William to quail. Success involved a contest which must let loose all the elements of European discord. The prophetic eye of genius and patriotism could see through the darkness of the present the brightness of the future; but the sybarite and the epicurean, the dainty Royalty bred in luxurious ease, whose ambition was an idle fancy cultivated to vary the monotony of unopposed power, whose only idea of heroism was in the past and in the future and never the dictate of the imperative *now*—he was not the man for the crisis—and Germany had none other. Her womb was barren of greatness. Her reproach was not taken away among nations. She remained as she was, divided, distracted, despised, the prey of petty despots, led as a silent captive to decorate a tyrant's triumph.

The fate of the constitution was sealed by the combination of the despotic powers. Yet the Parliament clung to its high mission, and the Regent still represented the imperishable existence of the unity which princes and people had created. The Parliament on the 4th of May, repeated by formal votes their assertion of the obligatory character and legal validity of the constitution, called on the several states to conform to its provisions, and convoked the first Constitutional and Federal Parliament to meet at Frankfort on the 15th of August. They provided for the refusal of the Imperial crown by Prussia by elevating the sovereign of the most populous state which should conform to its provisions, to the dignity of Regent of the Empire. But the man for the time was wanting. The solemn and heroic resolution not to despair of a great cause however admirable is worthless, unless supported by armed power against armed aggression: and nothing could secure the operation of such a constitution within the limits of states whose sovereigns were hostile to its existence—but a central army, strong enough to rally round it the masses of the country—and led by a man competent to deal with such a crisis. Neither army nor man existed. The King of Prussia could safely usurp the power of recalling the delegates his people had elected: and volunteer military aid to crush the outbreaks of the people which the faithlessness of their princes had provoked.

The people of Saxony and of Baden were too much in earnest to submit quietly to an outrage which justified force if force could be successful. The Saxon Assembly called on the King to acknowledge and submit to the Frankfort Constitution. The dissolution of the body was the remedy copied from the example of Austria and Prussia. The people of the capital rose and expelled their King: the people were masters of their own fate. Prussia rushed to the rescue, and by armed intervention prostrated the nation at the feet of its petty despot.—In Baden the disgust and discontent of the people encouraged the radical party to deeds of violence which again provoked or excused the intervention of Prussia: and after a sharp struggle, the people were there also crushed into quiet. But these disturbances were the direct result of the perfidious conduct of the princes of Germany, who excited by their promises and their acts expectations which they seized the first pretext to disappoint. Till they saw their hopes fall with the constitution, the conservative and reforming mass of the nation controlled, in the very tempest and fury of the revolutionary feeling, all serious breaches of public order, by radical violence. The progress of affairs was like the reform agitation of England rather than the madness of Parisian revolution: and the sovereigns of Germany must accuse their own bad faith for the blood of the struggle in Saxony and Baden. To them will history ascribe the untold horrors which must attend the revolution they have at once postponed and necessitated. They have laid up wrath against the day of wrath.

The Frankfort constitution fell before the combined cowardice and treachery of its chosen head, and the intrigues and menaces of its open enemies. It was denounced beforehand by Russia as "the day-dream of a democratic and levelling spirit of aggrandizement;" it was spurned by Austria as contaminated by its popular origin. The offspring of the will of the people, it was the centre of their affections and attracted to itself their united support. It had a source other than princely grace. Its title to rule was paramount the delegated authority of princes. The fear and the hatred of this firm and lofty title had driven the King of Prussia and the Emperor of Austria to dissolve and disperse the legislative assemblies which their people had chosen and they had convoked to make constitutions for their empires—that they might substitute charters emanating from the royal grace, which the people would not care to defend against the royal pleasure.

The King of Prussia played the same game in the affairs of United Germany. The four powers who had strangled the Frankfort constitution united to contrive a substitute, not infected by the contagion of the revolutionary plague, yet providing for the essential interests of the nation. It fills us with contempt for their incapacity, when we contemplate their work. Fresh from the destruction of one constitution, Prussia Saxony and Hanover promulgated, on the 30th of May, another, embodying every feature which had ensured the failure of the former—with the single exception of its origin. The essential demerits which proved fatal to the former were the elevation of Prussia to the supremacy formerly occupied by Austria—the substitution of a government for a confederation—the exclusion of the Austrian provinces or the division of the Austrian Empire. The minutiæ of organization, the more or fewer voters for the lower house, the existence of two or of three chambers, were matters of detail about which princes and people might differ but for which no one would fight. Yet *these* are the changes which the royal Solons supposed would make a constitution acceptable which had been already rejected because it placed an efficient control on arbitrary power and shifted a crown from one dynasty to another!! Bavaria participated in the conferences without committing herself to the result. The completed structure was at once and peremptorily rejected by both Austria and Bavaria—for the precise reasons which controlled their judgment on the work of the Frankfort Parliament. The embryo fell stillborn from the hands of the royal midwives.

In the brief time between the rejection of the first and the second constitution, Austria had tasted the sharpness of death and the sweetness of an unexpected resurrection.

The power of Austria was the real cause of the overthrow of both the constitutions. But for her intrigues backed by her own and the Russian arms, Germany could have succeeded in creating a powerful and constitutional government. Her power to speak with authority in the affairs of Germany depended on the fate of the Hungarian struggle. In April, 1849, that conflict had been closed by the entire success of the Hungarian arms. Between Hungary and Austria the impassable gulf had been fixed by the defeat of the Austrian army, their expulsion from the kingdom, and the declaration of Hungarian independence. The success of her arms dismembered the Austrian empire. If left to herself, Austria could no longer control the affairs of Germany. She could no longer defeat the strivings of the people for an efficient and central constitution. She would not have dared even were she able, with constitutional and independent Hungary in her rear, and the mass of her people clamorous for similar privileges, to support a threat by acts. Her negative would have been an idle breath. Prussia could safely, peacefully, quietly have so controlled the rest of the German states as to insure the Imperial crown to her sovereign, while United Germany under its guidance and armed with the constitutional power of the people would have taken her place among the powers of Europe.

In May, 1849, the Czar advanced to retrieve the waning fortunes of Austria.

It was the re-construction of the Austrian Empire, shattered by the Hungarian explosion, which restored her power for mischief, and made her menace effectual to seal the fate of constitutional freedom in Germany.

On the plains of Hungary shaken by the thunder of Russian battle let us seek the causes of this final disaster.

SECTION V.

THE REVOLT OF EUROPE IN 1848

AGAINST THE

HOLY CONSPIRATORS.

HUNGARY.

THE REVOLT OF EUROPE IN 1848

AGAINST THE

HOLY CONSPIRATORS.

HUNGARY.

THE fate of Hungary involved that of Europe. The revolution of 1848 was decided on the plains of Hungary. A crime was there committed which surpasses the annihilation of Poland in iniquity. A blow was there struck by Russia for universal empire in a single campaign more decisive than half a century of victory and robbery. One of those blunders was committed by England in her indifference which is worse than a crime: for the crime passes away with the perpetrator and the victim—while the blunder entails slavery and blood on untold generations. The principles of the Holy Alliance triumphed by promptness, energy, and logical consistency. The friends of liberty fell because of the lukewarmness, the selfishness, the indifference of the free nations of the world. The cause of Hungary deserves to be stated for our instruction and for our warning. It is rich in the prophecy of history. Happy the nation that shall read it aright!

The Hungarian war was at no time a revolution. It fell by accident in the era of revolutions—and was confounded with them. It was not a struggle for new rights, but a defensive war for old rights. It aimed at no change in the form of government—but sought to maintain the existing form against illegal alterations. It was not even to punish with deposition a king who traitorously assailed the constitution he had sworn to support. Without the consent of the National Diet, the King renounced his crown, abandoned the duties of government, and arbitrarily transferred them to Francis Joseph who was not even the legal heir apparent of the crown. He refused to accept it with its constitutional limitations, abrogated the constitution, arrogated to himself arbitrary power, and made war on the people of Hungary to enforce his daring usurpation. It was only *then*—in the absolute vacancy of the throne, and on the absolute refusal of the only crown known to the Kingdom of Hungary—that the National Diet drew the sword, not to expel a lawful incumbent of the throne, but to repel an insolent invader of the national independence. It was not till their arms had achieved victories which converted their right into a fact, that they announced that fact to the nations of the world—and by their declaration proclaimed the fall of the house of Hapsburg-Lorraine. If that house now wield the sceptre of Hungary, it is no sceptre known to the history of Europe. It is one made after the fashion of that of the Czar—

and by him placed in the hand that holds it. The national crown of Hungary ceased to exist from the 14th of April 1849. The title of her master is that of conquest. It is nothing more or better.

Hungary for a thousand years has been the seat of a constitutional and independent monarchy, coeval with the infancy of the nation, reared upon the feudal plan, and guarded with the feudal jealousy of arbitrary power. Her constitution out dates by centuries the royal house whose perjured hands have been lifted against it. It was venerable and mighty when Rudolph of Hapsburg was a petty prince with his crown to win. It was no bundle of musty charters wrung from the niggardly hands of absolute princes—but the birthright of the nation, the law whence their princes drew their rights, the limit which confined their powers. It was entwined around the very heart-strings of the nation, and could be ruined only by their destruction.

The Diet of Hungary was the assembly of the nation, vested with their supreme legislative powers. It was divided into two houses—the upper, wherein sat the magnates and prelates—the lower, corresponding to the English Commons, and composed of the representatives of the lesser nobility and the towns. This venerable body was the sole source of law known to the Hungarian constitution: and its convocation was imperatively required by the law every three years.

The delegates to the lower house were elected at the "congregations," or meetings of the nobility of the "comitat." The "comitat" is the county, the congregation the county court of the early English law. Nobility followed *descent*, not *race*. Men of every race might be and were of this class of nobles, and every child followed the condition of the parent. The Croat, the Servian, the Czech participated in the privileges and rank of the nobility, as well as the Magyar: while the vast majority of the Magyars as well as of the rest were not noble. One in every twenty of the whole population was noble, and consequently entitled to political privileges. Under the French charter of 1830, only one in about two hundred of her forty millions, held the right of suffrage. The nobility of Hungary were over five hundred thousand. The population of Magyar descent were over five millions. The whole population of the Kingdom were about fifteen millions. The whole political power was therefore confined to about five hundred thousand persons.

But the noble was not necessarily an aristocrat, nor even generally rich. The vast majority were men of the middle class in life, or else of the class of peasant nobles—the latter by birth, the former in cultivation and condition. Of these elements was the Diet composed which for centuries had given laws to Hungary, and which voted by acclamation the reforms of 1848 which provoked their ruin.

The crown of Hungary was for centuries elective—as were all the other crowns of Europe that now forget their lowly origin in their lofty claims to the right divine. The mists which hang round the morning of history have always been the refuge of royal pride to conceal the nakedness of its birth. It has ever aspired to draw its title to rule from the gift of God rather than the will of man; and the illusion of historic perspective which blends the heavens and the earth in the distance of the dim horizon has served to veil the fiction of a divine diploma for usurpations which time has half covered with the hoary emblems of right. This pestilent delusion has hitherto proved ineradicable save by the sword or the axe. But no such illusion conceals the source of the title to the Hungarian crown. The fatal day of Mohacs extinguished in 1526 the House of Jagellon. The Hungarians conferred the vacant crown on Ferdinand I. hedged around with the limitations of the constitution, the coronation oath, and the formal right of resistance to his illegal acts. He acquired no arbitrary power, nor even an hereditary title. It was not till 1687 that the crown was entailed, by a law of the Diet, on the heirs male of the House of Hapsburg: and the pragmatic sanction of 1723 first admitted the heirs female into the line of the succession. But these acts merely made the crown hereditary, they did not release it from its previous limitations. They were imposed anew, with additional limitations. The crown of Hungary had always been conferred upon conditions only. Upon their observance rested the obedience of the people: and five times in one century did they grasp their arms to repel or to punish the aggressions of their princes. In 1222 the Hungarians had forced the Golden Bull on Andreas II.—the Magna Charta of Hungary,—and it continued to the last day of the monarchy the authentic declaration of the rights of the nation. The pragmatic sanction, formally adopted by the Diet, reiterated—as a condition of the concession it contained—that ancient fundamental law, that Hungary should never be governed according to the laws of any other kingdom; that it was and should be independent of any other state, and should remain in continual union with the hereditary states of Austria; that every heir of the throne must be crowned before he ascended it, and before his coronation confirm the national liberties and laws, customs and privileges, in a formal diploma, and with the solemnities of an oath; and that till such oath should be taken, the title of the heir to the crown should have no validity. It was further provided that "all parts of the Kingdom of Hungary re-conquered or to be re-conquered should remain embodied in the kingdom;" and that on the extinction of the House of Hapsburg, the right of election should revert to the nation. So strict, so precise, so jealous, so inexorable were the Hungarians when committing their liberties to the guardianship of power. No crown in Europe is so clearly held only by a conditional title. If Hungary can be governed by her own laws only, any decree not sanctioned by the Diet is illegal. If Hungary is to be independent of every other state, she is entitled to a ministry for the conduct of her own affairs, responsible to herself alone—else she is not independent. If all the fragments of her territory are to be and remain integral parts of her kingdom, there exists no power in the crown to divide her territory without the consent of the Diet. These points bear directly on the struggle of 1848. They were wise far-sighted and practical provisions against the dangers to the independence of Hungary from the numerous and powerful states over which the House of Hapsburg reigned, by different titles, and with various powers.

The laws and usages of Hungary defined the prerogatives of her kings to be—the execution of the laws, the powers of war and peace, of coinage and the post, the administration of justice according to the laws and through the ordinary Courts, and the dispensing of mercy and of honor. With a change of name these words would describe the prerogatives of the constitutional kings of England.

The ambition of the House of Hapsburg had accumulated in the course of centuries on the heads of its princes the several crowns which now glitter in the constellation of the Austrian empire. The Counts of Hapsburg and Tyrol grew by conquest and diplomacy to be kings of Bohemia on the one side, and of Lombardy and Venice on the other, gradually united under the same rule all the intermediate territories, and under the forms of election rendered the Imperial crown of Germany hereditary in their house. The same *person* held, with the crown of Hungary, those of the other kingdoms and principalities: but they were held by different titles, they were politically foreign to each other, and their only union was in their common head. The king of Hungary gained no new powers over Hungary from his associated dignities—as George, Elector of Hanover brought no accession of power to George, King of England. He ruled in Hungary by her laws only; to her his other dominions were foreign: and she never in law or in fact formed any part of the German Empire. Her boundaries and her laws severed her from every other state, in isolated independence. There was a perpetual struggle of her kings to break down the wall of partition between the separate nationalities under their sway, and to blend them into one simple monarchy. But their resistance was as pertinacious and as ceaseless as the encroachment: and while Bohemia and Austria and the Tyrol gradually yielded to the incessant assaults of the Imperial head, and lost the substance while they retained the shadow of their original freedom and independence, Hungary, more resolute, more warlike, or more fortunate, never, for an instant succumbed to art or force. Her sturdy citizens foiled the one and broke the other on many a well fought field and by many a formal statute. The violation of their rights was made the occasion for their re-affirmance; as the Magna Charta of England was re-enacted and confirmed by the parliament as protests against its violations by their kings. In 1790, when Leopold succeeded Joseph II.—whose reign was one of despotic liberalism, and whose energies had been mainly bent towards the obliteration of Hungarian nationality,—the Diet re-enacted and imposed on him the declaration "that Hungary was a country free and independent in her entire system of legislation and government; that she was not subject to any other people or state; and that she should have her own separate existence and her own constitution, and be governed by kings crowned according to her national laws and customs."

This was the answer of the Hungarian Diet to the centralizing policy of the Imperial head. They cherished their national independence. They clung to their national laws. They forced on their princes perpetual recognitions of their prescriptive rights. They would know nothing of an Austrian Empire. They remained and were resolved to remain citizens of Hungary, subject to the constitutional king of Hungary. Their isolated position—in the midst of jealous despotisms, alone free—gave them the habit and imposed on them the burthen of perpetual vigilance. They were forced to defend the errors that they might not lose the defences of their antique bulwarks. They were heavy and frowning battlements of the feudal age; but they looked defiance on despotic power in the prince, and this excused their gloomy hostility to popular privileges. They were the only protection of the people, and the people loved and defended them. They would cheerfully have amended them, but they feared to pull down the old battlements to widen and deepen the foundations, lest while defenceless and in the process of repair, the powers of despotism should rush on and overwhelm them. The abuses of their constitution and laws were softened by usage, and were endeared to them by the blessings with which they were associated. But still the lapse of time was visible to the eye; and the patriots of Hungary felt the spirit of the age, and only awaited a propitious day to make the necessary changes.

Three parties struggled in the Diet, in the forms of constitutional debate, for the control of the policy of the country. One clung to the time-honored edifice as the perfection of human wisdom which alteration could ruin but not improve. They corresponded to the Tories of the English Parliament. Another sought by moderate reforms to remove the outgrown relics of a barbarous age, and to replace them by the institutions of the nineteenth century. A third represented the wishes and the intrigues of the Imperial court, consisted chiefly of the officers or dependents of government, were looked on as traitors to the country, and were powerless and despised.

The popular party, lead by Kossuth and Batthianyi, embodying all the ability of the legislature, sought no revolutionary changes in the dynasty, in the relations of the King to the Diet, or in the relations of the kingdom to the provinces of the empire. They strove by legislative acts, under the sanction of the King, for those reforms of their internal administration which should make their government in fact what it was already in law, to guard by fit defences the rights they already held, and by expanding the foundation to strengthen the structure of the political edifice. They had the substantial body of a free constitutional government—such an one as the English constitution prior to 1688. They aimed by peaceful and parliamentary reforms to introduce those changes which cost England two revolutions, twenty years of war, twelve of absolute despotic rule, a change of dynasty, a century and a half of embittered political strife, and which the reform bill of 1831 only half secured. They were no empirics, no demagogues, no destructives of the school of the Jacobins, no preachers of the Red Republic. They were statesmen trained in the great school of parliamentary politics, dealing with an old and venerated constitution so as to infuse new vigor into its body without destroying it. They did their work in an artist-like style.

The grievance to be redressed flowed from institutions which had outlived the reasons of their introduction. The feudal system still subjected the peasantry to the burthens of personal service. Their lands were held subject to oppressive tenures limiting the title and diminishing the value of the ownership. Out of fifteen millions of citizens only half a million of nobles held political privileges; and while they engrossed the power were exempt from the burthens of the state. To raise the peasant to the level of the citizen, all that was required was—to emancipate him from personal service—and his land from feudal burthens—and to extend the right of suffrage and the liability to taxation to all orders of the state. This was no revolution—but a great renovation. It was *this* that Kossuth and Batthianyi and their associates had struggled for in vain for years, against the hostilities, the corruptions, the pertinacious opposition of the court. The Hungarian affairs were conducted by the ministry at Vienna, who while in law responsible, were enabled to evade that responsibility by their position, by their connexion with the administration of the rest of the empire, and by the materials of which they were constituted. The indispensable condition of success in any effort at reform was—the obtaining of a national Hungarian ministry, in *fact* as well as in *law*. This was possible only by severing the Hungarian ministry from the irresponsible bureaucracy which guided the affairs of the empire at the nod of the court of Vienna. To the obtaining of this great end as the means of every other reform, the great leaders of the Diet devoted their sleepless and untiring energies.

The events of February 1848 in Paris were felt on the banks of the Danube, and in the halls of the Hungarian Diet. At the sound of that stirring voice, even the free Hungarian gathered new energy in the cause of freedom. Kossuth, even before the news from Paris had reached Pressburg, seemed inspired by the revolutionary air with prescience of the future, and had pronounced *him* worthy to be called the second founder of the house of Hapsburg who should reform the Austrian government on the basis of constitutional institutions; while he declared that Hungary could never be assured of the desired reforms, so long as the government of that monarchy, whose head was the same with that of Hungary, should stand in direct contradiction with the principles of her constitution—so long as that ministerial council of state, which conducted the common interests of the empire, should continue to exert a decisive though unconstitutional influence in the internal concerns of Hungary.

On the 3d of March—eight days after the overthrow of Louis Philippe had shaken Europe—Kossuth lifted his warning voice in tones of prophetic wisdom before the Diet, and their echo rang through the empire, far beyond the confines of Hungary, like the reverberations of thunder among the mountains. "I speak my firm convictions—he said—when I say that the clinging to the perverse policy which opposes at once the interests of the people and their rightful claims of national freedom, must compromise the future of the dynasty. Unnatural systems may sustain themselves long—for it is a long way between the patience and the despair of a people: but there are systems whose long endurance has diminished, not increased their strength, and the hour comes when it is dangerous to try to sustain them: for their long life has only ripened them for death; and death one can share, but not put off. The people is eternal: and eternal we wish the fatherland of this people, and the glory of the dynasty which rules over us. But the dynasty must choose between its welfare and the maintenance of its rotten system; and I fear, unless the loyal declarations of the people intervene, this ossified system will seek a short respite in the revival of the now slumbering Holy Alliance, at the Court of the dynasty."

The 13th of March followed his prophecy with the confirmation of history. The Court hypocritically bowed a reluctant and ambiguous compliance with the demands of the people, and calmly awaited the hour of reaction. The news of that day combined the floating thought of the Diet at Pressburg into a definite shape. A deputation to Vienna, headed by Esterhazy, Batthianyi and Kossuth, was immediately despatched to demand of the King a national and responsible ministry. Their demands were complied with on the 19th of March 1848. The Archduke

Stephen was commissioned as Viceroy, and Batthianyi was charged with the construction of a national ministry, which the pressing emergency required without delay. On the 23d the chief members were announced to the Diet and greeted with tumultuous joy—as the pledge of the fulfilment of the national hopes. The spirit of a new life seemed breathed over the Diet. It was filled with the representatives of a single class, men who enjoyed a monopoly of the powers of government and an exemption from its burthens, and were the chief possessors of those feudal rights which the progress of time had converted into irritating shackles on the industry of the nation and the freedom of her citizens. Every concession was a sacrifice of selfishness to patriotism, of the powerful to the powerless—not at the bidding but in spite of the hostility of the government. Yet this aristocratic body, this close corporation, this monopoly of the rights of sovereignty, in a week, strode over the space it had taken England a century and a half of painful conflict to accomplish by doubtful victories and niggardly concessions. By acclamation of the privileged orders—almost by unanimity—in the days between the 18th and 23d of March 1848, peacefully, quietly, legally and cheerfully, the Diet of Hungary achieved the results of 1688 and 1831 almost without a division of the Houses, and with the entire and grateful concurrence of the nation. These changes were the spontaneous gift of the privileged class to the requirement of justice and sound policy. They were not wrung from them by the external pressure of the mob, nor by the armed might of the country. They were the fruits of free government freely distributed to all by the few who had engrossed them. So utterly false is it that these great concessions were flung down by the greedy leaders of the aristocratic party, as necessary sacrifices in a critical hour, when the favor of the people must be bought at any cost.

The most important of these laws was that relative to the responsible ministry for Hungary. It was a great constitutional charter declaring anew the fundamental law of the state, and without which every other was waste paper. The law is comprehensive and statesmanlike, embracing a vast multitude of details that nothing might be left for inference or dispute in its execution—yet the fundamental principle on which all depended was comprised in a few simple words. Their power lay in the readiness of the nation to die for them.

The law affirmed the sacredness of the person of the King and of the Palatin when exercising his powers in his absence. It declared that his Majesty and the Palatin exercised the executive power in the sense of the laws, through the organ of the responsible ministry, without the signature of some one of whom resident at Pesth no order or command of the King should be of legal obligation. To the ministry resident in Pesth it committed all the affairs of the nation, civil, military, religious and financial, which hitherto had been conducted at Vienna through the various councils or chanceries. The appointment of ecclesiastical dignitaries, the conferring of titles and orders, the dispensations of grace, were confided to the personal will of the sovereign: but the disposal of the military force beyond the limits of the Kingdom could only be in accordance with orders signed by a responsible though non-resident minister: and the receipts and expenditures of each year were required to be reported to the Diet for their consideration in detail.

The other laws of these prolific days extended the elective franchise to every resident of Hungary and of the kingdoms united with her without distinction of class who paid a moderate tax; thus they destroyed the political monopoly of the noble class. They subjected the persons and property of every class to proportionate taxation—and abolished the exemption of the nobles. They repealed the soccage burthens and feudal rights—conferring on the peasantry at once personal freedom and absolute titles, while the landlords were partly compensated at the cost of the state. They abolished the titles and confiscated the lands of the ecclesiastics—but provided for their salaries out of the coffers of the state. They released the press from the censor's gag. They converted the mass of the citizens into a national guard for the maintenance of the internal peace.

On the 11th of April 1848 was celebrated the passing away of old things. The King of Hungary, surrounded by the magnates of the Kingdom and the constitutional ministry, appeared in the Hall of the Diet *at Pressburg* amid the clamorous greetings of a joyous assembly: and, in the presence of the august Diet of the realm, formally and solemnly signed and sanctioned the acts of the session which was about to close. The approval—an antique formulary—is worth translating.

"Having graciously heard and graciously approved the petitions of our Court and faithful Archbishops, Bishops, Abbots Magnates, Nobles, &c. &c., of Hungary and the united territories, we command that the above named articles of law which have been laid before us for our sanction be accordingly registered. We approve, confirm, and authorize them, and pronounce them valid as well word for word as in their whole extent. We extend to them our Kingly sanction; and, by this our royal Brief, we pronounce them good and sanction them; while we assure our faithful States that we will ourselves observe and cause to be observed by others the above laws which we have freely approved.

FERDINAND.
BATTHIANYI."

PRESSBURG, 11 April.

Those names and that date speak volumes. They still stand there a damning testimony against the iniquities that followed them—still witnessing the cry of Batthianyi's righteous blood from the ground to Heaven for vengeance against the deep damnation of his taking off.

These laws contained every thing the people of Hungary desired. They were stained by no blood, wrested by no violence, stripped the King of no legal prerogative. They were the peaceful, constitutional, regular enactments of the acknowledged Legislature of the Kingdom, freely approved by the King, and under his special sanction put into active operation. He came from Vienna to Pressburg—from Austria to Hungary—from beyond the kingdom within its limits—and therefore he freely came—for the purpose of approving them. Whether he liked them or not, is nothing to the purpose. He may have thought them ruinous—but he made no protest, he uttered no objection. We can listen to no mental reservations: to such a plea the only reply is an appeal to arms. These enactments were the legal results of a constitution equal in venerable age and dignity with that of England, and by them renovated with all the life of popular power. By them the nobles freely abrogated the invidious distinctions which consigned one half the people to the caprice and the power of the other, and by the breath of freedom created out of the dry bones of their serfs a nation of freemen, an army of heroes—ready at the voice of their country to devote themselves as an army of martyrs. Hungary was as England had been after Charles signed the Petition of Right. Whoever struck a blow at this law was the *revolutionist*—be he King or Jacobin.

But if these laws stood, they were fatal to the dream of Austrian unity. It were vain to talk of merging her various nationalities into one simple indivisible irresponsible despotism after the model of Russia. It was equally vain to suppose so cherished an idea would yield to any thing but inexorable necessity. It might be postponed—not abandoned. The question was merely one of time and means of regaining by fraud or force what an evil hour had lost.

Every province of the empire had claimed the rights of man. A Diet was sitting filled with their representatives under the Imperial sanction to contrive securities for those rights. The main army was busy in Italy. The home armies were disorganized, or of doubtful faith. The Hungarians were not a people to be trifled with. To strike and not kill would be worse than folly—it would be fatal. Fury furnished arms and Satan was prolific of devices. The clique who held the feeble Emperor in leading-strings while they controlled affairs in his name took refuge in the diversity of nationalities, whose adverse claims had shaken the Empire, and whose spirit they had devoted their utmost power to break. The Sclavonians might be encouraged to fight the battles of the Emperor for promised concessions—which the hour of victory would enable them to retract, or at least leave them equally able to combat. Jellachich was tempted, and proved a pliant instrument: treason, treachery, and rebellion were the honest implements of the warfare: and the actors were simple enough to suppose themselves concealed by the thin veil of the royal word and plighted faith.

The realm of Hungary, its crown, its Diet, and its constitution embrace four several kingdoms, those of Hungary, Croatia, Dalmatia, and Sclavonia, and the Grand Duchy of Transylvania—as England, Scotland, and Ireland, originally three several kingdoms, now form one united kingdom, under the same crown, and represented in the same parliament. For eight centuries these states had formed an integral part of the Hungarian kingdom, enjoying the equal protection of its constitution, represented in the Diet, having their voice in the administration; and it was a part of the coronation oath that this union should be maintained. Besides their representation in the

30

national Diet, they enjoyed their congregations of the comitats, and had local Diets for the regulation of their local concerns. The most important of these Diets met at Agram in Croatia. We have the authority of the Imperial proclamation of June 10 1840 confirming the voice of history, that for these eight centuries the national Diet had respected the rights of the united kingdoms, and that they were without reasonable grounds of complaint. They were included in all the great reforms of the Diet of 1848, *whether political, social, industrial, or financial.* The law was the same for them that it was for Hungary itself.

But, in Croatia and Sclavonia the inhabitants were chiefly of that Sclavonian race which spreads through the Turkish provinces of the Danube, and extends over the greater part of the Russian empire, and under various names peoples Bohemia and Moravia and the plains of Poland.

Croatia was the chief field of their activity in Austria, because there they were less mingled with other races that swarm through its agglomerated provinces, and the Diet of Agram and the habits of political life which the Hungarian constitution favored gave opportunity for the cultivation and expression of public opinion.

The versatility of Russian diplomacy has enabled the Czar, in the pursuit of universal empire, to substitute the feeling of *nationality* for the enthusiasm of *freedom;* and to draw to himself, by the deep feeling of relationship, the sympathies of the inhabitants of a third of the Austrian and half of the Turkish empires.

Russian agents, intrigues, and gold have given a universality and life to the Sclavonic nationality among all the provinces of the empires among which the vicissitudes of a thousand years have divided them, which has stripped Turkey of Bessarabia, has weakened her hold on Wallachia and Moldavia, and causes the inhabitants of Dalmatia, Croatia, and Servia to look with more affection to the Czar at St. Petersburg than to the constitutional crown of their King at Vienna. So Russia prepares far beforehand the march of her armies and the solid foundations of her fatal rule.

This feeling of nationality, based on community of origin, evidenced by community of language more or less nearly related, and looking for its realization beyond the political relations of the present, was directly antagonistical to the efforts of the Austrian court to obliterate all distinctive nationalities throughout its heterogeneous provinces, and to melt them all into one undivided empire. That court strove by every art to draw the eyes of the people away from the past, and fix them on the Imperial crown. The nobles were invited to Vienna, the German language was pressed on them, national memories were discouraged. The result of the effort was to make each people cling with greater pertinacity to their historical recollections and mother speech; and in all the departments of the Hungarian kingdom this tendency was strengthened by the thought that the assault on the language and the national feelings of the people was only the necessary preliminary to weaken first and then to destroy their time-honored constitution and their political freedom.

For the time being the Russian sympathies of the Sclavonians were quiescent. They did the work of Russia by dividing and dismembering and enervating Austria.

The only visible point of unity among these races was that of language. This feeling developed itself about 1835 in the vivid and active cultivation of the Sclavonian dialects. Nothing political seemed mingled with it, but it was implicitly involved in the concentration of the ideas of the people on historical and ethnological relations of the past, to the exclusion of, or in hostility to the political relations of the present, as the ground of nationality. Between 1840 and 1848 the seed sown brought forth bitter fruits.

One of the results of the opposing efforts of Austria to centralize the empire and of the Hungarians to preserve their national rights was the adoption by the Diet of the Magyaric language as that of official intercourse. This chiefly served as the pretext, it certainly was the occasion for the development of the hostility of the inhabitants of Croatia and Sclavonia against Hungary, as well as against the central Imperial government. Sclavonia and Croatia were parts of the kingdom of Hungary chiefly inhabited by the Sclavonian race speaking dialects of the Sclavonian language. Croatia had about five hundred and thirty-one thousand five hundred Sclavonia about three hundred and fifty-two thousand seven hundred inhabitants—together only about eight hundred and eighty-four thousand two hundred souls. They formed part of a kingdom of about fourteen or fifteen millions of people—speaking thirteen substantially different languages. The languages were more numerous than the races, and many spoke the Magyaric language who were not of Magyar origin. Divided according to races, the kingdom of Hungary held about five millions and a half of Magyars, five millions and a half of Sclavonic origin, three millions of Wallachs, one million four hundred thousand Germans, and three hundred and eighty thousand of various other races and languages. But there was no one Sclavonic tongue common to all the races of Sclavonic origin. Those who spoke Croatian did not amount to a million in the whole Kingdom, those who spoke Servian, scarcely to a million, the Slovack language was spoken by about half a million, the Ruthenes language by about six hundred thousand, and three hundred thousand Jews spoke a language of their own. German was spoken by about two millions, and Magyaric by over six millions of the people of the Kingdom. Sclavonian was not even the exclusive language of Sclavonia and of Croatia. The rest of the people of Hungary spoke the babel of tongues whose very names are known only to the ethnologist, and whose political weight was insignificant.

The judicial and legislative proceedings the debates and the laws of the land were all in Latin. A change from a dead language, spoken only by the learned, and utterly unknown to the mass of the people, to some one living language was the dictate of the highest statesmanship as well as of the simplest common sense. It was one of the cherished designs of the cabinet of Vienna to procure the substitution of German; for the strongest link of national unity has often been proved to be language. Nationality is a communion of thoughts, feelings, sentiments, and pursuits: and community in neither of them is possible when a diversity of tongues is an absolute barrier to easy and frequent interchange of ideas. The proud Magyar spurned the suggestion: the wise defender of the national liberties repelled it as an insidious assault: the statesman rejected it as a remedy not meeting the disease. There was but one language which at all answered the essential conditions of being sufficiently developed and cultivated, of being spoken by a majority of the people of Hungary and by a large plurality of the people in the united kingdoms, of being the language of the leading and most powerful and influential class, and of being spoken by three times as many inhabitants as any one other language in the realm.

Moved by such considerations the Diet, in a series of acts extending from 1830 to 1844, declared the Magyaric the language of debate in the Diet of the kingdom, of the authentic public laws, and for the conduct of public affairs by the high public functionaries.

The law of 1839–1840 went rather beyond what the case required in exacting of all priests a knowledge of Magyaric, and in requiring it to be taught in the schools of Hungary.

The latter as oppressive to the Slovacks was repealed in 1847–1848. The former remained and gave occasion to some effervescence of feeling in Sclavonia and Croatia. But *all* were formally approved and sanctioned as formal and valid laws, not oppressive or impolitic, by Ferdinand V. the King of Hungary. They were the formal peaceful laws of the land. They were never the causes of national estrangement—but only the pretext behind which designing and ambitious men screened their insubordination. In the absence of any grievances they were made the pretext for the revolt of the Croats, under the lead of Jellachich—against the Imperial crown and the government of Hungary. It was as if the Welsh and Irish, merely because they are of Celtic race and their language of Celtic origin, without any other grievance, should revolt against the English government, and assert their right to dismember the British empire in order to gratify their historic pride and national sympathies of race. But it must never be forgotten that this was not a question *between the Imperial court and the Hungarians.* They stood on the same side. The Emperor had signed and sanctioned the laws of the Diet. It was a revolt of the *Croats* against *both* the Emperor and the Hungarian government to dismember Hungary without a grievance laid to her charge.

The claim put forth by the Croatians to a separation from the crown of Hungary rested on no specified grievance. It had no foundation in the history the laws or the traditions of the people. It is by no means certain that the whole people felt any great interest in the demand. They who chiefly pressed it were men of ambitious views, connected with the government, of no special power, and probably conscious that they could play a first part on the small theatre of Croatian nationality, but that they would always be insignificant before the united Diet and in the presence of the great leaders of the Hungarian nation. On the basis of legality, of national right, and of justice, there was no sort of pretext for the clamor for national separation. The case of South Carolina for secession was strong and irresistible compared with it.

Yet as matter of high policy, if the great events of 1849 could have been foreseen, if it could have been known that Austria when humbled would sink so low as to accept the aid of Russia in her domestic difficulties, it might have been wise to conciliate even the unreasonable pretensions of Croatia by yielding the separation. But the refusal, if a blunder, was no wrong.

The storm of 1848 blew the embers of discontent into the flames of rebellion—which an artful intriguer contrived to divert from the cracked and tottering edifice of Metternich's policy against the renovated structure of the Hungarian constitution.

Among the deputations which in March 1848 crowded Vienna none were more clamorous and importunate than the Croatian. They asked nothing less than the dignity of Ban for Jellachich—the chief agitator against the imperial government—and the erection of Croatia, Dalmatia, and Sclavonia, into a kingdom disconnected with Hungary. This was placed on the ground of community of race. By some diplomatic legerdemain, after interviews with the court clique, the main head vanished from their petition; yet the leaders boasted that the Austrian ministry had conceded all they asked; and Jellachich, invested with the dignity of Ban, returned to Agram, to fill the country with the novel watchword,—"The Unity of the Monarchy"—while every where the note of preparation was sounded against the Hungarians as separatists to be put down by arms. The unity of the South Sclavonian kingdoms had suddenly become merged in some higher and invisible unity. The imperial general Nugent stood quietly by in the midst of the preparations. Batthianyi, instead of arming, sought accommodation by negotiation. Jellachich vouchsafed not even a reply to the invitation of the Palatin to a seat in the Council of State. The Hungarian ministry invoked the mediation of the court at Innspruck. Yet not till June and after being thrice required did Jellachich appear. He was received with apparent coldness—and dismissed in peace. The Imperial proclamation of the 10th of June followed him with the charge of treason against the Emperor, of rebellious purposes against Hungary, and ambitious views for himself; and stripped him of all his dignities. The proclamation ascribed the fears of the Croatians for their nationality to *the seditious slanders of interested agitators,* recalled the lapse of eight hundred years of peaceful union with Hungary, the uniform justice of the Diet, and its recent extension to them simultaneously with the Hungarians of the great political reforms of March, as the best assurance of their entire safety; and reminding them of his coronation oath to maintain the integrity of the Hungarian crown, he vowed a new oath for the observance of the old.

This proclamation emanated from Innspruck, bore the name of Ferdinand, and covers by its sanction every act of the Hungarian ministry and Diet to its date. Yet not the slightest regard was paid to it by Jellachich. He proceeded in the face of the imperial court and army and officers with his preparations for war. He even refused to allow the Croatian regiment to march for Italy at the order of the ministry of war. He openly appeared, on the 19th June, nine days after the proclamation denounced him as a traitor, in *Vienna*, was recognized and treated with by the ministry, arranged with Latour the plan of operations, and returned in peace to Agram, apparently a traitor, secretly confirmed in his dignities, and worshipped as the saviour of the Imperial house. But the proclamation still stood unrevoked—a snare for the Hungarians, to entrap them into the belief that the court was on their side and would afford them the requisite aid to suppress the rebellion. Jellachich was secretly provided with money, and arms, and all the munitions of war by Latour from Vienna. Hrabrowsky was ordered to stand neutral. When for appearance sake he was compelled to rebuke the preparations of Jellachich, he on the 6th of August threw off the mask, declared the proclamation of the 10th of June to have been revoked, and announced himself as the defender of the Imperial court against the *faction* which used Hungary for the division of the monarchy. Batthianyi again repeated his efforts at peaceful adjustment; but Jellachich insisted on the separation of Croatia, Sclavonia, and Dalmatia from the Hungarian crown. That condition was inadmissible; and the leaders parted with fierce words and defiances to be adjusted by arms on the banks of the Drave.—It was sufficiently plain that the demand of the deputation of March was suspended not abandoned, and one need not be very conversant with public affairs to divine the terms Jellachich had wrung from the distresses of the court. The price of laying Hungary at their feet was to be—the concession of the Croatian claim to separation.

Hungary now awoke when almost too late to the truth of Kossuth's prophetic words, and eagerly grasped her arms. Jellachich was not yet quite ready. Art must win yet a little delay. The Emperor on the 21st of August peremptorily insisted that the Palatin should accommodate matters with the Croatians; but conditions were suggested which were inadmissible; and the trick shown out through the preliminary requirement that the Hungarians should suspend their tardy military preparations. This artifice was too transparent to be successful, and the Hungarians pushed on their preparations, till Ferdinand's letter of the 4th of September removed all doubt from every mind for whom Jellachich was arming. In that letter the Emperor confesses his error in having supposed Jellachich ever intended *to divide the territories of the Hungarian crown*—revokes the proclamation of June the 10th—restores him to his dignities—and assures him of the Imperial confidence in his exertions for the benefit of the whole monarchy, the integrity of the Hungarian crown, and the development of the associated territories. Not a word alludes to his warlike preparations, to the aid of the Viennese ministry, to the view taken by the court of his purposes; but Jellachich is assured that the Emperor is convinced he never intended to divide the Hungarian Kingdom—though that had been the express demand on which the last attempt at reconciliation between Batthianyi and the Ban had failed!!

On the 11th of September Jellachich crossed the Drave, on a pontoon bridge furnished by Latour from Vienna, and marched on Pesth the capital of Hungary.

If preparations could not be postponed, at least they could be retarded by changing the persons at the head of affairs. On the 24th of September, when Jellachich was almost in sight of the capital, the Archduke Stephen, the commander-in-chief of the Hungarian army, received orders to vacate his post of Palatin. Instead of reporting the illegal order to the Diet, he secretly, at night, like a criminal, slunk from the capital and fled the country. Even this could not confuse the affairs of a government conducted by the trained statesmen of Hungary. This blow was followed up on the 27th of September by an order dismissing the Batthianyi ministry, commissioning Vay to form another, appointing Lemberg royal commissioner for Hungary with the command of the Hungarian army, and commanding the obedience of citizens and officers, civil and military. Neither order was signed by any responsible minister; and Lemberg was appointed to an office unknown to the laws. The Diet instantly declared the orders illegal and unconstitutional, forbade obedience to them, and required the people to follow the orders of the president of the ministry and the committee of public defence. On the 28th, Lemberg was barbarously murdered by a rabble—whose deed was condemned and mourned by the Diet.

On the 29th, this riddle of fraud and treachery was solved on the field of Velencze, where the Hungarian peasants half armed, undisciplined, under the lukewarm command of an Austrian General, Moga, but inspired with devotion for the land which secured them the rights of man, met and foiled Jellachich's superior and well appointed army. To him a check was equivalent to a defeat. He represented no nation; he was without a reserve; his whole resources were exhausted by that one blow; and he violated a truce, which he was driven to ask or accept, by hastily retreating—not towards *Croatia*—but to the nearest point on the *Austrian* frontier—on the direct road to the court whose authority he had been apparently defying.

The Hungarians stopped the pursuit at the frontier. However convinced of the guilt of the court, they resolutely shut their eyes to the fact, and acted as if the question were between them and the Croatians. They were guilty of a great folly in pausing in their pursuit till they had annihilated Jellachich's army. The hour of victory was the best time for negotiations. They feared the reputation of revolutionists,—and played into the hands of the most unscrupulous of counter-revolutionists.

The court tricks had been exposed and their plans defeated. Secrecy was no longer possible.

The proclamation of the 3d of October threw off the mask and denounced war to the knife against Hungary and her freedom. It was as unambiguous and as significant as the attempt of Charles I. to arrest the five members in the House of Commons. Nothing remained but an appeal to the sword—not between Croatia, under whose mask Jellachich had been commissioned to destroy the Hungarian constitution—but between Hungary and the house of Hapsburg Lorraine, in whose name the war was now waged.

That insolent proclamation assumed the right to dissolve the Diet, a gross and impudent usurpation—annulled the measures it had taken for the defence of the kingdom—created Jellachich, then in arms against the Hungarians, and dripping with their blood, the commander-in-chief of the Hungarian armies—declared all Hungary under martial law, which meant the substitution of despotic for legal authority—and confided to Jellachich the entire executive power of the kingdom in the absence of the King, in gross violation of the plain law of the land.

The revolutionary outbreak of the 5th of October was the answer of the people to the proclamation, and shewed the deep sense of the danger to the newly acquired liberties of the empire which this outrage on Hungary occasioned. The people of Vienna rose to defend what they had acquired—for they knew that the fall of Hungary would drag them down. Still the Hungarian Diet and the Austrian assembly higgled over legal formalities for more than two weeks; and the march of the Hungarian army was resolved on only after the imperialists were fully prepared to repel them.

The battle of Schwechat arrested the advance of the Hungarians on the 30th of October, and compelled them to leave Vienna to her fate. She surrendered on the 31st: and Hungary lost by her delay an opportunity of changing, by a vigorous blow, the course of European politics. She gained only a month to arm. She might have gained a victory which would have made arming needless.

That month was devoted to formal preparation for a struggle which all parties recognized as one for life and death.

The court of Austria transferred the Diet to Kremsir—that they might be dependent on its pleasure. The Emperor was at Olmutz. The control of affairs was in the hands of the reactionist party of the Imperial family, the Archduke Ludwig and the Archduchess Sophie, mother of the present Emperor. The emergency called for energy unscrupulous in its means, reckless of moral and legal obstacles in reaching its objects, relentless in vengeance, and not sick at the sight of righteous blood. There were only two possible courses. They must honestly accept and maintain the popular institutions which the Imperial word had conceded to the prayers of the people; or they must openly or secretly undermine or overthrow them, eradicate every trace of provincial nationalities, and by force of arms march straight across the fragments of every constitutional and legal barrier to the establishment of a simple indivisible irresponsible despotism. The voice of the people, the cry of humanity, the whispers of conscience must be silenced, and will and the sword stand in the place of law and right. He who could not rise to the height of this pure iniquity was not the man for the crisis. He cumbered the field of battle, and must be removed. The Emperor Ferdinand V. was old and weak. Bred up under the shadow of Metternich's influence, he knew not how to act but at the dictation of stronger spirits around him. He was not very scrupulous even for a King, but he had some human feelings left. He was not darkly bent on annihilating Hungary, for his mind could not comprehend that liberty and despotism cannot lie down side by side in friendly embraces. He did not comprehend that the time had come to choose between them. He might have been induced to accept reasonable terms of adjustment—which would have brought quiet for the present at the expense of certain liberty to Austria for the future. The clique who guided affairs in his name, therefore, secluded him from the public—put in his mouth his official replies to deputations—and cut off all communication between him and the Hungarian ministry. But when urged openly to abrogate the constitution of Hungary, his superstitious mind recalled the tenure by which he held her crown—and he yielded no other answer to their urgency than that touching remonstrance—"But my oath—but my oath!" One so incapable of appreciating the rights of a necessity was forthwith pronounced in family conclave unfit to rule. He was discovered to have a rudimentary conscience, and was at once declared not to belong to the royal species. They who wielded the power behind the throne resolved that the empire needed a youthful head, and a less scrupulous conscience, unentangled by the sin and snare of constitutional oaths, who, free from duties might conquer rights and realize the idea of unity which had haunted Joseph II. The crown was torn from the aged brow of Ferdinand V. by family strife, and transferred to the head of a boy, who would prove a pliant tool, and might be educated in the virtues of a Nero under the auspices of an Agrippina.

The abdication of the 2d of December was known on the 6th at Pesth. On the 7th the Diet declared that the crown was held only under conditions, and could not be abdicated or transferred but by their consent; that their law recognized no secret family arrangements as entitled to dispose of their national crown; but that the Diet alone were authorized to provide for the regency or the succession. They therefore commanded the people and the officers of the kingdom to adhere to the constitution, to refuse obedience to the illegal usurpation which had been perpetrated against their liberties, and branded as a traitor him who should do otherwise.

In the absence of a legal king, and of a legal ministry, the Diet provided for the exercise of the powers of government by electing a ministry; and placed at its head Lewis Kossuth. The people greeted with joy the resolutions of the Diet; and Görgey and the army under his command formally gave in their adhesion to the national government.

On the 16th of December Windeschgratz crossed the Leitha, on the crusade of despotism against Hungarian liberty. The miraculous efforts, the heroic struggles of this momentous campaign belong to another pen than mine. They stand with those of Poland alone on the page of modern history. I deal with their results.

The Hungarian army retreated fighting, with their face to the foe, across the Danube. Their government sought safety in Debreczin. The day of Kapolna—the 26th of February—gave the Austrian army, by the divisions of the Hungarian generals and the traitorous inactivity of Görgey, what the court considered their crowning victory. They thought the power of Hungary broken, and the spell of the revolutionary spirit dissolved. They breathed more freely, and stepped boldly to their object. They dealt summarily with the Diet of Kremsir and the constitution of Hungary. Only eight days after the battle, on the 4th of March, the charte octroyée of Stadion was published at Olmutz. It was proclaimed at Vienna on the 7th of March 1849.

By a single stroke of the pen, it dissolved the Diet of Kremsir, because too slow in its movements for the popular zeal of the Court—it *abrogated the Hungarian constitution*—it *divided Croatia, Dalmatia and Sclavonia from all connection with Hungary*—it combined all the territories over which the house of Hapsburg ruled into one great consolidated and centralized empire, under the forms of a constitution, but under the reality of a despotism. It was a fit successor to those shadows of free institutions whose substance had withered away beneath the touch of Austrian despotism. It reserved to the monarch the right to make the decrees requisite to its operation; and till then all things were to remain as they were.

This act of audacious insolence reveals the depth and blackness of the perfidy of the court. History affords no parallel to it in modern times. It can only be illustrated by saying, it is as if George, Elector of Hanover, on his falling heir to the British crown, but even before he had set foot on English soil, had promulgated a constitution razing to its foundation the bulwarks of English freedom, and blending in one empire under new forms England and Scotland, Ireland and Hanover and Canada, with such rights as he saw fit to concede—during his good pleasure. It would not be a grosser outrage for the President to annul the state constitutions, proclaim the United States supreme and absolute, and himself their hereditary and imperial head.

The constitutional structure thus summarily dealt with was no mushroom growth of yesterday—but a sturdy oak of ages, beneath whose boughs generations had risen, reposed, found shelter, and a grave. If this Hungarian constitution, imbued with the life of the nation—hoary with venerable age, yet vigorous pliant and expansive as youth—outdating every one of the upstart sovereignties which crowded around it for its ruin—alone the frontier and guardian of Europe while they were petty principalities or semi-barbarous and wandering hordes—bearding the imperious Turk while Austria was a subordinate dukedom and ere Russia was half a match for Poland or for Sweden—if this time-honored growth could not escape the assassinating hands of those who hypocritically plead for time-worn and prescriptive governments, how shall those of newer date and less deep and spreading roots abide the whirlwind that will rush over them when this barrier is swept away?

This "charte octroyée" of Count Stadion, arbitrary in its origin, unsatisfactory in its details, was a castle of cards piled up by a child to be blown down by his capricious breath. It was introduced by the dispersion of the Diet of Kremsir—which sat by a higher authority than any Diet this constitution could assemble: and its fate must ever impend over any successor having no independent power, no popular origin—and subject to be revoked by the paramount sovereignty which granted it. Its concessions to freedom were revocable graces emanating from the crown and only pending its pleasure. To call this liberty, and such waste paper a constitution is trifling on grave subjects and making a mock of things holy.

That was precisely what the wily despots desired. If they could substitute these Sibylline leaves for the deep solid often defended and always impregnable barriers of the Hungarian constitution, founded in the hearts and inscribed all over with the proudest memories of the people—not only could the same power which gave them, revoke them; but while they remained, they would be a mere veil for the convenient concealment of the arcana of despotism beneath popular forms. It could offer no firm resistance to any design of the monarch: for there would be no terrible looking for of fiery indignation for the violations of a constitution forced on a crowd of reluctant races. It must remain a piece of lifeless mechanism, moving at the nod of the central autocrat, with puppets for actors treading its stage in dumb mimickry of the acts and contests of popular rule—having the form without the power thereof.

Its very existence would be a perpetual protest against the existence of any inherent independent original power of sovereignty in the nation—that rottenness at the heart which made the French charter a mockery till 1830, and not much better from that time till 1848. It would have reared itself aloft—a stupendous fraud by which despotism, foiled in the field, had gained the reality of victory by consenting to the formal humiliations of defeat.

What all men foresaw as the consequence of the defeat of Hungary has come to pass even while I write. The issue which trembled in the scale of battle was not the substitution of the "charte octroyée" for the Hungarian constitution. It was the substitution of despotic power for constitutional freedom of a thousand years in Hungary, or the triumph of popular power over the whole of Europe. That issue was tried and decided on the plains of Hungary, in 1849. Murder and rapine reigned till 1850. Late in 1851 an imperial decree sounded the passing bell of the languishing constitution—in declaring that the responsible ministry were thenceforth responsible only to their Imperial master: and now while I write, another edict has declared that the whole baseless fabric has passed away—leaving a naked despotism, unveiled by even the drapery of freedom.

The feet of those who carried out Hungarian Liberty have returned—and carried out its successor also.

While the court at Olmutz gloried in their victory, and their generals reposed in fancied security on their laurels, Lewis Kossuth organized with rapid energy a vast army, inspired with the hopes of heroes and the resolution of martyrs. On the 23rd of March, a month from the battle of Kapolna, the Hungarians resumed the offensive along the whole line of the Theiss. A series of rapid movements exploding in ruinous blows, and crowned by brilliant victories, in ten days, drove the Austrian army, along the whole line, from the Theiss to the right bank of the Danube, shattered its power, despoiled it of the prestige of victory, and freed the central plains of Hungary from the presence of a foe.

This was the glorious result of ten days of continued battle. Austria was again prostrated at the feet of Hungary: another blow which Hungary was able to strike, which Görgey was ordered to strike, but which he traitorously neglected to strike, would have ended the war.

This was the hour to proclaim to the world the political result of these victories. Hungary had been stripped of her constitution, invaded by an usurper, and her very existence threatened by military violence. She had prostrated the assassin. She would no longer recognize his blood-stained brow as fit to bear her diadem. On the 14th of April the Hungarian Diet solemnly pronounced the deposition of the house of Hapsburg from the throne of Hungary. This was merely the declaration of a fact. But there were those who were interested to make the fact otherwise at any cost.

That sword which was red with the blood of Poland had been freely tendered to Francis Joseph, in February, and again in March—but was refused. Thousands of Russian troops crowded the borders of Austrian-Poland ready for marching at a word. The overthrow of the Austrians in April first convinced the court that Hungary was more than their match. They were driven to choose between surrender or Russian intervention. They preferred that Francis Joseph should rule as the viceroy of a despot, rather than be the constitutional king of a free people. Schwartzenburg took the place of Count Stadion—and flung himself into the arms of the Czar.

The 10th of April had settled the fate of Windeschgratz: on the 17th the line of the Danube was free from the presence of the enemy; and Welden, on assuming the command, had no alternative but a precipitate retreat to the Austrian frontier. His army was disorganized, dispirited, demoralized, and broken. The orders of the ministry, the dictates of military science, the settled plan of the campaign which Dembinski had advised and Görgey had approved, alike imperatively required the prompt unintermitting pursuit of the retreating Austrians, and promised as its fruits their utter annihilation. Vienna was exposed—Görgey's rear was unthreatened—a single battle would have ended the war—and the Hungarians could have dictated peace at Vienna before Russia could have been even summoned to the rescue. Yet Görgey held his main army idle on the left bank of the Danube from the 21st of April till the 20th of May—amusing his own and the national vanity with freeing the unimportant fortress of Buda from its Austrian garrison; and then he whiled away the precious hours on the banks of the Waag, in the presence of an inferior enemy, till the middle of June—while the net was being drawn round his native land and the destroyers preparing in quiet their deadly blow.

On the 27th of April the proclamation of Nicholas announced his intervention in the affairs of Hungary—for his own defence. The terms were arranged at Warsaw, where the young Emperor repaired to plot, amid the ruins of Poland, under the auspices of its destroyer, the murder of another nation, her equal in heroic grandeur, in historic renown, in priceless services to Europe in the past, and in importance to its safety for the future.

From the 4th to the 11th of May the Russian corps crossed the several frontiers of Hungary. On the 12th the Imperial proclamation summoned the free Hungarians to unconditional slavery. On the 3d of June the first Russians reached Pressburg. Not till the middle of June did the general advance of the invaders begin. Görgey quietly awaited their readiness.

The early days of June were consumed in sharp but detached and insignificant conflicts on the line of the Waag—usually resulting in favor of the Hungarians, but deciding nothing. They introduced the inevitable hour of ripe preparation.

Hungary is a great plain surrounded by the Carpathians and penetrated by the Danube—whose exit and entrance make two gates through the mountains. Around this mountain barrier lay the masses of Russian and Austrian troops, ready to pour through the passes on the plains beneath.

The children of Hungary, at bay within the fated circle, concentrated their power across the paths of their foes, and opposed their breasts to the threatening onset.

The hour for advance having been wasted at the end of the campaign of April, the plan of the second campaign was confined to the defensive. The Hungarian troops were to retreat—if driven back—from the frontier to the centre. Their united power would overmatch the enemy at any given point. They occupying the centre of a circle round which their enemies were disposed, could choose their time and point of attack with all their power, and thus defeat in detail the armies whose combined power they could not oppose. This plan also was sacrificed by Görgey's traitorous disobedience.

Haynau with the main Austrian army advanced along the Danube—Görgey lay across his path.

Paskewitch crossed the northern frontier with the main Russian army, to descend the vale of the Theiss and its tributaries. Dembinski opposed him.

Jellachich, recovered from his castigation, threatened the southern frontier. Guyon and Vetter bade him defiance.

Luders from Wallachia invaded Transylvania.

Bem created the force with which he harrassed his advance, and hemmed in his activity.

With chivalrous folly, or with treacherous faith, Görgey waited the readiness of his foes—and then with Quixotic madness assayed an impossibility

Not till the middle of June, when Haynau was fully prepared, did Görgey cross the Waag. He proved, by his incipient success, how decisive might have been an earlier activity—but at Pered and Zsigard the victory was wrested from his grasp by the fatal appearance of the Russians on the field. He was defeated, driven over the Waag, and when Haynau on the 27th of June, at last in the fulness of time, began his advance, Görgey was compelled to retreat to Comorn.

On the 1st of July he repulsed the assault of Haynau, and on the 2d he assailed the Austrians, but failed to drive them from their positions.

At this critical moment he was informed of the elevation of Meszaros to the command in chief—whom he was ordered to obey. His wounded vanity vowed revenge, and he peremptorily refused obedience to the government, declined to unite his forces with the central army, and proceeded to act out his independent course.

He wasted from the 3d to the 10th of July in inactivity—and then learned the advance of the Russians in his rear, threatening to cut him off from the Theiss. Necessity drove him to do what he had refused to duty and patriotism.

Under cover of a feigned attack, on the 11th he fell back on Waitzen, only to encounter the Russians.

Paskewitch had begun his advance on the 18th of June, had pushed as far south as Gyöngyös, and had sent a corps to Waitzen to cut off the communication of Görgey with Dembinski.

Görgey assailed them fiercely on the 16th of July under the walls of Waitzen, and under cover of the battle maintained by Nagy Sandor, he drew off his main army to the north by the valley of the Eupel, and away from the rest of the Hungarian forces. Perczel was distant only a few miles with a strong force, yet Görgey gave him no notice to unite against the enemy.

Grabbe crossed his path and cut short his northern tour at Losonez. By bold manœuvring he evaded his antagonist, turned to the south, and suddenly presented himself at Gyöngyös, directly in the rear of the Russian army, on the 22d of July—on that very day engaged with a corps of Dembinski's army at Aszod. The Russians were defeated, and Görgey enjoyed the exemption from attack which it secured him, but neglected the opportunity of at once annihilating a large body of the enemy, and effecting his union with the central army.

Perversely flinging away his advantages, he turned again to the north, sought strong positions secured by skilful strategy amid the meanders and marshes of the Sajo, the Hermad and the Theiss, repelled repeated assaults of the Russians in the neighborhood of Tokay, and on the 25th of July gained such decisive advantages as opened once more a communication by Tessa Fured with the main army. His delay of three days lost the chance, and his victory of the 28th of July was rendered fruitless by Paskewitch's crossing the Theiss — which compelled Görgey to fall back to the left on Nyiregyhaza on the 31st, on the road to Arad.

The plan of the Imperialists to invade Hungary by Paskewitch on the north and by Haynau on the west—to penetrate to the central plains, divide Görgey from Dembinski, and with united forces crush the rebellion in detail, was now on the point of accomplishment. Paskewitch divided Dembinski from Görgey.

Dembinski despairing of union, withdrew from the upper Theiss to cover Szegedin, on which Haynau was rushing with overwhelming masses.

His outposts were in sight when the Government retired to Arad.

On the 2d of August Haynau occupied without resistance the fortress of Szegedin: on the 3d crossed the Theiss; on the 5th defeated Dembinski at Szoreg.

The Hungarians retreated to Temesvar, instead of to Arad—another blunder; but yet there was hope. Around Temesvar, to the south of Arad was concentrated the combined power of Vetter and Guyon and Dembinski; and the name of Bem lent its power to the array.

The latter had come from his mountain home in Transylvania to take the command in chief at the summons of Kossuth, while Vetter and Guyon after scattering the thrice beaten hosts of the treacherous Ban, the boasted saviour of the dynasty, had hastened to join Dembinski, shared the defeat of Szoreg, and now were ready for the fatal day of Temesvar. Görgey's column alone was absent from that field. The treason of Görgey, inflicting many a stab on his native land, prepared from afar the final blow of that decisive day.

He was retreating in two columns on Arad, when on the 2d of August Nagy Sandor was assailed at Debreczin by the Russians, and called for aid. He received laconic orders to retreat—and after a fight of ruinous bravery met Görgey at Grosswardein. There three precious days fled in idleness, while Haynau was shattering the Hungarian force at Szoreg on the 5th; and not till the 7th of August did he advance on Arad—where Nagy Sandor arrived on the 8th and Görgey on the evening of the 10th.

Görgey was ordered instantly to advance to Temesvar for the final conflict—but when the order was given the day was decided. His delay had been fatal. His languid preparations were abruptly broken off by the fugitives from the stricken field.

On the 10th of August Haynau had attacked Bem, who displayed the full power of his genius, and was confident of success. The Austrian force was already broken—when the Russian and Austrian reserves opportunely reached the field, and snatched from him the half gotten victory.

The overthrow was decisive and final. The last Hungarian army was annihilated, and its fragments were scattered in flight and dismay.

Görgey's three days in Grosswardein were the fitting conclusion of his whole campaign. He could have reached Arad on the 7th, Temesvar on the 8th, rested his troops on the 9th, and with Bem have crushed the Austrian main army at a blow on the 10th. He would have held the option of meeting the Russians, or of retreating on an open road to the south for time and reinforcements.

On the night of the 11th when all was over, Kossuth, under the moral and physical coercion of the generals and representatives assembled at Arad, laid down his power which treachery had rendered useless, and placed his life in the keeping of the hospitable Sultan, that he might dedicate its future to his country. Görgey held the only army on foot and between Arad and the enemy. He was entitled to the fruits of his villany. He assumed the dignity of Dictator for a day—that his country might fall by a worthy hand.

Görgey at Villagos attained the height of his ambition—an immortality of infamy.

The fourth battle of light and darkness was closed on the plains of Hungary.

Her fall was as that of the apocalyptic star which turned the third part of the waters to wormwood—of which many died because they were bitter.—

Four times in less than thirty years have four nations of Europe risen after free institutions, wrested them from their rulers, and maintained them intact against their assaults—and as many times have those nations been prostrated at the feet of their tyrants, by foreign military power, inspired by satanic hate of liberty, and commissioned by the Holy Alliance for its extinction. In every instance the voice of the only two free nations of Europe has been silent. Their sword has clung to its scabbard. They have hugged the delusive phantom of selfish security, and closed their eyes and ears to the inevitable day when alone they must defy or obey the powers whose insolence they failed to punish. That day is at hand.

The overthrow of Hungary closed the revolutionary era of 1848.

It left Nicholas the arbiter of Europe. Under his protectorate the petty princes of Germany resumed the airs and vexations of irresponsible power. Beneath the blight of his frown the visions of German Union faded away. Austria, strong in his support, and with Hungary at her feet, disdainfully rejected the federal constitution proposed by Prussia and Saxony on the 30th of May 1849.

The King of Prussia, as ambitious as weak, summoned Germany to Erfurt on the 20th of March 1850, to consult for a constitution, which his horror of revolutionary affinities and his fear of separation from his royal cousins caused him to reject when tendered by the people with the assurances of their support. But any union other than that of the *Princes* stood condemned as savoring of that "material unity" which Russia had denounced. Austria neither desired nor dared to think otherwise than Russia. Her power was at stake in any change of the Diet and its plenum, where her influence was supreme. Secure of aid from abroad, and fearing no serious opposition at home from Princes whose power she was protecting with her own against the people, their common foe, Austria forgot or disregarded the events of the last three years, her active participation in the creation of a central power, her recognition of its legitimate title to the attributes of an established government, and the incompatibility of those facts with the continued existence of the confederation of 1815. She wanted a power to oppose and if possible to crush the dangerous innovations, and the revolutionary agitations of Prussia. She was not sure of consent, if the Princes were consulted; but she was sure of acquiescence, if she assumed the responsibility of summoning the Diet into renewed existence. All Germany was startled by the resumption of her vacant presidency, the call of the Diet of the confederation to Frankfort, and the demand for its recognition by the foreign diplomatists.

Germany seemed threatened by two governments. Energy and resolution decided the supremacy. The Erfurt Assembly yielded to the Frankfort Diet—because Austria in arms audaciously supported the usurpations of the one, while Prussia in defence of the other, weakly entangled herself in the meshes of a technical legality, and met aggression only by argument. The issue was made and decided, under the dictatorial mediation of Russia, in the affairs of Hesse Cassel.

A free constitution, the offspring of 1830, sheltered Hesse Cassel from the storm of 1848. Her Elector repaid his people by invading their rights in the reactionary period of 1850. Their constitution required, as preliminary to a vote of money, a ministerial budget in detail, specifying the purposes to which the money was applicable. This is indispensable to the existence of ministerial responsibility. The Elector had resolved on freeing himself from that control. His minister demanded the taxes without a budget. The Diet refused them—and was dissolved. The taxes were decreed by the Elector—and payment refused by the people. The officers would not collect them, the troops would not enforce obedience. Haynau, red with Hungarian butchery, was invested with the command as a terror to well doers. The officers refused obedience and threw up their commissions—which their subalterns disdained to accept. In his extremity the Elector appealed to Austria. The refusal of taxes was forbidden by the construction put on the 25th and 26th articles of the Final Act of Vienna in 1832: and Austria eagerly seized at so opportune an occasion of enforcing the articles of the confederation, which she wished to re-instate, while she dealt a blow at a free constitution for which the people would fight. Russia played the mediator in this domestic quarrel, and *Austria* and *Prussia* were invited to *Warsaw*, to settle the internal affairs of the *German* government.

The invitation itself was of sinister significance. The government of Germany had passed north of the Vistula, and the conspiracy against the last relic of her freedom was conducted where the ruin of Poland had been consummated, and that of Hungary plotted. It was as if the constitution of the United States were debated at Quebec, under the mediation of England!!

Terms of arrangement were ostensibly mediated. Yet the conference was followed by the occupation of the Electorate by the armies of Austria and Bavaria in the name of the confederation; and martial law substituted the sword for the constitution.

Even the patience of Prussia was outraged. Her population armed and rose en masse at the summons of the King; and Austria yielded to his armed demands the "free conferences" of Dresden.

They resulted in nothing but the submission of Prussia, the continued occupation of Hesse Cassel, and the march of an Austrian corps to Hamburg. Germany lay at the feet of Austria—the slave of the Czar, and Prussia stood silent, irresolute, dangling her military ornaments, and clattering her useless sword.

Such is the result of the revolution in Germany.

Despotism crossed the Rhine at the election of Louis Napoleon to the presidency of France. His ambitious eye was fixed on the memories of the Empire. He longed for arbitrary power; and turned in reverence to the Mecca of despotism. He gave earnest of sincerity by crushing the infant freedom of Rome beneath the spiritual and temporal omnipotence of the Pope. Two short years have fled, and now the constitution of France is a thing of the past. Absolute power, seized by the sword, covered by the sanction of a sham election, and cheered by the assurances of Russian support as it was usurped by its example, now chills the banks of the Seine by its gloomy shade. The example of the Czar supports the position, and inspires the policy of Louis Napoleon. Wherever a hand is lifted against liberty, there is the Czar to support, to aid, to encourage, to inspire, prodigal of his resources in the crusade on freedom, and defending his frontiers from the approach of danger by meeting and repelling it far from his threshold.

But Louis Napoleon cannot stand still. He must advance or fall. His equilibrium can only be preserved by action. Russia insists on the treaties of 1815, and that excludes the Rhine from his ambition. But England is hateful because powerful, and dangerous because free. To cripple her resources would be the most acceptable sacrifice the neophyte could lay on the altars of the northern Moloch. Rumor points to that quarter: the note of preparation seems to confess the reality of the danger; and we do not hear that the treaties of 1815 are invoked in the north for *her* protection.—

Three months have elapsed since the above was written—and already the northern powers are preparing to reduce France to conformity with their despotic theories of the divine and hereditary right.

Louis Napoleon was welcome when he arose—to stay the plague. He was greeted with favor when he forced the bit between the teeth of rampant France, and prevented her from dashing to atoms their tottering empires—while they struggled with the revolutionary maniacs at home.

But height has recalled high thoughts—security has banished fear—and the useful tool may now be treated as a dangerous weapon. Safely enthroned amid the ruins of the suppressed revolution, they feel strong enough to renew the alliance for the restoration of monarchy in France.

If the communication in the London Times may be relied on for substantial accuracy, the condescending visit of Nicholas early in 1852 to Vienna and Berlin was no idle courtesy. It was a political mission of union, conciliation, preparation, and conference. The diplomatic notes interchanged between the courts related directly and ostensibly to the personal ambition of Louis Napoleon; but the principles and purposes avowed or foreshadowed plainly import a renewal of the Holy Alliance in spirit and in substance for the restoration of absolute monarchy in France—leaving the time and mode to be settled by the exigencies of the future.

The northern powers assume the right to dictate or to declare the public law of Europe: and in their diplomatic notes, Europe and the despotic powers are convertible terms.

They confess and recognize *the fact* that Louis Napoleon is possessed of supreme power—but they hint that it involves a violation of the treaties of 1814 and 1815. They contemplate the possibility of his assumption of the Imperial dignity, and declare in advance how it will be received. Whether voluntarily assumed or conferred by the will of the French nation, in either case it is equally reprobated as an infraction of what they are pleased to term the fundamental maxims of the public law of Europe. Their conduct may be different according to the circumstances attending the change—but they deny the right of either the president or the nation to make the change. They assert for the first time in explicit terms, that they recognize no power to create a new dynasty, hereditary and legitimate, ruling over the French people. They scoff at the caprices of universal suffrage in a tone which might lead them to impeach the legitimacy of our presidential elections. They recognize no government as *de jure* unless it claim by inheritance; and the only inheritable crown of France which they will recognize or accept is—*that of the Bourbons.* Its assumption by any one else is—*an usurpation.*

They justly regard the assumption of the Imperial title by Louis Napoleon for life as merely a *verbal* change: but to claim it by inheritance from his uncle would be a grave usurpation. That would be an assertion of a *right* which they would feel called on to resist and resent—for it would involve the integrity of their central principle—the assertion of a fountain of rightful sovereignty elsewhere than in the breast of a legitimate and anointed ruler.

All other authority they treat as temporary—as passing and exceptional in its nature—to be respected or expelled according to circumstances—but never for a moment as clothed with the incommunicable attributes of heaven-descended sovereignty. They liken it to the authority of Cromwell—as if his title was not as good as that of the tyrant he expelled. They even have the impudence to class it with that of Napoleon—their master and scourge—as if they had never bent the knee before his legitimate might. They venture to assimilate it to the authority of the kings of Poland—as if centuries of elective dignity consecrated by the national devotion could confer no sanctity. Or did they mean to shelter their bloody extermination of that magnificent realm under their modern principles—that an elective crown is only tolerated till the advent of the first armed usurper who conquers in the name of absolute and hereditary right?

The principles therefore of these recent conferences plainly indicate that the northern powers regard the rule of Louis Napoleon as illegal in its origin—an infraction of the treaties of 1815—outlawed by the common law of Europe—and liable without any iniquity to be swept away at the pleasure and by the arms of the despotic powers.

That if they tolerate the continuance of his authority, it is only in the interest of peace, dependent on his civil and peaceful conduct, and accompanied by a protest that it is accepted as a fact, not regarded as a right.

That the right appertains only to the line of the Bourbons—over whom even in exile the halo of the crown hovers till it shall descend and settle upon their triumphant heads.

That they recognize the power of Louis Napoleon as only *de facto*—which means, they will seize the first and best opportunity to make it *not a fact*.

That it may endure, under certain humiliating conditions, during his life, but not beyond; it must be a barren sceptre—no son of his succeeding: but while a dark silence rests on what shall follow in his room, that silence is pregnant with meaning.

If Louis Napoleon, though proclaimed Emperor by the unanimous voice of France, will yet be allowed to hold only a temporary authority not transmissible—then *at his death*—or sooner, if he violate the limits imposed on his ambition—some other authority is to fill his place vacated by death or by armed expulsion. The northern powers have declared that the crown of France appertains of right perpetually and exclusively to the Bourbons—surviving every change—undying in the midst of murderous revolutions—and calmly waiting the passing away of every temporary revolutionary possessor of their legitimate and indefeasible sovereignty.

They therefore mean that the Bourbons shall again—sooner or later—by peaceful or by forcible means—by armed interventions or by the capricious nature of universal suffrage—so soon as it may be convenient and at the death of Louis Napoleon at the farthest, remount the throne of the restoration and link France once more to the car of despotism.

The Bourbon princes of either branch look for this mighty deliverance—are burying their domestic feuds which the usurpation of 1830 engendered—and preparing to cross once more the French frontier at the head of an army of deliverance. The heir of the elder branch now counts his partizans by the hundred thousand—insolently issues his bulletins to regulate their conduct and marshal their forces—interdicting the oath of office to the usurping president—and pointing to the bright day of their approaching advent.

Whether this bold iniquity shall succeed or fail—rests with God. Louis Napoleon can utter no voice of complaint. But France will speak in tones not easily to be forgotten.

I only mark the event as proof of the consistent assertion by the despotic powers of the universality of their principles, of their deadly hostility to every form of *national* sovereignty—of their deep conviction that the *principle* must be extingushed as their only safety.—

No man can tell what a day may bring forth. It behooves wise men not to shut their eyes to disagreeable truths, nor to put far from them a danger which may be at the door. Wisdom demands that we of this western world anxiously inquire the import of these startling events of our day, which outstrip the calculations of political sagacity, and heap up in weeks the events of a century—all bearing in one direction, inspired by one spirit and backed by powers which act as one man—the powers of despotism banded and sworn for the ruin of liberty.

If Russia grasp the dictatorship of Europe she must wield her power for the overthrow of this Republic. The law of necessity will compel her: and the hatred and the fear of freedom will make it a grateful task.

What then is the position of Russia and of her allied despots in the affairs of Europe—is the question it behooves us gravely to consider. Let us not shrink from the investigation—nor refuse to accept the conclusion which reason and history may force on our conviction.

SECTION VI.

THE DICTATORSHIP OF RUSSIA IN EUROPE.

THE DICTATORSHIP OF RUSSIA IN EUROPE.

The revolution of 1848 has recoiled with disastrous ruin on the cause of human freedom. It lies crushed beneath the fragments created by its own explosion.

The result of that stupendous outburst is now before us, real, palpable, complete. The victors have secured their footing—and already look for the signal of a new onset.

What that result is, who have gained by it, against whom is the power of the victors directed, are momentous inquiries for the free people of the world.

I insist—

That the issue of that eventful struggle has been to upset the balance of power in Europe in favor of Russia:

That it has decisively overthrown the cause of popular liberty, and driven for their security all the despotic powers of Europe under the protectorate of Russia:

That this union in her hands of preponderating power, and of the recognized lead of the despotic powers in the war of freedom has inaugurated the Dictatorship of Russia in Europe:

That this power must from necessity, on principle, and by inclination, be devoted to the ruin of all free governments: that it is absolutely inconsistent with the existence of the English monarchy and the American Republic as free popular representative governments: and that they will be compelled sooner or later to defend by force of arms their freedom and independence against the intrigues, the diplomacy, the legislation, the hostilities of the despotic powers of Europe:

That it is, therefore, the part of wisdom to be prepared for the advent of the inevitable day, and ready to seize the first favorable conjuncture to strike in common the first blow, and so to strike that it may be the last:

That such a course is the dictate of sound policy—the policy followed by our foes and the cause of their present triumph:

That this is the policy of President Washington—illustrated by his conduct, and consecrated by his parting address—adopted by President Monroe—re-affirmed by President Adams—reiterated by President Polk—the traditional policy and the only safe policy of this Republic:

That the question we have to decide is—not whether we will live in peace and repose, or gratuitously go on a crusade for liberty throughout the world, but—the absolute certainty of a contest with the combined powers of despotism being apparent—shall we wait till those powers, having utterly rooted out free governments from Europe, shall turn their might for our destruction, alone and without allies;—or shall we now seize the first opportunity of a decisive outbreak in Europe to aid the cause of freedom with arms and money, fight our battle by the armies of European revolutionists on the field of Europe, and by the aid of our allies for ever settle the question between freedom and despotism.

The only alternatives are war, in Europe, now, with allies—and war hereafter, on our own soil, without allies.—

Thrice since the days of Charlemagne has Europe been threatened with universal empire:—but never has the danger been so immediate, so threatening, so irresistible as now.

Charles V. united beneath his massive sceptre Spain and Italy and Germany and the Netherlands, and supported his mighty armies from the gold and the commerce of the colonies of the Eastern and the Western Indies. England and France alone existed to oppose him. But the reformation divided his people, and raised foes of his household, and opened the door to foreign intervention which was used with decisive effect. His death divided his empire. The wars of the reformation impaired the unity of power in the hands of his successors. After the death of Philip II. the cloud melted away from the sky of Europe and men breathed more freely. The great war of opinion in matters of religion in Germany, aided by the arms of France and England, rescued the liberties of Europe from the fate of those of Castile. The spirit of bigotry and the wasting hand of despotism exhausted the strength of the empire of Spain. At the death of Charles IV. it had been deprived of some of its fairest provinces. What remained was lethargic, spiritless, dead in political power, a *hereditas jacens* for the first or the strongest comer. One danger had departed. Another was at hand.

France and the fortune of Louis XIV. filled the haughty place of Spain. The Spanish dominions, still majestic though in ruins, were bequeathed by their childless monarch to the grandson of Louis. This was to bestow them on him. His ambition was armed with the double power of the French and the Spanish monarchy. He swayed the sceptre over France and Spain and the Netherlands and the two Sicilies and the Milanese. Powerless in the imbecil hands of Charles, these vast dominions in the energetic control of Louis and supported by the genius and military science of France—if once consolidated—made an end of the independence of Europe.

The courage and far-sighted statesmanship of William of Orange united the arms of England, Holland, and Germany, to shatter this stupendous but ill-compacted empire, ere it should be too late. He died—and left the execution of his plans to Marlborough, who vindicated on the field of battle the independence of Europe. The second danger fled.

Napoleon united in his grasp the scattered energies of the revolution and turned its madness into the docile minister of his ambition. He dragged at his chariot wheels the monarchs of continental Europe.

He dictated the law from the Baltic to the Euxine. He assembled in stupendous masses the whole military power of western Europe for the overthrow of the colossal empire of the north. But his power had no deep foundations. It rested on opinion. It vanished with its change. England and Russia alone bade him defiance: but it was only when the enthusiasm of Germany and Austria rose on his retreating armies that Europe was free. For the government of a conqueror is necessarily that of a despot. Military power replaces the will of the people. Freedom and law can have no sure abiding place. The people rose at the call of their kings—because national independence is indispensable to national liberty. Napoleon fell—his foes sat in his seat. Europe was delivered from the hands of one, to those of many tyrants. The third danger passed.

Yet it did not pass without dragging us into a war for our independence and our neutral rights. That war would have been waged ten years before, but for our feebleness. The provocations, the insults, the injuries existed, accumulated, were repeated during long years—till strength was substituted for endurance; and we entered the lists of armed nations because the two tyrannies, which divided and contended for the mastery of Europe, with impartial hate depredated on our commerce under the decrees of Berlin and Milan and the Orders in Council, and invaded the security of our citizens under the assumed right of search for absconding sailors.

The fourth peril now exists. It is greater and more grievous than the others, and has attained what they only threatened to attain. Russia at this moment dictates the law to Europe from the Ural to the Bay of Biscay.

Her power is more permanent and stable in its foundations than that of either of the preceding aspirants for universal dominion.

It is not composed—like that of Charles V.—of divers discordant states united only by the crown he wore. It is one great central empire, compact in shape, vast in dimensions, inexhaustible in resources, moving as one man at the word of its master. His will is hampered by no feudal privileges. His orders are disputed by no proud and powerful vassals. No national immunities withdraw the resources of his people from his reach. No Cortes, deeply seated in the national affections and interwoven with the history of the people, bids him defiance in his usurpations, and summons him to a civil war ere he can dispose of his arms for foreign aggression. No religious dispute rouses the stubbornness of conscientious resistance; but the religious zeal of his people conspires with his ambition and with the expansive tendencies of his empire. The ideas of human liberty and popular power are to this age what those of conscience and faith were to that of Charles V. But armed and organized governments, fired with devotion for the cause of the reformation, met Charles on many a field; when inactive, their arms lay ready to repel aggression; and the consciousness of their power compelled the respectful consideration of the Emperor and his bigots. His own vassals were divided against him, and France and England lent them countenance and "material aid." Nicholas is troubled by no internal dissensions on liberal ideas. His people are far behind that point—quiescent in the faith of their fathers, and glorying in their Czar as the vicegerent of God, the father of all his people. *Without*, all governments are on his side. He is their protector against their domestic foes. By his arms alone can the petty tyrants of Europe maintain their tottering thrones. He is the head and leader of the conspiracy of princes against the people. The Emperor of Austria, the rabble of German princes, the besotted and foresworn King of Naples, the trembling Pope, the Austrian tools of Tuscany and the Italian principalities, are one and all his slaves, pensioners on his bounty, eager to do his bidding, covetous of his favors, absolutely dependent on his power. Through *them* he rules Europe. Without him *they* are nothing. Their thrones are held by no tenure but obedience to his dictation: for his aid would be withdrawn from the refractory, and the people can deal with their domestic tyrants when freed from the weight of Russian arms. The only issue in Europe now is freedom or slavery. On that question all the princes of Europe are of one mind and of one heart. They make common cause, have a common purse, swear by and invoke the same devil, and ply with rival skill his borrowed flames.

The Czar is relatively to his opponents more powerful than Louis XIV. in all the might of the Spanish monarchy. He was forced to guide discordant kingdoms under the forms of domestic rule. They were jealous of foreign domination. His power was not consolidated ere it was shattered by the coalition. It had no central idea, rested on no tradition, was inspired by no grand purpose. It was the idol of his ambition, the monument of his egotism. Devoid of all hold in the affections of the people whom the will of a dotard delivered to the rule of a boy, his vast dominions were a lifeless corps over which heroes contended, while it was careless and unconscious of the maddening conflict. A few years of grace and respite would have made a difference. But William was too prompt to shape the weapon, and Marlborough too hasty to ply it.

The Russian dictatorship is more absolute, more powerful, more dangerous than that of Napoleon, when all Europe followed his eagles to Moscow. His followers were his vassals, outraged at his upstart domination, and driven like eastern slaves to the battle by the terrors of threatened castigation. The heart of neither kings nor people was in it. They moved like automata at his bidding. They covered his flanks, kept open his communications, and formed corps of reserve. His power for action centred in the troops of France. The first check chilled the devotion of his allies or revealed their discontent. The first retreat loosed the bands of authority, released the struggling and reluctant vassals from their restraints, and arrayed them in open hostility against the standard they had followed. Nicholas has the absolute control of his own people and the absolute devotion of his vassal crowns. Before him every head is bowed low—for by him alone are they decorated with a crown and tolerated on a throne.

Without him they are nothing. They are therefore the slaves of his will. There is no fear of defection. Adversity will only strengthen the bonds. Defeat will only make protection more necessary, and union more indispensable for the common cause. The kings and nations whom Napoleon hurled on Alexander reluctantly, sluggishly, and against their will, Nicholas now arrays as with a magician's wand in the cause of human slavery. Napoleon's fall was involved in the very nature of his empire. It rested on his military genius—but its only object was his personal aggrandizement. To that the independence of his neighbors was unhesitatingly sacrificed. Kings and people were alike interested in its overthrow. Kings could not brook the rank and humiliations of Viceroys. The people felt that freedom was impossible without independence. Liberty must find its security in the responsibility of the domestic government to the people of the state. Their rulers were beyond their control so long as they were coerced by the fear or supported by the countenance of a foreign power. Kings became agitators in favor of freedom, that they might break a galling yoke. Their people were partly deceived by their promises, partly conscious of the necessity of national independence to domestic liberty. They joined against the common oppressor, and adjourned the question between themselves and their rulers to a more convenient season. *Now*, large masses of every nation support the governments. They are surrounded with highly organized armies, officered with a view to revolutionary disturbances. All the powers of government are sedulously devoted to the great cause of kings, and the leader of that cause is the Czar.

Napoleon was the soldier of a revolution which he betrayed, the champion of a liberty he chained. The powers by which he rose were his fiercest foes. The cause in which he fleshed his maiden sword was the victim of his success, and its partisans shed no tears at his fall. Nicholas reigns with quiet unquestioned accepted authority over a docile people. His title is hereditary and unquestioned. His purposes are those of national aggrandizement. His people associate themselves to his glories. His authority is looked on as divine throughout the great majority of his people, and the disquieted provinces of Poland are held in obedience by the immovable mass of the empire.

The centre and body of the empire of Napoleon was vulnerable at every point. Spain and Germany and Italy and the ocean surrounded it. His power was divided in his assaults by the necessity of defence. His rear was always exposed, and while contending with the allied arms on the German frontier, Wellington penetrated his territory from south to north, and only closed his career on the field of Waterloo.

The empire of Russia occupies the northern and eastern extremities of Europe. Eternal snow and ice are the unassailable bulwarks of its rear. Its eastern flank skirts far and wide into the dim confines of Asia—free from the chances of assault, and prolific in the materials for the best cavalry in the world.

Its vast plains slope to the south, and tend to precipitate the mass of the empire on the fated walls of Constantinople. On the west alone is it assailable, and there only during three months of the year. Retreat can hide disaster behind inaccessible snows till the favorable moment summons new armies to activity. They march to soft and sunny climes, allured by the splendors of art and the luxuries of civilization, where no month can numb their frames enured to the ices of the pole, and the campaign and the year are conterminous. This colossal and invulnerable power Napoleon well declared the "Antæus of the fable which cannot be overcome but by seizing it by the middle and stifling it in the arms." "But where," he asked after his own melancholy failure—"is the Hercules to be found who will attempt such an enterprise. Show me an Emperor of Russia, brave, able, and impetuous, in a word a Czar worthy of his situation, and Europe is at his feet. He may begin his operations at the distance of only one hundred leagues from the two capitals of Vienna and Berlin, the sovereigns of which are the only obstacles he has to apprehend. He gains the one by seduction, subdues the other by force, and he is soon in the midst of the lesser princes of Germany, most of whom are his relations or dependants. A few words on liberation and independence will set Italy on fire. Assuredly in such a situation I should arrive at Calais by fixed stages, and be the arbiter of the fate of Europe."

A generation do not yet sleep in their graves—and the vision of the seer has become the fact of history.

†

Alexander—"faux fin et foube comme un Grec du bas Empire"—is replaced by Nicholas—"brave, able, and impetuous,"—but also calm, prudent, far-sighted, and inexorable. Events which properly used should have broken his power have permanently consolidated it. Europe is at his feet. Those whom Napoleon contemplated as the enemies to be overcome are now the suppliants for his favor. He now may begin his operation—not at only one hundred leagues from the two capitals of Vienna and Berlin—but at the Rhine. Those sovereigns, the only obstacles to be feared, are his accomplices or his slaves. The Emperor of Austria owes him the rescue, the preservation, the possession of his crown—twice lost in the Hungarian war. Without the aid of Russia he falls to-morrow. Russian aid was invoked to conquer Hungary. Russian troops now again are invoked to keep down the rebellious population, and the plains and fortresses of Hungary have been garrisoned by the Czar at the humble request of the Austrian Emperor. The Empire of Austria is not only out of the way of Russian conquest—it is the dependant of the Czar. Its territory is the basis of his operations. Its resources are at his disposal. Its Emperor rules by his permission, and is little better than his vicegerent. He is a willing slave, imbued with the principles and devoted to the cause of despotic power, and cheerfully aiding in the great crusade against liberty.

Prussia, the other obstacle, has ceased to be a stumbling block. The King has repented him of his imperial dreams and popular ambition. He has failed in energy for a great game, and has sunk to a second rate place. He no longer leads Germany whose sceptre he flung away and whose people he disappointed, disgusted, and betrayed. He stands before them in confessed impotency, bearded on his frontiers by Austrian arms, driven from his great scheme of German regeneration within the meshes of Austrian intrigue and beneath the Diet of the treaties of Vienna. He has danced attendance on the Czar and the Emperor at Warsaw, to debate the internal affairs of Germany and settle by the interested mediation of Russia her government on its narrow and tottering base. He has allowed the only free constitution of Germany to be crushed by Austria at his very door. He has compelled his troops to retire before the advancing Austrians, and to allow Hamburg and the north of Germany to be occupied, brow-beaten, and insulted in the name of the abandoned and fallen Diet. The capital of Germany is at St. Petersburg.

The usurpation of Louis Napoleon has stricken from the map of Europe the only free power capable of bidding defiance to Russia. His policy from his election has been reactionary. His feelings are with the counter-revolutionists. He held the fiery spirit of the French in check till despotism had won decisive triumphs. He discountenanced and repressed every sign of sympathy. He signalized under false pretexts his devotion to the cause of despots by assailing the Roman republic and crushing its infant freedom. He calmly waited the day of factious violence to merge dissensions in his absolute power, confident of impunity in the midst of factions too hostile to each other to unite for his overthrow, and singly not a match for his partisans backed by the arms and power of the government. His usurpation has thus far been successful. It has stricken France from the list of free governments. It has ranged her in the ranks of despotisms. With them only can Louis Napoleon sympathize—from them alone can he hope for support—and by them alone can he hope to maintain his usurpation. With his usurpation end for the present the hopes of European freedom. The Kings of the north were clamorous with exultation and joy. Austria and Russia hastened to greet the converted revolutionist in the cause of royalty. German tyrants breathed freely, when relieved from the frown of French democracy at their unrighteous deeds. Prompt acknowledgments met his accession to the holy cause. Secret assurances of aid and comfort must have encouraged his nascent treason. By this usurpation France changed sides on the day of battle. Whether the usurper pursue a subservient or an independent policy the weight of France is lost to the liberal cause. He cannot encourage the spirit of the revolution without sounding the signal for his overthrow. He may be inclined to defy the schemes of Russian ambition; but he cannot with safety to himself attack the foundation of her power. That rests on her sole ability to repress the revolution and to maintain the princes on their thrones. Louis Napoleon will hardly venture to appeal to the people of Germany and Italy while oppressing those of France. He will scarcely speak of constitutions and popular guarantees, while yet smoking with the heat of his contest with both. His private interest to maintain his power is greater than his public interest to preserve the dignity of France. His position is not a little like that of Louis Philippe; and similar causes may induce him to stifle the voice of France in the affairs of Europe.

He would doubtless prefer an independent and a brilliant policy—one which should gratify the pride of France and decorate his own name with the laurels of high deeds. But the first question is—the preservation of his power; and that rests on the suppression of the spirit of revolution and the extinction of the idea of free government. The friendship of Russia is the best security for the success of that effort: and such aid is worth many sacrifices of dignity and of national benefits. His sympathies are on that side; and his interests seem to run in the same channels. It is scarcely possible for any war against Russia not to assume the shape of a revolutionary appeal to the people against their rulers. They are all in the interest of Russia: and France would scarcely dare the contest without allies. She must therefore be still, or seek allies at the hands of the revolutionists: and *that* would ill comport with the position of Louis Napoleon as the tamer of the spirit of Jacobin France. An easier game would seem to be—a Russian alliance with a hostile aspect towards England, and based on such partitions of European and Turkish territory as the parties might be satisfied with.

A revolution in France must, therefore, precede any hopes of her aid to the cause of liberty; and without her there is no power on the continent able to stay the march of Russia to universal empire.

The Czar is not only the arbiter of Christian Europe—he is also at his pleasure the master of Mohammedan Europe. The last barrier between his eager hand and the glittering dome of St. Sophia has been swept away.

The two great problems of European politics in the nineteenth century are—the fate of the Ottoman Empire and the fate of free principles. The events of the last three years have solved both in favor of Russia.

The flood of Mohammedan conquest rolled at the two extremes of Europe to the foot of the Pyrenees and of the Carpathians. Before those mighty barriers were its proud waves staid. Ferdinand the Catholic drove them across the Straits of Gibraltar three centuries and a half ago. Nicholas would have driven them across the Bosphorus thirty years ago—but for the armed veto of united Europe. The Ottoman is still camped at Constantinople by favor of the dispute for the possession of his spoils. There was only one nation able at once to seize and to govern the provinces of the Turk. But such an accession to the power of Russia was too dangerous to be permitted; and England, France, and Austria were sharpsighted to spy out her insidious advances, and more than once united to forbid her progress. But the contest has been between jealous allies, distant from the scene and having discordant interests, uniting only for a negative object—and one despotic power on the scene of action, taking advantage of every emergency, with every thing to gain and out of reach of possible loss, retiring from every contest with some fragment of the prey, and each time leaving the victim more enfeebled and more defenceless.

The Mohammedan power has reached its term of life and is now fading away. The only question is what shall fill its place. The mode of its removal is immaterial. It is already dead, and awaits those who shall carry it out and bury it. Its expulsion from Europe and Western Asia is natural, moral, and necessary. It is a tyranny of the fiercest character, compensated by no advanced civilization, and destitute of promise for the future. The civilization of which it was the representative has run its cycle of rise, perfection, and decline, and its naked stump now only cumbers the ground and excludes better occupants. It covers the earliest seats of Christianity and of civilization with the fragments of an infidel and a semi-barbarous empire. Of its population only one-third in the European provinces are Mohammedans, and only two-fifths of that in the Asiatic dominions. The rest is almost wholly Christian, held in the most abject subjection, and ready at any moment to receive with open arms their Christian brethren. The despotism of the Czar would be a mitigation of that of the Turk. The most fertile provinces of Europe would be regained to the arts of civilization and the faith of the Christian, and its desert places would blossom as the rose beneath the touch of modern energy and the breath of modern improvement. The power which reposes in those delightful regions won them by the sword, but has not naturalized itself by taking root in the soil. Its continuance is an outrage on the faith and feelings of the vast majority of the people. It is fading away from the scene of its glory as did the Greek empire of Constantinople before the splendor of the ascending crescent. It treads the path of the grave with the even step of fate—pushed onward by a power that looks like Providence, in its calm, steady, deliberate, but ceaseless and fatal advance.

The consistent policy of Russia has been met only by the vacillating schemes and the shifting expedients of her opponents; and the history of the world is one long comment on the fate of such a contest.

The Greek revolution stripped the Turk of his most celebrated provinces, and set the fatal example of internal dissolution.

The battle of Navarino in 1827 destroyed the Ottoman fleet—for the benefit of Russia.

Nicholas seized the moment of exhaustion in 1828 to pick a quarrel. Debitsch forced the passes of the Balkan, scattered the Turkish armies, and Constantinople was exposed without a defender. His march was staid at Adrianople by the threat that France and England would cross his path; and his master contented himself with the treaty of Adrianople in 1829, which surrendered the mouths of the Danube, opened the Bosphorus and Dardanelles, virtually severed Wallachia and Moldavia, and vested Russia with pretexts for perpetual intermeddling, and a right to make war whenever it might be convenient.

The genius of Mehemet Ali had gradually augmented his power in Egypt till he could defy his master, and was more than a match for the sluggish mass to which he was nominally subject. Egypt was lost to the Porte.

Syria is the necessary outwork and dependent of Egypt, and the Taurus the first barrier fit for the frontier of an empire. Mehemet Ali coveted that mountain rampart; and in 1831 his son marched to the conquest of Syria. Ibrahim captured Acre; and he followed up his success by scattering the armies of the Porte at Homs, at Beylan, at Kouiah, in rapid succession. In 1832 Constantinople was naked and trembling before his sword. Russian armies promptly responded to the Sultan's piteous cry for aid, crossed to the Asiatic side of the Bosphorus, and interposed between the powerful vassal and the powerless lord. The treaty of Unkiar Skellessi formally inaugurated the Russian protectorate. The terrified and feeble Sultan secured the right of Russian aid; and Nicholas knew that to ask protection was a confession of dependence, and cheerfully assumed the duty of guarding his future dominions against a more formidable occupant. Protection covered the insidious advances of the Macedonian, the Roman, the British empires; and Russia only availed herself of the traditional and customary forms of incipient conquest.

Russia had rescued Constantinople; but Syria still lay in the grasp of Mehemet Ali.

In 1839 the Porte renewed its struggle for its lost province. The battle of Nezib stretched it again prostrate before Ibrahim. Again Russian arms were ready. Nothing but the sudden and brilliant descent of Napier and the English squadron on the coasts of Syria, and the threatened bombardment of Alexandria, scared the rapacious Egyptian from his prey, and spared the Porte a second precedent of the dangerous presence of the Russians.

Languid and exhausted, the Ottoman empire, unable to stand erect even before domestic foes, lay at the mercy of European diplomacy and arms. The joint treaty of England, Austria, Prussia, and Russia, embodied the jealousy of the former powers, and secured their common intervention. It alone stood between Nicholas and his fated victim. He was not hasty or impatient. He used the treaty to break the alliance of England and France,—and secured by their division future impunity. Turkey was fallen from the list of powers. Her place was vacant—awaiting an occupant. There was only one power which could occupy it. That power, sure of the future, confident in the course of events, rich in the promises of time and accident, waived for a season the occupation of her inheritance. The blood of the princes of the Greek empire transmits to the Czar a specious pretext of title, which has been nurtured into a national tradition, and confirmed by ancient prophecies. The religion of Russia is that of the majority of the population of the Turkish dominions. Their advance to the conquest of Constantinople would be a holy war to the Russians; while the Christians of Turkey would greet their advent as a great deliverance. Superstition and policy, national tradition and hereditary ambition conspire to fix the destiny of Constantinople. The events of 1848 and 1849 have removed or lessened the obstacles which hitherto have postponed and impeded the accomplishment of those darling dreams; and any day we may be called on to listen to the trumpet call of Christian Russia to a crusade for the extermination of the religion and the empire of Mahomet on the soil of Europe.

What stands in the way of its speedy, easy, entire triumph?

Certainly not the most serious of the obstacles which have hitherto retarded it. That has been the opposition of united Europe. All the great powers have been on one side and against Russia, however diverse their peculiar interests might be. France may have been for a partition; Austria for the integrity of the Ottoman power; while England may have seen in its weakness the best security for her East India communications: yet all felt and acknowledged that the possession of the wide domain of the Turk and the port of Constantinople by Russia would destroy the balance of power in Europe for ever, place the fate of Asia in her hands, and subject the world to her dictatorship. They therefore tried every species of political combination and military protest to hinder the consummation of the hopes of the Czar. Austria was most deeply and directly interested of all. The Ottoman dominions form her southern border. Moldavia alone divides Russia from her eastern line. On the north from Cracow eastward Russia is her conterminous neighbor. To allow her to seize and appropriate the spoils of the

Turk would be to permit Austria to be completely wrapped round by the coils of this constrictor. She would lie in the embrace of death. Metternich was, therefore, the most prompt, pertinacious, and uncompromising enemy to Russian aggrandizement on the side of Turkey. He more than once lined the Hungarian frontier with troops ready for action, and was willing to fling to the winds the hopes and blessings of the Holy Alliance, and bid defiance to its head, rather than submit to the inevitable fate which the conquest of Turkey involved. Austria, while an independent power, was, alone of all the great powers, directly interested in checking the Russian advance. Her independence, her power, her very existence were at stake. No scheme of partition could reconcile her—for her discordant provinces were her greatest difficulty; and a part of the spoil would increase the difficulty more than it would add to her strength.

But all this is now changed. Austria is held together by the weight of Russian power. Her prestige is lost among the powers. Her domestic difficulties are beyond her control. She was indebted to Nicholas for her existence as an empire. His arms still support its tottering fabric. The relation of equals in the Holy Alliance has been changed into that of protector and dependent. Nicholas is the master of the Austrian empire. Austria, therefore, will be no worse off with Turkey in the hands of Russia than she is now. Wallachia and Moldavia are now practically Russian provinces; and they line the greater portion of her Turkish frontier. Wallachia was, on the south, the basis of Russian military operations against Hungary in the cause of the Emperor. It was found convenient to have that spirited nation compressed on all sides by the powerful protector of the Imperial feebleness. The Russian occupation of those provinces is now the greatest obstacle to a Hungarian rebellion. Such is the miserable exhaustion of Austria that her danger is her safety. She cannot, therefore, if she would, arrest the march of Nicholas to Constantinople. She has not the will any more than the power to do it. Hungary and the Carpathians have ceased to be barriers: and Russian troops under Austrian leave can penetrate through them into every province of Turkey, divide her feeble forces, distract her defence by multitudinous attacks, and prostrate her at pleasure. But the difficulty has not for thirty years been of a military, but a diplomatic character. Russia was always able to crush the Turks; European arms and diplomacy stood in the way. But only three powers were at once interested in the question and able to speak with authority. They were England, France, and Austria. All were equally threatened by Russian preponderance. Each had a separate and special interest. England must keep open her communications with India over the Isthmus of Suez and by the Red Sea. Egypt must, therefore, be in the hands of a power dependent on England and not on Russia or any other strong power. France has always aspired to influence in Egypt, partly inspired by hostility to England, partly by her interest in her African provinces, and the desire safely to extend them. She has always longed to call the Mediterranean a French lake, and Russia would be a dangerous rival. Austria shrunk from absorption in the spreading flood of Russian conquest.

On Austria the brunt of the conflict must fall. England and France were too far off to operate either promptly or efficiently with bodies of troops adequate to the encounter of the Russian armies. The Egyptian expedition of Napoleon was as decisively overthrown as that to Russia. One to Constantinople would meet a more speedy and inevitable fate. Men of war might force the Dardanelles—but Sebastopol is at the door. Russian fleets could meet them or anticipate them, and Russian armies could fortify those straights so as to make them impassable to any fleet. She could at less expense put tenfold greater masses of troops at any given point of the Turkish empire than France and England combined. The great majority of the population would be indifferent or on the side of Russia, and that alone would be decisive.

The only power which could act with effect was Austria. She was nearer than Russia. Her military resources were on the flanks of the Russian operations, and as they progressed they would be liable to have their communications cut off from the east of Hungary, and to be assailed in rear by Austria, while opposed in the front by Turkish armies, commanded by French or English officers, and supported by foreign troops. So long as Austria was an independent power, and chose to forbid the occupation of Turkey, it was impossible.

But the events of 1848 and 1849 have made her dependent on Russia. Her territory is protected by Russian troops, and would form the base of their operations against Turkey. She cannot forbid it—for the withdrawal of their aid would leave her at the mercy of the outraged and inflamed Hungarians, who stand ready to clutch their weapons at a moment's warning. Austria must acquiesce in whatever policy Nicholas may see fit to dictate, for her military strength always resided in Hungary. The genius, spirit and devotion of the Hungarians alone rescued the empire from dismemberment on more than one occasion; and now the Hungarian is at once the bitterest and the most dangerous enemy of that house which clung to him for protection in the hour of need, and repaid his services in treachery, slavery, and blood. When the Emperor invoked the power of Russia to crush the liberties of Hungary, he for ever alienated the people who alone could defend him. He could sink to no lower or more humiliating condition. From that day there was no possibility of arraying any force against Russia adequate to protect Constantinople from occupation at her pleasure.

It is by no means certain that France, under her present usurper, would even strive to prevent it. Louis Napoleon is too ambitious of permanent alliance with the legitimate despotisms to incur the hostility of the leader of them. French vanity and ambition could be pacified by concessions in Egypt which would strengthen and extend the African empire. French hate would be the more grateful for an opportunity of cutting off the English communication with India. The policy of Napoleon has become a national idea. Louis Napoleon could carry the nation with him in any arrangement which should deliver European and Asiatic Turkey to Russia and Austria in such proportions as the former might designate, while it secured to the French the African provinces of the Ottoman empire from Alexandria to Algiers. The quadruple treaty of 1840 foreshadowed such a partition of influence, if not of empire, between England and Russia. But that treaty was a blow aimed at constitutional France and the English alliance. France under a despotic head would be entitled to very different consideration. Her ruler would strive to rouse the national ambition and fire the national hatred against England. Her eastern empire is her vulnerable point, and Russia and France would easily unite to humble a common and dangerous rival. The partition of the spoils of the Ottoman empire would cement their hate of England into an alliance for her ruin; and the geographical position of Russia and of France indicates the proportions of the partition.

Turkey in Europe is, therefore, under the existing relations of the European governments, at the mercy of Russia. What future and unforeseen contingencies may arise human ken knows not. We must base our calculations on the only elements of calculation—the existing relations of the Powers on which the fate of Europe depends. On that basis, European Turkey may be regarded as—a province of Russia.

If so—the time of occupation may be postponed for a while—but only that it may be easily and safely effected.

The addition to the Russian Empire of the rich provinces of Turkey, stretching from the Euxine to the Adriatic, and from the borders of Hungary to the Bosphorus and the Egean—sparsely populated by ten millions of people, and capable of supporting thrice that number in affluence—embracing half the course of the Danube, whose mouths she now already holds, and along whose banks the peaceful and the warlike march of nations has always found their natural and easy entrance to western Europe—the power of Russia would be finally consolidated. Austria would be enclosed by her iron folds. She would be the neighbor of Italy. She would hold the Euxine as a Russian lake, and dispute with France the possession of the Mediterranean. She would have the control of the centre of European commerce: and by her influence in Italy and Sicily, while consolidating the reign of despotism, she could bar the path of England to the east and cut off or harrass her commerce at her pleasure. Asia Minor, Syria, and Egypt would be at her control: and Suez would soon be a Russian or a French Gibraltar. These are the inevitable results of the occupation of Turkey by Russia. They are involved in the relations of powers and of places, they flow from the political dynamics which must give the law to the consequences of the occupation. They are the results of the most consistent of all logics—the logic of historic consequences.

But if this be so—then, Europe is delivered over to the dictation of the Czar and his dependent empires. England stands isolated and alone—with nothing but her sturdy yeomanry and heroic tars between her and ruin. Her eastern empire depends on her European power, on her ability to open her communications across the isthmus of Suez, and on her ability to throw a greater military force into her distant possessions than Russia, by her intrigues and her arms can bring to bear on the vulnerable points of her expanded but ill consolidated dominion. The Russian eagle has already flown farther from St. Petersburg than its resting place is from British India, and the Czar already murmurs of a treaty of Calcutta.

The result therefore, seems to point to the isolation of England in Europe, and to reduce the question of her fate to a calculation of the chances of her being able to maintain herself at Suez and on the Euphrates *alone*, against the power of Russia and the states which are her vassals or confederates.

On the continent the dictatorship of Russia has now been inaugurated. From St. Petersburg go forth the decrees which control the destinies of Europe. The question of power and political aggrandizement seems to have reached this solution.

The other problem for solution in the nineteenth century is—the relation of the people to the sovereignty. The conflict of free ideas against despotic rule ushered in the century, and for fifty years it has shaken Europe with the noise of battle. Whether power descended from the Eternal Throne on the anointed heads of kings, or emanated from the people, a trust for their benefit—whether the people were by Providence delivered into the hands of their rulers, bound to unquestioning obedience, or were vested by God with a right to dispose of their own destinies, and to dictate the law to those whom they set over their affairs—this has been the great question debated in the council and in the field, between kings and people during the first half of the nineteenth century.

The American revolution first introduced the idea of liberty, as an absolute right of man, on the field of battle. France caught the inspiration, and her example and her arms propagated the enthusiasm of liberty from the Straits of Gibraltar to the Vistula. The triumph or defeat of this principle involves the total reconstruction of the states and politics of Europe. It has therefore been the centre round which all events of moment have grouped themselves. They have been judged and estimated according to their bearing on this problem. The ambition of states and individuals has disguised itself in devotion or hostility to this principle, and men have sought to enlist the power of the opponents or the partisans of liberty for the purposes of vulgar ambition—as kings arrayed Protestants and Catholics in adverse ranks to decide under the name of a religious war the political empire of Europe. But the principle of liberty and popular power strikes by its very nature at the root of every authority claiming any other source than the popular will. Invoked as a tool, it soon becomes a chief actor on the scene. Rulers are therefore driven to choose between friendship and enmity. They must admit and act on its principles—or they must oppose and defeat its partisans—or they must submit to defeat and ruin in the inevitable encounter. Neutrality is impossible—or it is ruin.

Kings were long in discovering this necessity—and still longer in uniting to act on it consistently. But bitter experience has taught wisdom. The spirit of liberty has shone on many a field of battle, and tried the extremes of fortune. It has shaken thrones by its triumphs, and from defeat it has risen in defiance of death—like a spiritual essence incapable of decay, and stood a spectre frighting kings from their propriety at the banquet and on the couch.

The apparition when last it rose spread ruin over Europe, and struck terror into the stoutest hearts of kings—and for a while it held undisputed mastery. But its foes recovered from their fright, resumed the fallen sword, and, in the absence of a leader fit for the crisis, smote and overthrew its scattered and disorganized power. It triumphed in every state over its domestic tyrants. In every state it was overthrown by the intervention of foreign powers, and those foreign powers in the last resort found their ultimate reliance and support in Russia. To Russia it was the crisis of life or death, of ruin or of universal empire. The sword of Nicholas decided the contest. Every crown north of the Pyrenees is worn by virtue of his arms. Every government is in his interest, linked to his policy and empire by dependence, by gratitude, by hopes of safety, by the consciousness of feebleness if deserted. Every army and every government, France included, is now in the hands of despots and in the interest of despotism, leagued to keep down the spirit of liberty which they have overthrown: and the leader of the league is Nicholas.

The fate of liberty has been that of the prince of the Genii, whom the fisherman ignorantly released from his vase.

A rebellious and defiant spirit, it had for centuries been oppressed by princes in the name and with the seal of God.

France fished in troubled waters for means of annoying England. She found on these western shores in the English colonies, something as promising in secret riches, as innocent of threatened danger, as the fisherman's vase. She broke the seal—and forth streamed the smoke which spread over the heavens—and assumed the terrible form of the Spirit of Liberty—wearied with promising for centuries in vain, as the price of liberation, riches endless—the hidden treasures of the caves—the glories of princely power—and now, when freed by an accident, maddened with disappointment and despair, threatening death to its deliverer. For years it held the princes of Europe in mortal terror—till fraud supplied the place of might—and the spirit before which they trembled was coaxed, cajoled, and deceived into submission to their power. It dissolved again into thin smoke—it laid aside its terrible form—it surrendered its arms to the hands of its deceiver—it voluntarily quieted the terrors it created by changing the form of armed defiance for that of peaceful and submissive citizenship—trusting that its freedom would be restored. But the day of submission was the last of liberty, and the terrified princes hasted to place the seal of fate guarded by military power over the place of confinement of the terrific phantom.

This is the present result of the great revolution of 1848. Europe has fallen back—pressed beneath the heel of its masters more heavily than before. The liberal cause has been decided definitively—for the present at least—in favor of despotism.

It has been decided under such circumstances as forbid the hope of any voluntary mitigation of the severity and exclusiveness of despotic rule. The terror was too imminent and too mortal for princes to forget it. The fashion of liberal ideas has proved too costly a luxury even for royal palaces; and it is prudently abandoned and forbidden. Liberty might before have been hoped for in some moderate form of concession; but royal souls can never forgive the arrogance of demanding as a right what they considered a royal grace. To beard and defy them in such a cause was unpardonable: but how shall they wipe out the humiliating memory of flight and exile, concessions wrung from terror and safety bought with tears, the ungraceful sight of royal backs and trembling knees, the deep and smarting wound to the pride of kingly independence compelled to seek safety by foreign aid, the pledges, the oaths, the perjuries, the treacheries which have exposed royalty to the hate as its cowardice did to the contempt of the people. These are the fruits of liberty to kings: they all unite in deprecating the agitation and stifling the discussion of topics so dangerous: and if they did not unite voluntarily, their dependence on Russia would compel submission. She demands as the price of protection the avoidance of exciting topics and of all encouragements to popular commotion. She will not tolerate the submitting of the prerogatives of the right divine to the impertinent curiosity and irreverent discussion of popular assemblies. Europe will be no more troubled with volunteer constitutions from royal hands—while Russia is the guarantor of despotism.

The revolution of 1848 has thus strengthened the power, and expanded the field of action of Russia; it has elevated her to the dictatorship of Europe in the great controversy of the age: and the permanence of that dictation is secured by the dependence of all the despotic powers of Europe on her arms for the compression and extermination of the revolutionary spirit. The first necessity of the prince is the existence of his power: the mode and extent of it are secondary considerations. It is only by the union of all princes for the defence of each that the power of any can be insured: and the only effectual combination for this purpose of first necessity is that under the guidance and dictation of Russia. Her power therefore is as permanent as the revolutionary agitation. It must rest on its present basis, so long at the least as the spirit of liberty shall animate the masses of the people of Europe with the resolution to arm for the attainment of power. Every purpose of individual aggrandizement, of personal ambition, of territorial enlargement, is subordinate to the maintenance of monarchical absolutism: and the power of the people is the external force which drives all the princes of continental Europe cowering beneath the Gorgon ægis of Russia. Before the fierce eyes of their people terror expels every repining thought and every ambitious aspiration. It deadens the sting of humbled royalty, as the passions of men sink into calm at the presence of death. To resist is to deliver themselves naked to their outraged, insulted, exasperated, and merciless subjects. At their hands, after the perjuries of 1848 and the bloody proscriptions which stained the victory of royalty, small grace could be expected in the hour of triumph. The majesty of monarchs would be soiled in the dust: and their prerogatives, if they existed at all, would be mocking shadows of their former power. The Russian dictatorship, therefore, rests on its necessity for the defence of those who claim despotic power and spurn the moderate prerogatives of constitutional rule.

But even constitutional monarchy would not now content the outraged people of Germany, Austria, Hungary, or Italy. They would have been satisfied with it in 1848. They actually accepted it, modeled their constitutions in monarchical forms, surmounted them with a crown emblasoned with ample and honorable prerogatives, and armed with powers adequate to its own protection, to the maintenance of order under the guardianship of liberty, and subjected to only such control as is necessary to secure the nation some safe guarantee of its rights. These constitutions were either voted by popular assemblies elected in the height of the revolutionary fever and representing the utmost demands of the mass of the nations, or they were accepted and acquiesced in by such bodies on the voluntary grants of the sovereigns. That mighty upheaval of Europe was not a revolt of Jacobins, nor of the red republicans, fiercely threatening royalty with death, and repelling any thing short of a republic as the form of European government. It was the fair, calm, and irresistible expression of the great mass of the people, *declaring their confidence in monarchy, if surrounded with popular institutions* The legislative assemblies, the responsible ministry, the national guard, the freedom of the press, the administration of the laws by independent judges equally to all—these were the great central ideas around which the whole movement circled. For their attainment the masses of Europe rose with one consent, and, except small factions of madmen, the slaves of democratic or of monarchical despotism, these were the limits of the popular demands. They left the king on the throne, armed with prerogatives as ample as those which guard and decorate the crown of Victoria. How these constitutions were gotten rid of it has been my painful task to narrate.

The people of Europe *now* would not be content with such moderation. Their kings have destroyed their own cause. They have repelled popular and moderate constitutions and have clung to irresponsible power—in the face of pledges, promises, and oaths—in defiance of the almost unanimous cry of their people—in utter forgetfulness of the magnanimous moderation of their victorious subjects.

They have made their election, and repelled moderation from their council chambers. While cringing before the indignant wrath of their people, they hastily yielded to every demand, and confirmed it by a royal oath, to get time for a perjury. They plotted with a foreign despot the perjury they have committed, laid the national independence at the mercy of the Czar as the price of his assistance in regaining their despotic power, and humbled their dignity before a master rather than consent to rule with moderate sway over a free yet loyal people. That people is disgusted with the faithlessness of those who rule over them. They despise the cowardice which fled and would not fight for the power clutched after so eagerly. They have learned that despotic power is now in the hands of men disgraced by every vice, faithless to every obligation, and not redeemed by personal courage in the defence of their usurpations. They have seen royal heads bowing humbly before the people, suing for time to betray them, fly in terror from their capitals, and return at the head of foreign armies to revoke and annul their solemn acts. Their people feel that even the rule of their master is no longer a national government—but that it represents a foreign domination. The love of freedom, the sense of nationality, the devotion to the independence of the country, all conspire to rouse the hatred and contempt of the people towards their masters. Their cruel proscriptions, the martyrdoms of the children of liberty, the holy blood shed by a brutal soldiery at the order of a court martial, in insolent defiance of the popular disgust, have sunk deep in their minds. They no longer rest in the faith of their fathers, nor will they be content that creatures thus defiled by blood and iniquity, faithless, cowardly, cruel, and cringing, shall rule over a free people. They cannot be trusted with the powers requisite for the good of the state to be placed in the executive hand: for those powers have once already been turned to the destruction of the constitutions which gave them, and to the oppression of the people who in the honesty of their hearts confided in the faith of their rulers. If the people rise again, and again have the power in their hands, they will make short and sharp work with kings and crowns and thrones. Their wrath has been taught little moderation by those who have shewn no mercy and have known no faith. The blood of murdered heroes cries from the ground at Arad, against Haynau and his hell-cats, and the heartless and remorseless despots who let them loose. Aulich, Poltenberg, Lemingen, Nagy Sandor, Damianich, martyrs of liberty, heroes on the field of battle, struggling in honorable warfare for their nation's rights, betrayed by the traitorous Görgey, and vilely done to death by the shooting party or the tree of shame, have laid up untold wrath against the terrible day of account. The noble blood of Batthianyi stains the tyrant's hands so deeply that it will not be washed out. The Hungarian plains decorated with the gallows trees—like telegraph posts on a highway—are one eternal summons to vengeance. Germany, delivered to the insults of a foreign soldiery, her men of heroic mould shot down at the word of a court martial, her very groan of agony stifled by the steel gauntlet of a strange master, pants for vengeance and sighs for the leader and the hour. The fate of Charles I. and of Louis XVI., the terrors of Robespierre and Danton, the madness and ruin of the Great Deliverance are the bitter fruits stored up for the day of retribution by those crowned scourges of their kind who have imitated and exceeded the cruelties, the blood, and the phrenzy of the worst of the evil Genii of the Revolution. An avenging God will visit them by the hands of their people with the fit rewards of their perjuries and their bloody deeds. The dogs of Austria which licked the righteous blood of Batthianyi shall yet lick that of those who shed it.

By these terrors, by this necessity, by this threatened scourge are the despots of Europe bound to the Czar. He alone is able to protect them. He alone rules a people untainted by the revolutionary plague, docile in obedience, devoted to their master, and powerful and ready for every enterprise of arms. His power can be applied beyond his frontiers for the suppression of liberty: for no serious fear of internal disturbance restrains his arm from giving efficient aid. He defends himself by aiding them: and their union with him and submission to his will is their great security and their wisest policy.

On these principles, it is not rash to say, that the centre of gravity of Europe has passed north of the Vistula: and St. Petersburg has become—the Capital of Europe.

SECTION VII.

THE RELATIONS OF

AMERICAN AND ENGLISH LIBERTY

TO THE

RUSSIAN DICTATORSHIP.

THE RELATIONS OF

AMERICAN AND ENGLISH LIBERTY

TO THE

RUSSIAN DICTATORSHIP.

THE events of 1848 have placed in the hand of Russia no barren sceptre. It is not the unmeaning bauble that decorates the feeble hands of other princes—but a mace of crushing weight, lifted by a giant arm, in a cause where aggression is the only defence, in a contest which cannot be declined, and where the existence of the combatants is staked on the issue.

It is of vital moment to this Republic to ascertain if she do not stand in the line of its destructive descent.

It is in no spirit of vain bravado, nor at the dictation of a blind fanaticism, nor from any capricious hostility to liberal improvements, that the Autocrats of Russia have freely poured out their treasure and the blood of their soldiers in the defence of despotism. They feel that they are fighting their own battle, and that it is one which is inevitable.

They have calmly, deliberately, and justly come to the conclusion that popular sovereignty is absolutely incompatible with royal sovereignty; that there cannot be two co-equal sovereign powers in one state; that the claim of the people has pushed them to the wall; and that they are driven to elect between a popular constitution and their absolute power.

They have elected in favor of absolute power in their own hands.

Experience has also convinced them that liberal ideas are contagious. They have ascertained that to encourage or to tolerate them is fatal—so congenial are they to the mind of man, so rapid is their spread, so vigorous is their working, so suddenly do they pass from speculation to action, from the mind to the field of battle. If, therefore, despotic power be incompatible with popular sovereignty, and if popular sovereignty be the legitimate fruit, the universal and necessary product of liberty of thought, of speech, and of action—of any participation in the high acts of government by the people—it is only consistent, wise, and logical, to war down and exterminate every thing that looks like, or leads to, or advocates popular government. The despotic powers of Europe—triumphant over the revolt of 1848—have every where shewn the utmost resolution in acting on those views. They tolerate nothing that savors of liberty.

But it is the peculiarity of liberty that it tends to spread. It radiates like light from a centre, and destroys darkness within its reach. Its influence does not stop at the lines of foreign states. Regardless of laws and of limits, it spreads like an etherial essence, in spite of political and legal barriers. It shines into the heart of man wherever he may be, and finds a congenial reception. It wakes the slumberer from the incubus of despotism, and breathes life into the dead in slavery. So long as a spark of it exists any where, it is ready to break into a flame.

It is not enough to extinguish the spirit of liberty at home. It is almost as dangerous in a neighbor. It spreads across the bounds, and flashes conviction into benighted minds, and nerves the soul to high thoughts and daring deeds. If therefore the despots will maintain their power intact and undivided over their own subjects, it directly concerns them that their neighbor be as despotic as themselves. *This* is the foundation of the Holy Alliance. *This* it is which rouses the Czar to such strenuous hostility against every step towards liberty in any neighboring country. It is the great law of self-preservation logically applied to the destruction of a principle, unquiet, aggressive, propagandist, by its very nature—always tending to stir up the people to war against despotism, and if left to itself absolutely sure of success.

If Germany could be free, if Hungary could be a republic, without disquieting the subjects of Nicholas, assuredly we should not have seen Russian armies crossing the Carpathians. If Spain could have enjoyed the blessings of constitutional liberty and her example had not tended to make France restive under the fraudulent mockery of her charter, we should have been spared the expedition to Cadiz. If Italy could be free and raise no longing after freedom in the Austrian people, Metternich would hardly have concerned himself to reinstate, at the head of a hundred thousand men, a dotard on the throne of Naples, which he had proved himself unable to hold.

They felt that liberty *any where* was dangerous to despots *every where*, and they resolutely set to work to root it out.

Nicholas is the devotee of this new faith, for in it alone can he find the salvation of his power, his crown, his empire of rich promise. He knows, if western Europe be democratic, Russia must cease to be despotic; and its despotism is its union, the centre of its might, the very principle of its expanding dominion. Free government, were the people fit for it, is as absolutely incompatible with the unity of Russia as it is with that of Austria. If Germany and Hungary were free, ideas of liberty must migrate across the border, and sooner or later enter the very penetralia of Russian despotism. Had they succeeded in 1848, there must have been an end of Russian dominion in the Polish provinces. A quarter, the most flourishing quarter, of the empire of Nicholas would have been lost. Any form of popular government on the borders of Russia would have lighted up a conflagration which could have been extinguished only in the ashes of the empire: for Poland is a great and ill-protected magazine of explosive material, which any day, by a chance spark, would explode with irresistible fury, and shatter down the last home of despotism on the continent of Europe.

This Nicholas knew: and with logical consistency he called the invasion of Hungary a *defensive war*. With statesmanlike resolution he dared the worst, rather than tolerate a successful revolution on the side of his Polish provinces. If he were indifferent, the revolution must have been successful and the consequences to him ruinous. If he lent Austria his arms and she failed, he was little worse off than if he had been quiescent; some money, a few men, were well paid for by the damage they did; and the humiliation of the defeat chiefly attached to the principal in the contest. If he succeeded, he delivered himself at once from an ever present terror, fatal in its influence, and sure in its workings. He knew that on the Hungarian plains he fought the battle for his crown; and fortune rewarded the resolution and the daring of the despot according to his merits.

It is this deep conviction of the fatal contagion of liberty, founded on a true analysis of its nature and powers, which lies at the foundation of the alliance of sovereigns under the Dictatorship of Russia, for its extermination.

This alliance has now endured the shocks of political strife for more than thirty years, with various activity and success, but never broken down nor abandoned, and now triumphant in the cabinet and in the field. It has pursued its object under various disguises, under shifting pretexts with infinite art and endless activity. It has moved under the cloak of religion, and called itself holy. It has clamored for social order, and leagued the quiet and peaceful under its banner. It has strenuously defended whatever existed, and arrogated to itself the epithet of conservative; and aristocratic traitors and mushroom rich civilians have sheltered their ignoble heads beneath its ægis. It has called self-defence an assault, and punished it by confiscation of a nation's freedom. It has pronounced the oaths of sovereigns void when wrung from them by the national will—and armed to release them from the obligation, and to restore their yielded prerogatives. It has encouraged the abrogation by the monarch of a free constitution peacefully established, and in quiet and sedate operation; and it has punished as revolution and rebellion the arming of the people to restore it. Swearing by things old, yet when a nation took up arms to maintain the constitution of a thousand years against the innovations of their sovereign, the sword of the chief of this alliance was swift to strike them down. The treaties of 1815 are the shibboleth of the league; yet the constitution of Poland and the independence of Cracow, guaranteed by their most solemn provisions, have been unscrupulously suppressed. Aghast with horror at the blood and phrenzy of the revolution, it has looked calmly on while its generals have desolated realms in its cause. Shocked at the sight of a crownless or of a headless king, it has delighted in the sacrifice of hecatombs of noble souls on the altars of its ambition. Wherever the issue has been between the nation and the king, whatever the point of dispute, whatever the merits of the parties, the Holly Allies have never taken but one side—that of the king against the nation. With the words of religion, social order, conservative government, on their lips, they have warred on only one thing—the spirit of liberty, in every form, under every pretext, and without pretext when one was wanting. It has consistently pursued to its extremest conclusions the principle of their politics—that liberty any where is incompatible with the quiet repose of despotism every where—and therefore it must be exterminated.

This is a new thing under the sun. No previous age has witnessed or dreamed of it. Former politicians derided such an alliance as impracticable, and predicted its speedy dissolution. Yet this has survived unbroken and triumphant, still pursuing with unrelenting hostility the spirit of liberty, but never dragged aside by temporary advantages, never hurried into premature assaults, calm, wise, slow, and patient, biding its time till the hour to strike.

The people have repeatedly every where proved themselves masters of their destiny against their domestic rulers. In Italy more than once, in Spain, in every state of Germany, in glorious and heroic Hungary, in France, in Lombardy, in Venice of old renown, have the people proved themselves by deeds of arms equal to the high task of wresting liberty from their oppressors. They have every where given this indispensable proof of their fitness for the freedom they sighed for. It is only possible when the power of the country is on its side, and, till that day, the powers of government are properly in other hands: for government is the power of the nation, and should be with those who can wield it. It is for this reason that no people can be said to be fit for freedom till they are able to cope with and control any domestic government which may oppress or oppose them. Every nation in Europe but Russia has given this proof, and most of them more than once. But they have always been flung back beneath the rod of their masters by a power from abroad.

The contest between a people and their government is always a difficult and doubtful one. Large masses of the population cling to whatever exists: many are too indifferent to risk life in battle or ignominy on the scaffold. All fight with a rope round their neck, and in the face of all the powers of organized government, usually armed with regular troops, and amply provided with the sinews of war. The government can never be overthrown till a decided majority of the nation are, not merely discontented, but actively, earnestly, and resolutely hostile to its continuance, and united on the substitute to fill its place. But when even all this exists, the contest is always so close that slight aid to either party is decisive.

The genius of Cromwell is indebted to the absence of a standing army for the splendor of his triumph; and Charles would have died king of England peacefully on his couch had foreign arms or a domestic army seconded his endeavors. The endurance and the wisdom of Washington, the patriotism and courage of our fathers would have fainted before the oppressive masses of foreign troops that more than once have been thrown into the contest for freedom of the nations of Europe. Even the elastic courage of France has confessed the burthen of this hostility. After twenty years of the wars of the giants the expelled Bourbons were forced on her. Reluctantly endured for fifteen years, they were expelled by a new revolution, and the faction of the legitimists remained as a root of bitterness with those of the republic and the empire. Louis Philippe disgusted the people, pampered his partizans, and was expelled, leaving another faction. These four factions, the fruit of the wars of the allies against the liberty of France, disputed the mastery from 1848 till the usurpation of Louis Napoleon silenced them all. He now rules France with an iron rod, amid the exultations and cheers, with the support and countenance of the despotic powers—only because the people are wearied and worn out with incessant revolutions—each necessary—each imposed by the iniquities of the despotic powers directly or indirectly—yet each serving to lead only to a new necessity. The allies have for the present triumphed over France—not in the field, not by open violence, but by the moral and political effects of pertinacious hostility on the minds of the French people. They are disheartened, exhausted, and in despair, that such stupendous exertions and ruinous sacrifices have proved fruitless by the perfidy of their rulers, which leaves them no alternative but submission or an appeal to arms and civil strife. It has thus been the plan of the despotic powers to wait the hour of exhaustion, or to anticipate the hour of readiness: they march ere the children of liberty have nerved themselves for battle, or clothed themselves in armor—they watch the hour of nascent rebellion, and strike while liberty is naked and defenceless. Thus have they smitten it down all over Europe when triumphant over those who alone were entitled to draw the sword in the contest.

Where—as in France—armed and enthroned, it could defy direct assault, there they have poisoned liberty at the fountain, so that those who taste of it die. They have broken the cisterns and cumbered the streams with the fragments so that marshes and pools of water exhaled pestilence from their stagnation, while weeds of rank and poisonous growth cover the soft vale watered by its flow. Men sicken, where they sought salubrious airs, amid its mephitic exhalations, and despots mock bitterly at these—the sweets and fruits of boasted freedom ! !

For the first time in the history of the world has freedom been thus attacked, by an universal conspiracy, in the cradle. Ere it had yet done good or evil it was fiercely set on; and, though its Herculean infancy strangled those who sought its life, its youth and manhood have been pursued with unrelenting hate, by fraud and force, by temptation and defiance, by the poignard and the bowl, till overthrown, fainting, and dispirited, it threatens to vanish from the earth.

Let no one boast its immortality; for spirits as immortal have yielded up the ghost to the faggot and the sword. Religion, fired by persecution into fanaticism, sank beneath relentless bigotry and the civil sword in Belgium. The reformation in France was stifled in the blood of St. Bartholomew's day, and cast out by the repeal of the edict of Nantes. In Italy and in Spain its rising powers and spreading promise were cut short by the fires of the inquisition; and in half of Germany it yielded its spirit to similar weapons. The powers of persecution have thus often at least extinguished the most resolute of all rebellions—that of the conscience in the cause of religion; and surely the same powers which combined against it may now with equal success, under more favorable circumstances, trample down the spirit of liberty. We at this day of its humiliation and defeat—at least—ought not to be skeptical as to the possibility of its extinction. It now lies prostrate, powerless—giving small signs of life and less promise of resurrection. If it live and rise again, it will be to meet a like and final fate, unless it be succored and defended after a very different fashion from that cold indifference which greeted its last resurrection.

But if the genius of liberty may be extinguished like the freedom of religion, it never is effectually done while it breathes any where. Religion metamorphosed into bigotry and superstition, and burnt into the minds of a people, becomes a positive power—not merely repelling with horror and shrinking from, as sacrilege, the purest spirit of Christianity—but ready at any moment cheerfully to volunteer in a crusade for its destruction. Dominic and De Montfort led no reluctant or indifferent slaves to desolate Provence.

But the love of liberty speaks in soft and winning accents to the heart of man—which leaps in spontaneous sympathy to her voice. Despotism may rest on contented heads—but as such it wakes no enthusiasm, and its dominion is ever ready to vanish with the dawning light. If it is to be permanent, it must dwell in darkness. Men must know of nothing better—lest they desire it.

The Holy Allies cannot ever rest in peace till liberty has ceased from the world. They dare not lay their armor aside till there is nothing more of light and liberty to conquer. It is not enough to prove it mortal, they can celebrate no final triumph but over its grave. They cannot rest quietly on their thrones, till the spirit of Liberty in its last agony, shall in yielding up the ghost cry aloud—it is finished!

It may strike us with horror to indulge the thought of such an iniquity as an assault on English liberty: but Hungary was as free, as venerable, and as virtuous—yet it fell; and at some day not distant measured by the life of nations, in some mode not difficult to indicate, such an assault is not only possible—but sure as the flight of time.

On the confines of European darkness, so thick that it may be felt—still flames the Pharos of English liberty: and against it are the scowl and hate of tyrants bent. They must extinguish it—or be themselves consumed. They have no choice left. They have chosen their part and they must act it out—and the penalty of failure or faltering is—death.

So long as England exists resplendent in all the glories of liberty, despotism can find no safe and quiet abode on the continent of Europe. In form a monarchy—her crown is a shadow of a departed power—so thin that the stars which lead the coming day shine through it—yet paling before a more effulgent light. Her aristocracy—once the strength, now little more than the ornament of the throne,—has deeper roots and more inherent power. It is of sturdy growth and might deliver serious battle for its existence: but before the real power of the state it is—nothing. A breath—and it is gone. But behind and beneath all, the foundation and the wall of that glorious fortress "formed to freedom's hands," stand the great mass of the people of England, her indomitable and heroic yeomanry—the democracy militant—in fact though not in form, the governing power of the country. Their free ideas, their bold spirit of independence, their sturdy hatred of tyranny, their deep sympathy for the oppressed, will ever speak in trumpet tones—enough to wake the dead beneath the pall of despotism, and sound the advent of the judgment day. The miracles of their art and industry, the ceaseless activity of their enterprise, the smile of happiness that shines over their land—all perpetually personify and proclaim the blessings of liberty. No nation is so distant that they cannot see this light in the sky—none so dull that they cannot confess the majesty of this example—none so besotted as not to feel the waking longing after its nameless, endless, priceless, blessings. Vain, while it exists, are custom-house barriers—paper blockades—literary censorships—inexorable exclusions—laws of non-intercourse. They might as well decree eternal night, and veil the sun at his going forth—as leave the giant of English liberty unbound—and forbid him to run his course. They must smite him, or—he will smite them.

That the *will* exists, who so simple as to doubt—if only it may be safely and successfully done. They who have laid liberty low on the continent feel and know that the busy hum of English liberty is ever exciting their oppressed subjects to rise, and that the plain spoken words of indignation at their doings are holding them up to the hatred and contempt of their people. Their war is against liberty as incompatible with despotism: and what so dangerous as the example and the power of free England. Her freedom is not older than that of Hungary—but infinitely more dangerous. Her example is more contagious than that of Spain—for her liberty imbrued its hands in the blood of her kings, and they who now rule over her are there by the choice of the people. With her boisterous and turbulent sons, fierce in tongue and resolute in act—tenacious of legal rights and defiant of official encroachments—irreverent towards foreign royalty and not very respectful of that at home—jealous of absolute freedom of speech, and proud to signalize it in the High Court of Parliament by language that from no other quarter of Europe rings so loudly in the ears of princes—how can she be left to stand, if she may be stricken down. She stands in the direct line of precedents—she is guilty of every liberal sin—bristling with every danger that terrifies ambitious despotism. It were scarcely worth the while to stain the hand with Spanish, or German, or Hungarian blood, if England may live, and breathe the words of freedom.

How and when the assault may be made, is—for the prophet or the historian. I claim to be neither. I use the facts of the past to calculate the dangers of the future—for the guidance of the men of this day. It is enough to shew the will, the existence of a deeply seated plan of policy—hitherto pursued consistently, resolutely, and unfalteringly—but never rashly or hastily—guiding the power of the mightiest military monarchies of Europe—and that England stands in the way of that policy, is its chief, it may be its only obstacle to entire success,—for statesman to foresee and provide against the collision which time must develope.

No man may predict the mode of that attack. Amid the infinite combinations which the politics of this troublous era present, pretexts will not be wanting. What if Russia and France agree to assign to the former Constantinople and Turkey in Europe, to the latter the line of the Rhine, or Egypt; or Russia arm Persia and Afghanistan and the Tartar hordes against British India? If Russia march on Constantinople, England must meet her *there*—or wait, and meet her with augmented power, and a more disciplined and efficient navy, at Suez, a few years later. If France in alliance with Russia grasp at Egypt and assert the mastery of the Red Sea and the line of the Euphrates, England cannot decline the battle, unless she is prepared to surrender her Indian empire. It is at these indispensable points that England is most vulnerable. We are not driven to the necessity of calculating the chances of a successful invasion. England on her own soil, now, united, and fresh, is a match for all Europe. The clamors of French invasion may have good foundation in the ambitious daring of the upstart usurper. It is no part of the profound Philippic policy of the Autocrat of Russia. That policy will hazard no ruinous defeats—no discrediting failures. It will seek no rash and barely possible triumphs. Time is for it, and its haste is slow. It will strike vital points at the extremities, worry and weary by long, and vexatious, and distant contests, compel the putting forth of every power to maintain dependencies which are as necessary channels of English industry as veins are for the blood. If they be cut off, the ruin of the centre is slowly but surely consummated. Russia is rapidly spreading her actual government over Asia, and her influence spreads far in advance of her government. She is the neighbor of Persia, which is the neighbor of England in India. Her agents flit like demons of the night around the skirts of the English dominions. They were felt and seen in the Afghan war. They can discipline, organize, arm, and direct the Tartar, the Persian, the Belooch, the Sikh,—better materials for an army than the native troops which under English officers form the mass of her Indian army. Russia may thus meet England in her own dominions with troops drawn from her borders, and compel her to fight on her own soil for her empire. How the populations of India would side, it is vain to conjecture: but it would be more strange for her recently conquered provinces to be faithful, than that they should eagerly join any standard adequate to support them. Russia is the only military power that can support an army at Constantinople or in Egypt, without the aid of a navy. She now holds the passes of the Caucasus, and her territory eats far down into Armenia. She can coax or coerce a free passage over the Dardanelles: or, subject only to the necessity of defending them, she can in safety land on the Turkish shore of the Euxine, as many troops as she needs for operations on the Euphrates or in Egypt, and march them unopposed by any adequate force to their destination. If therefore Russia retain the dictatorship of Europe, the fate of the English empire depends upon her ability to measure swords with Russia, without European allies, in Asia Minor, in Egypt, and in India; and *failure* is to England ruinous, without a blow struck on English soil.

But we are not entitled to predict eternal quiet to England at home. Elements of discord are there brewing. Civil disturbances lie concealed in her dense population, and the discontents and suffering, occasional or perpetual, of large masses. The democratic spirit is rife, and radicals clamor for concessions, and might be induced to urge their claims in arms. The red republic has its representatives, and the socialist theory will flourish with rank luxuriance in her manufacturing districts. It will not be the first time nor the only place that despotic powers have agitated in the name of liberty for the cause of despotism. Russia has signalized her art in this department more than once at the expense of Turkey; and the seeds of the Greek revolution were scattered by her hand, that their growth might unsettle the walls of the empire. A civil war for republican institutions in England is by no means a distant contingency. The discontents of Ireland are an ever open door for foreign interference; and steam navies change the whole conditions of the problem as to the possibility of exciting or aiding them. By this policy, under the dictatorship of Russia, wielding the power of Europe, or of the whole north of the Rhine, the fall of England is not only no remote contingency, but it is the natural result of the continuance of causes and a policy now existing, successful for thirty years, with continued motives for perseverance, and now stronger, more united, and more under the control of a central head than ever before.

The power of England is to Europe now, what that of the Dutch was formerly: and similar causes but of greater intensity may bring her proud head to as great humiliation. England's strength, like that of the Dutch Republic when Van Tromp and De Ruyter swept the Channel—lies in her colonies, her dependencies, and her marine. Never a first rate military power on the continent, she has played her part there by subsidies, by alliances, by the genius of her generals at the head of allied troops with small bodies of her own. Her size is contracted—her population pressing the confines of its possible limits—while the expanse of Russia offers room for additional millions, and her continental neighbors may double theirs with comparative convenience. The advance of the rest of Europe tends directly and inevitably to the relative decline of English power and influence. Her genius and industry and commercial enterprise may keep up the unequal contest for a long time; but she must see across the channel in the Dutch Republic the foreshadowing of her own fate, and one as speedy as it is unavoidable, if Russian counsels are to dictate the policy of Europe.

She must expect to be assailed by arts and intrigues as well as arms—traitors will worm their way into high places—feed orators may stir up sedition—paid patriots may prefer Russian aid for the introduction of the republic to English independence under aristocratic forms—dearth of military genius may fall on her, and sterility prepare the way for defeat—fierce factions may drink in bitterness in civil feuds, and invoke an arbiter from abroad. The power of corruption, intrigue, and force, at the control of the man who dictates the policy of the chief continental nations, in this revolutionary era, in a country so filled with elements of discord as England, are beyond the reach of calculation. How efficient they may prove in a critical emergency—when national existence may depend on one man—the traitors of heroic Hungary and Poland may illustrate. With a Charles or a James on the throne—a Strafford at the head of affairs veiling his designs with popular art—some English Görgey in command of her army or navy—the Czar lavishing his resources to aid his royal cousin in yoking his rebellious subjects, wearied with an exhausting war for India, and divided in the great struggle between numbers and property at home—these things, within the experiences of this age, are sufficient to render a final account of English empire and English freedom.

Grecian genius has left the model of liberty for the inspiration of future ages. It has also left the plan by which it may be encountered and destroyed. Every usurpation of later day effected by any thing but barbarous force has been a coarse and distant imitation of the classic art with which Philip subjugated the fierce and turbulent democracy of

Greece. The rise of the Russian Empire, and its march to the control of Europe is the closest imitation history furnishes of the great model.

Europe—like Greece—is a peninsula jutting out from a great continent—whose southern portion is occupied by numerous highly civilized, populous, powerful, but jealous and discordant governments. North of these in both cases stretched a wide expanse, inhabited by semi-barbarous tribes scattered over a sparsely populated country of great but undeveloped resources. In both cases a prince unlike any of his predecessors arose, of far-reaching genius and indomitable energy, the impetus of whose activity urged the course of improvement within, and the power of his arms and diplomacy without, so rapidly, that in a brief space the northern wilds were the seat of a flourishing empire, powerful in arts and arms, of martial spirit and aggressive tendency—pursuing with steady policy and regular success aggrandizement on all sides at the expense of his neighbors.

Both empires were cut off from the two seas which stretched on each side of them: and Thessaly and Poland respectively lay between the growing and aggressive power and the southern and civilized states.

Athens, with her dependencies scattered far as the Euxine and the Bosphorus, her naval power and commercial activity, was the England—as Sparta with her military might and lofty spirit was the France of that system: while Bœotia, interposed between them and the northern power,—alternately the ally, the stumbling block, the foe, and the victim of the Autocrat Philip—was the Germany of Greece.

While Athens was entangled in the social war and Sparta struggling to regain her ascendency in the Peloponnesus, Philip seized Pæonia, dismembered Illyria, fooled Athens out of Amphipolis; and thus doubling his power while he touched the Hadriatic by his dependencies and the Ægean by his territory, he came in contact with the naval empire of Athens and acquired the resources requisite to emulate her power on the sea.

Thessaly excluded Philip from the affairs of Greece, as Poland barred Russia from Europe: factions and tyrants and civil discord invited his intervention: and the people delivered from many oppressors cheerfully yielded to the dictation of a mild and skilful ruler, who was content to have the freedoms and the benefits apart from the burthens of its government. Philip become master of Thessaly—as Russia, of Poland—while the southern states were immersed in domestic discords or private ambition: and his conquest was perfected without a protest or an opposition. He had become a Grecian power, stationed at the cntrance of Thermopylæ: Athens looked on in silence, engrossed in her games and shows, her theatrical scenes and the rhetorical struggles of the Agora.

With infinite address he stirred up dissensions in Eubœa—the Ireland of Athens—he assailed covertly her allies, her dependencies, points essential to her trade, with professions of friendship on his lips, apologies for his encroachments, often compensation for his conquests. He cheated Athens out of the Olynthian alliance—cajoled 'Olynthus with promises and caresses—and then struck her confederacy to the ground,—while Athens debated their deliverance, weighed the arguments of his advocates against the patriotic remonstrances of Demosthenes, and sent inadequate forces under false and incompetent leaders in time to witness a fall they were too late to prevent and too feeble to restore.

The Amphictyonic council under the dictation of Thebes denounced high penalties against Phocis and Sparta, and all Greece was convulsed with the sacred war. It spread to Thessaly—and Philip covered himself with glory and the reputation of the defender of the faith, while consolidating his power at the expense of the state whose territory held Thermopylæ. He followed up his success by marching on the pass; but *that* was too palpable for Athenian indifference to fail to understand. She flew to arms, garrisoned the straits, and Philip paused,—as Nicholas did at Adrianople, before the English.

The Holy Alliance is the Amphictyonic council of Europe: it speaks in the name and fights for the cause of religion and social order: and Nicholas uses it as Philip did the Amphictyons of Greece.

By bribery he opened the pass of Thermopylæ—obtained a decree for the extermination of the sacrilegious Phocians—and executed the orders of the Amphictyons with fire and sword—till Greece stood aghast at the horrible sack, and Athens stricken with terror laid aside her arms and sunk her protest into a plea for peace. Philip was within the sacred bounds of Grecian liberty—oppressing by the terror of his presence his most powerful opponents—who feared to call down on them the anathemas of the sacred council whose voice he inspired. Yet he made no haste to snatch prematurely at the prize—for combination among his enemies might yet convert his victims into his masters. Europe, within thirty years has seen her Amphictyonic decrees executed with fire and sword on Naples, on Spain, on Germany, on Poland, and on Hungary. The free powers have murmured, protested, and acquiesced—terror stricken before the visitation, divided in councils, bewildered by intrigues, and paralyzed between the adverse terrors of the revolution and its sworn exterminator. Where Nicholas prostrated Hungary in the cause of Austria he laid open the only Thermopylæ which barred his march to Constantinople—and to the mastery of Europe.

The Bosphorus and Byzantium were to Athens what the Bosphorus and Constantinople and Egypt and the Euphrates are to England.

Philip withdrew himself from Greece, and struck at the distant but vital points in the naval empire of Athens. Again the Agora resounded with the conflict between Demosthenes, unveiling the future and exposing the artifices of the great agitator—and his spies and abettors, who extenuated his acts and pleaded his cause before the Athenians. But they armed in earnest, and their alacrity foiled Philip before Byzantium—somewhat as England, though in alliance with Russia, saved Constantinople by her prompt operations in Syria and Egypt: for Mehemet Ali, while the enemy of the Porte, played into the hands of Russia.

Biding his time, Philip withdrew from the face of a power he could not oppose into the wilds of Scythia—while his emissaries plotted new treasons—stirred up new sacred wars—got new Amphictyonic decrees of extermination. Then he made their languid execution by his creatures the pretext for investing him with—the leadership of the Amphictyonic army to execute their behest.

Armed with the authority of its central power, Philip stood in the midst of Greece—invested with all the terrors of superstition—firm in the resolution to abide the worst—secure in the dissensions of the states—in the jealousy of the minor republics towards Athens and Sparta—in the enfeeblement of the latter by his Peloponnesian expedition—in the activity of his partizans among the clamorous democracies that would not combine for his overthrow.

He seized Elatea—and a shudder of approaching fate thrilled through Greece. He marched to Chæronea—and the land of Leonidas and Miltiades—committed to the folly of Lysicles, and the effeminate vices of Chares, and the faithlessness of Theagenes, while Phocion remained in obscurity—in a single day passed under the dominion of Philip.

Europe awaits her Chæronea.

There was no moment of Philip's career up to the day of Chæronea that Athens in arms under competent leaders was not more than his match. Had Sparta and Athens united, the conflict would have been speedily and easily decided. But sloth, and division, and hesitation, and boastful confidence, and the short-sightedness of democracy, which will never anticipate and repel danger at a distance, allowed Philip to hem in their dependencies, cut off their resources, sow dissensions among their allies, and defeat in detail powers which united would have been irresistible.

The lesson is full of instruction in our day for Europe and for America. The same game is being played with consummate skill—under more favorable auspices—hitherto without check—already centering a dictatorial power in the hands of Russia, which only waits a favorable opportunity to shew itself as the governing power of Europe.

We neglect the lesson if we wait till Russia take the form and assume the functions of municipal government. That is not to be expected—if her effort be successful—within the limits of a century. It is not the form but the reality to which statesmen look. The effort of a conquering power is always to conceal while it grasps the control of affairs—to withdraw from the popular gaze any striking alterations—to deceive the eye with the sameness of external forms—to lull the passions by respect for usages and customs—to cheat the people, by freedom in municipal affairs, into acquiescence in the entire withdrawal of public and foreign affairs from them.

Philip changed—after the battle of Chæronea—no government in Greece. He did not even occupy Athens. The Greek republics all retained their forms, their laws, their courts, their assemblies. The rights of peace and war were not even taken away. Their relations among each other were not altered. They were dependent on a common power which by its unity controlled them to its purposes, dictated their external relations, disposed of their military power, occupied their strong positions so as to hold them in check: but the forms of municipal government, the freedom of legislative and judicial proceedings, the laws of commerce and intercourse were not changed. Athens retained the symbols of sovereignty as fully when her citizens listened to Demosthenes in the splendid oration concerning the crown, as when they condemned Socrates to the hemlock. The relation of Philip to Greece was that of leader to dependent. It is the initiative form of every conquering power. So Italy and the Confederation of the Rhine and the Kingdom of Prussia followed Napoleon to Moscow. Rome led her allies before she converted them into provincial subjects. England dictated the law in India far beyond her legal frontiers, in anticipation of the assumption of the forms of actual sovereignty.

This is what now exists over all the north of Europe, and which threatens to be universal—if it be not arrested. It is the first stage of universal empire; and, for all the purposes of aggressive ambition, it is as pregnant with danger to the independence of nations.

The power of Russia is the more dangerous at this stage—because her domination rests on the interests of the governments she controls: and their interests are hostile to the spirit of freedom and to the advance of popular government. They combine from necessity and from choice to defeat a common enemy: and the power of Russia over their movements rests on the sure and permanent foundation of their defencelessness and her sole ability to defend them.

The dictatorship of Russia, therefore, is not to be looked for in the shape of an actual government—but of an invisible power operating through diplomatic forms, and supported by military power—speaking through the voice of domestic rulers words she has put there—and standing guaranty for the enforcement of whatever they may resolve. In this form, this generation has seen Europe governed by Napoleon. But his power was from its very origin transitory as it was absolute and irresistible for the time. That of Russia is founded on what Napoleon had to defy—the domestic governments of Europe. It has the central empire of Russia as its nucleus and support—an undisputed monarchy as its head—a martial population as its soldiery—despotic will as its guide—and unity of thought and action to direct its activity. It is animated by one spirit and policy. Its great object is the extinction of liberty in the world: and on this is founded its claim and its hope of universal empire.

Like the power of Philip, it owes its increase to the supineness, the divisions, the indifference, the timidity of those interested to oppose it. All Europe has stood silently by—prating about the balance of power—ready to tear each other to pieces for a strip of territory on the Rhine—and allowed vast empires to be absorbed into the colossal mass of Russia.

Worse than that—the free powers of Europe have stood silent and inactive while a crusade has been preached against liberty, and Russia has assumed the lead of its powers, and again and again, in outrageous violation of the laws of nations, stricken down people struggling for their national rights, and augmented her power by the divisions and the weaknesses of her natural opponents.

England is guilty of sins of commission and of omission against the cause of liberty of deep malignity. She has been—

> Although no tyrant, one
> Who shielded tyrants.

Her arms joined and animated the coalition which turned the revolution of France to blood, and condensed her freedom into a despotism which shook Europe to its foundations. She is stained by association in the scheme of the Holy Alliance.—Though she has repented and turned from that iniquity, she has brought forth no fruits meet for repentance. Naples fell without even a protest. She faintly protested against the iniquitous blow at Spain—but did not arm to prevent it. She spoke sternly only when she hoped to break the barriers which excluded her from the Spanish American markets. She protested against the occupation of Cracow. She protested against the annihilation of Poland in 1830. But she did not draw the sword in the cause of right when sound policy imperatively required it—when the alliance of Austria and Russia could have been forever broken—when Poland could have been reinstated among the powers of Europe—when the integrity of Russia could have been shattered and a limit placed to her aggression.

She did not aid the revolutions which she encouraged in 1848. She stood by, a silent and inactive spectator while freedom was extinguished in every land. She looked calmly on while Hungary was trodden down—when prompt action, the loan of money, the advance of arms, the peremptory protest under penalty of war, would have changed her fate. Again she flung away the chance of raising Poland, restoring its independence, dismembering the empire of Russia, and delivering Europe from her dictation, and her Indian Empire from its most formidable assailant. She was blind alike to her own interests and to the requirements of high policy.

She was fettered by a temporizing spirit, by the aversion of her aristocracy to revolutions, by the clamorous imputations of socialism and red-republicanism to the revolutionary leaders, by the sympathies of her rulers and aristocrats for the governments of Europe more than by the sympathies of her people for the liberties of mankind. She has laid up in store bitter fruits for herself and her people. She has from these motives permitted the golden hours of 1848 to pass, the friends of freedom, her natural allies, to be overwhelmed for lack of her aid. She has resigned Europe to the dictatorship of Russia, and isolated herself in its midst. She stands a solitary and tempting prize for the cupidity and the ambition of Russia—more dangerous if let alone than if assailed—and promising rewards to triumph more than equal to the risk of the attempt. England must either be the accomplice, the victim, or the conqueror, of the allied despots.

Across the Atlantic there is another people allied in blood, in institutions, and in character, which must share the fate of England. That power is more dangerous, more hateful, and more hostile, to the coalition of the foes of freedom. Is it the Rome of the modern world?

The Republic of the United States is the first born of the revolution. She is the oldest, the most powerful, the most consistent, the most uncompromising assertor of the right of man to self-government. Her children are born free, and their birth-right is its enjoyment. Their earliest lesson is the hatred of tyranny, the love of their revolutionary forefathers, the duty to hold life second to liberty. Their riper years are initiated into the holy mysteries of self-government; and their life is spent in its exercise and enjoyment. There is no difference of feeling or opinion. No schism cleaves the fabric of our political edifice from the turrets to the foundation. On this point it is a unit. Freedom of speech and of the press, the universality of education and of reading habituate the people to the formation and the expression of bold and resolute opinions on all matters of public moment. After the particular business of each, that which most occupies their thoughts and words, and studious hours is—the blessings, the hopes, the dangers of the liberty they enjoy. Their sympathies are as wide as the world. Their hatred of oppression follows the oppressor to its confines. No where is a blow struck for freedom without their prayers for its success—their cheers for its triumph—their tears for its failure. They utter in no measured terms their detestation of its enemies, and fly to greet the exile on their hospitable shores. The sufferings of the Irish, convicted of ill-advised patriotism,—the heroic countrymen of Kosciusko, escaping from the ruins of their falling country,—the heroes of Hungary, betrayed by those they trusted and hasting to save their enemies the stain of their blood—all are met with outstretched arms: and people and government delight in doing honor to the persecuted children of liberty. No revolution shakes the despotic thrones of Europe that our hearts do not beat high as they totter. We sway to and fro with the wavering conflict; and when the fires of battle are extinguished in the blood of the victims, we go mourning to our homes—as if some national calamity spread its pall over our land. The muttered curse betrays the fire within; and youth sighs for an opportunity to strike or to bleed in the holy cause. They symbolize their devotion in the persons of those who have suffered in its cause; and the people roll after him whose name is forever blended with Hungarian freedom—like some tidal wave that swells from shore to shore.

The name of the American Republic is potent among the nations. It is the watchword around the camp-fire, it is the model in the senate, it is the hope of struggling humanity. Its proud elevation, its peaceful splendor, its military prowess hitherto signalized only in defence, the plenty that rewards its industry, its wide asylum for the exile and the wanderer, the simple majesty of its government that like the power divine "spreads undivided and operates unspent," mighty at the extremity as at the centre, swaying with a silent omnipotence, powerful to punish yet powerless to oppress, unshaken in seventy years alone of all the nations by civil discord, unstained by fraternal blood, so mild in its rule that no treason has ever lifted its hand against its authority—these its glories cover with shame and cast into the shade the gaudy and blood-stained idols that elsewhere crush humanity in their course, and boast themselves the sole possessors on earth of the right divine to rule. Who would not fly to its shelter and cheerfully defy death and the grave to secure its blessings for his children's children?—Englishmen, justly enamored of their venerable and glorious government, yet pronounce this the most perfect government ever devised by the wisdom of man. The wisdom of Germany in parliament assembled could contrive nothing better, and humbly copied the model. The people of Europe, wearied with their struggles, or fearful of their safety, or oppressed in their pursuits, flock by the million beneath its shield; and they who remain meditate on its beauties, and sigh for its blessings, till the peasant's arm is nerved with the strength of the hero for the war to obtain them. No art, no power, no tyranny can banish its name or destroy its memory. It has stamped the name of liberty on the minds of the people of this generation. It is the perpetual pleading by example for the rights and the blessings of legal constitutional liberty. It is one vast organized society de libertate propaganda. While it breathes and moves and has being no despotic power on earth can quietly rest or securely repose. Its life must be one of vigilance, of eternal readiness, of merciless coercion, of stern, relentless, bloody war, within or without, against its influences, its ideas, its existence, its very memory.

Such is its moral power, the penetrating influence of its peaceful example.

But the nation which is thus resplendent in the arts of peace and the light of liberty wears its gorgeous robes over armor of steel.

This people, so ardent, so sympathetic, so devoted, has passed in seventy years from the gristle of unformed youth to the bone and sinew, the developed form and well knit limbs of perfect manhood. Its territory is no aggregate of conquered districts, filled with hostile and lukewarm nations. It has expanded from less than a million to more than three millions of square miles, washed by the lakes and the gulf on the north and the south, and by the two great oceans on the east and the west—and embraces the body of the continent in its domain. Its merchant vessels whiten every sea, and its commercial marine equals or surpasses that of any other nation—inexhaustible in materials for the best and most powerful navy in the world. A population such as the world cannot equal fills with the hum of industry this vast territory. Its cultivation, its thought, its language and literature, its habits and manners are the same, and so strong is its individuality and so powerful is its faculty of assimilation, that the hundreds of thousands of European emigrants of every nation, language, and condition sink into its bosom—like rain drops into the rivers, swelling their current while indissolubly blending with their waves. This people has swollen within the limits of the life of man from three to more than twenty-three millions—a population such as France could not boast when she prostrated Europe before her march. More than two millions of armed men—soldiers by birth, by nature, by early education, by manliness of spirit, by habitude of self-reliance and self-defence—who are fitted to obey because accustomed to the obedience of liberty and the laws, whom a campaign of a month converts into the regular soldier, and the word of command in his country's cause elevates to a hero—these men—the cheap yet priceless defence of the nation—stand ever ready to guard their hearths and their altars from hostile feet whether near or remote. They laugh to scorn the thought of subjugation, and rather court the attempt that they may be forced to free the world from the terror of the only power that threatens them.

This republic rose in this new world like a pale star glimmering on the distant horizon, whose strange beams fixed the gaze of the wise men of Europe and attracted every eye as it announced the dawn of that day when men should no longer slumber. Earnest eyes watched and worshipped its augmenting splendor—till now it has mounted to the zenith and blazes in the heavens, the sun of the day of Liberty: and to it are the kings and the people turned—in hatred or in hope.

What land so distant, what eye so dull, what soul so dead, as not to confess its genial power? Where sighs the oppressed under the whole heavens who does not turn to its rising, and adore while he longs for its peaceful and heavenly light?

Where scowls the despot who does not feel and hate its glory—which may not be hidden?

Even now, Nicholas of evil omen stands—as Satan on his mission of sin from Hell to Eden—and pale with ire, envy, and despair, thus proclaims his hate—

> "Oh Thou that with surpassing glory crowned,
> Look'st from thy sole dominion like the God
> Of this new world; at whose sight all the stars
> Hide their diminished heads: to Thee I call,
> But with no friendly voice—and add Thy name,
> Oh Sun! to tell Thee how I hate Thy beams—"

And shall he not add—when the prophetic scales hang out on high which weigh his waning power—

> "That bring to my remembrance from what state
> I fell—how glorious once above thy sphere,
> Till pride and worse ambition threw me down."

But shall he be reduced to this humiliating boast of his vanished greatness? Or shall he—even though failing of the full fruits of his mission—while declining that final contest which would shake the pillars of the world, yet by his arts and arms reduce this new world so near the semblance of his hell as to obscure its glory and banish its dangerous influence?

That the quiet reign of despotism in Europe is incompatible with liberty here has been demonstrated. That every motive of self-preservation forces the despotic powers to assail us in self-defence is plain.

That the concentration of the power of Europe for external aggression in the hands of one despotic dictator must seriously menace our peace and safety, and in the hands of Russia that it would be directed to that end, is only the teaching of the history of our own day: and that contingency is sufficiently near to fix the anxious eye of every statesman.

The subjection of Europe permanently to any one power would be an event of serious import to this country. It would be the creation of a power military and naval before which our utmost strength would be as nothing. Our safety would be dependent on its mercy or its justice. A struggle now single handed with the English navy would strain our resources to the utmost, and years would not heal the wounds of such a war; but what would *that* be to a struggle against all Europe?

Still, the most serious consideration is not—the union of Europe under one power. It is the nature of that subjection—the spirit which actuates it—the purposes it avows or pursues—and the power which shall grasp that dictatorship.

In the hands of Russia, with all its energies bent on the extermination of the intractable spirit of liberty, and the founding of a perpetual and universal despotism, such a power must menace the liberties, the safety, the very existence of this government.

The probabilities of that dictatorship, its threatened advent, its incipient organization, have been already explained.

It remains to trace its probable or its possible policy towards this republic—when once firmly seated on its

European dominion. An adequate motive of policy, and a possibility of doing mischief are sufficient to put the statesman on his guard against their results: for security is the most deadly of dangers, and the besetting sin, the fatal poison of democracies.

Is confidence reposed in the ability of our citizens on their own soil if united to repel the invasion of united Europe? That would not shew it to be unwise to anticipate and defeat the union rather than encounter its matured strength. We might in any direct attack maintain our national independence: but that is a sad state of affairs when the question at issue is existence. When we have satisfied ourselves of our ability to repel any open and direct invasion from any quarter—we have only proved ourselves impregnable against an attack not likely to be made. If we confide in our distant position, it must be conceded to be a serious impediment to direct invasion, a great difficulty to be overcome, but by no means a defence against ultimate ruin—still less a shelter against serious damage. The possibility of a successful defence is scarcely an argument against making that defence with allies rather than without, a few years sooner with powerful auxiliaries rather than a few years later alone. Still less is it any fair basis for the security of a statesman—that a direct attack openly made can be repelled under favorable circumstances. It is his high calling to foresee the future and provide against the most unpropitious combination, to insure the nation against certain evil in great and dangerous crises; so to defend it by alliances and by arms that the most critical emergencies shall find the nation prepared, not merely to maintain its existence and independence, but to repel the most powerful combination possible without permanent loss, without serious injury to its resources—so that it shall not come from the conflict scarred, enfeebled, and crippled, safe for the present, but languishing and ready to fall before the next assault.

We need anticipate no rash and hasty attempts, terrible at the moment—but sure to recoil on the assailant. The work of ruin will be one of art, of intrigue, of bribery, of hostile legislation, of worrying restrictions and exclusions. This century has seen the whole coast of Europe blockaded and neutral commerce almost driven from the ocean. With Europe under the dictation of a power bent on our gradual ruin, exclusion from the continent would be a simple, a possible, and an effectual expedient.

The day of our union and strength would not be selected for the onset: but when measures of enfeeblement begin to work and shew their workings; when domestic discontents spring from outward adversity; when a crowding population feel the general hostility, and, in vain seeking employment, grasp arms rather than endure starvation; when fierce factions dispute the mastery, and nicely balanced parties quarrel over the spoils; when public virtue shall have sunk below its present level and men arise who work for gold without inquiring whence it comes—these are the times and these the crises of danger. They are the things laid up in store for us. The forms of democratic government admit of no concealment—the quarrels are as open as the unity, the peace, and the love. Interested partizans may plead the cause of ruin before the people for a fee, yet in colors so specious and with tongue so soft that the poison will be instilled and working before it is felt or known. There are vital questions where a vote will decide the fate of great measures. One vote decided the admission of Texas: and on it depended war or peace—events which might have brought a foreign fleet to New York. That vote might have been bribed by a power lavish of means and unscrupulous in pursuit of its object. An Arnold once already jeoparded our liberties on small temptation: but temptations may assume the shape of virtue. The north is filled with the fanatics of liberty, as the south is with the Quixotes of slavery. The ground still shakes with the shock of their collision. Proud states threatened war as the alternative of a refused concession: and nothing but mild forbearance and wonderful moderation dispelled the cloud. The great measures of peace were carried by small majorities. In every case they were carried by votes consisting of the great mass of the south converted into a majority by a few votes from the north—where the concession was to the south: and by the whole northern vote with the addition of a few stragglers from the south, where the measure was one demanded by the north. The significant fact stands out, that on these sectional disputes the great mass of each section adheres to its own extremest demands. The balance is turned by a small minority of moderate men. The fate of the country—union or disunion—peace or war—depends on these few. The time may come—and we shall be a strange exception to the course of human affairs if it do not in fact come—when on some such question, that small party of peace may not exist, or that balance of power may be held by a Russian faction. It was thus that Poland fell: and we are not more lofty, more heroic, nor more pure than her illustrious patriots.

But put far from us the supposition of corruption. Fanaticism is not less dangerous because it is honest. There are fanatics at both ends of this Union. It is a fatal error to suppose that the compromise bills have laid the infernal spirit of sectional agitation. The teterrima causa belli exists, expands, and grows with every year. With the increase of the slave interest and the slave power does the prize to be defended at the south, the iniquity and the oppression to be removed by the north, increase in importance: and the passions of the assault and defence increase in a fearfully greater ratio. The day of final collision is adjourned, it is not gotten rid of. Many years may elapse, many partial settlements may postpone an open contest: but if the population continue in our midst to multiply as it has done, the day must come when half measures, palliatives, and compromises must cease. Emancipation or disunion may be the only alternatives. It is vain to deny that this day may be hastened by events from abroad. There were recently factious men, neither few nor insignificant, who complacently calculated the blessings of an English alliance. The resources of the south were carefully estimated and ostentatiously paraded. The basis of her prosperity was to be a direct European trade; and that could not but hold out temptations to a protective alliance after a disunion. But motives might well exist to induce foreign aid for the accomplishment of the severance: and we know too much of the bitterness of civil factions, the utter alienation of feeling engendered by the war of words and interests, by the wrongs and retaliations, which precede the explosion of domestic hostilities, to entertain any doubt as to the possibility of its introduction to support the family quarrel.

When minds are verging to that state of fierce excitement, fury ministers and seeks for arms. Men may shrink in an hour of coolness from accepting the aid of the stranger; but once convinced that they are oppressed at home, and foreign aid is a blessing. The tender of assistance is greeted as a kindness and accepted as a providential resource. The discontented do not scrutinize the source of the suggestions which chime in with their feelings, nor see in the burning patriot the traitor and the spy of an ambitious power. There have been periods in the history of this government when foreign assistance would not have been repelled as an insidious insult. Had the sword been drawn by South Carolina and Mississippi, Russian gold or cannon or ships would not have been rejected. There may be discontents which, if left free from the inflammations of foreign instigation and hopeless of foreign arms, would subside. But the inspiration of hope, the prospect of success, the certainty of not standing alone, these things even in the chivalrous south will deeply and it may be decisively influence the final question of peace or war—submission or secession.

It is unwise to shut the eye to contingencies such as these. We may see southern or northern madmen preaching with adverse lungs the glories or the iniquities of slavery; or with mutual and bitter recriminations exaggerate the aggressions and wrongs on southern rights, or the sin of holding souls in slavery against the higher law. Each party may—as they now do—cast defiance in the teeth of the other, scorn and loathe the tolerant republic that embraces them both, and cling as to a benefactor to any power from abroad which will shield their weakness in the day of rebellion.

Can we suppose that the eagle eye of Russia, triumphant in Europe, will, for the first time in her history, fail to mark such an opportunity? Will she not be swift to poison the wound, to rend wider the breach, to madden the hostile sections? When did not her vulture scent detect the tainted spot in every nation she would make her victim? And if secure against division and attack at home, how ready, lavish, and unbounded would be the money, the arms, the supplies, which openly or secretly she would pour into the bosom of the oppressed, whose merit would be their rebellion. Two years have not passed since the voice of one man averted a calamity which might have even now made this speculation an historical fact. Every year only increases the chances of some combination of internal discord, servile rebellion, and foreign war, which will make the continuance of this republic among the great powers of the world to depend on other elements than her power when united, in harmony, to repel a foreign foe. Our generation has seen Poland fall before the combined power of gold and arms. Our own day has seen Hungary shaken by a war of races, instigated by an ambition as iniquitous as any assault on our own independence could be. We have now in our own midst, in full and fierce activity, elements of discord greater than either of those which were so deadly in the hands of skilful enemies. It is, therefore, the height of madness and of folly to rest our safety and to estimate our power on calculations which omit these sinister elements.

Nor are these the only sources of foreign danger. We are surrounded by feeble and factious republics—the prey of eternal war, delivered over to the horrors of civil discord, and the very points an ambitious, active, and malicious power would seize on, to annoy us. The protection of distance is destroyed when nations at our door sufficiently numerous and powerful of themselves seriously to harrass if not seriously to endanger us, may be stirred up by foreign intrigues, armed by foreign money, led by European science. Wc found the invasion of Mexico no child's play: and from it we may estimate how troublesome would have been her accession to an armed league of Europe.

Through her territory lies our shortest and best practicable route to our Pacific states. The possession of the Tehuantepec, the Panama, the Nicaragua routes is to us what Suez and the Euphrates are to England. The wisdom of Congress leaves our connections with our western states to depend on the strongest naval power. It makes no domestic military road, but drives its mails and its troops through a foreign territory, over a distant voyage, running the gauntlet of every navy which may happen to be hostile to us, where every material point is now in the hands of great naval powers, or their dependents whom intrigue and force can render inimical to us. Russia is on our western coast an *American power*—nearer to our possessions than we ourselves—and capable of attacking them with superior naval force ere we can even hear of the contemplated hostilities. Her possessions on our continent now stretch from the straits of Behring down to within two degrees of Oregon. On the Asiatic side they touch the limits of China at a lower latitude. These possessions are not treated as distant, outlying, and unimportant districts. They have already been the subject of sharp diplomatic discussion, and the basis on the part of Russia of a claim so arrogant and insolent that the attempted enforcement of it would leave no alternative but disgrace or war. Possessing a portion of the opposite coasts of America and Asia of undefined limits—occupied at a single point by an insignificant settlement of Russian adventurers—she expanded her claim over the North Pacific and the desolate and uninhabited region of North America down to the 51° of north latitude—where the fishermen of all the world had pursued their calling for centuries, and the ocean rolled four thousand miles from shore to shore.

From this vast expanse of land and water the ukase of 1821 arrogantly presumed to banish the industry and enterprise of the world.

This rapacious usurpation was defended against the remonstrances of President Monroe with characteristic insolence. The open ocean rolling between the shores of Asia and America was treated as a mare clausum—the private and peculiar domain of the Czar. The exclusion of our citizens was placed on the ground of their evil example in stirring up sedition among his loyal subjects, and furnishing their discontent with arms: and the perpetual hostility of the two systems of government was darkly shadowed forth in the polite and formal disclaiming of any imputation on the faith of the Republic for her failure to suppress such irregularities.

"The imperial government"—said De Poletica—"respecting the *intentions* of the American government, has always abstained from attributing the ill success of its remonstrances to any other motives than those which flow, *if I may be allowed the expression, from the very nature of the institutions which govern the national affairs of the American Federation!!*"

The nature of our institutions is not likely to change. This declaration is the formal announcement that these institutions cannot stand side by side in peaceful contact with those of Russia. It means that we cannot control our own citizens from interfering with our neighbors—not from any accidental and temporary excitement but—from a disability inherent in our system. It proclaims the principle that *exclusion* is the only method of peace—

that commercial intercourse must be restricted to the last degree, lest contact with our citizens contaminate the docile submissiveness of the Russian slaves. It treats American citizens as—South Carolina would treat an abolitionist.

Such reasoning in defence of such an ukase was more than our patience could stand. An exchange of diplomatic notes ensued, resulting in a treaty adjusting the existing dispute, but involving the seeds of future difficulty.

The treaty stipulated for the freedom of the Pacific, and of resort to its coasts on points not then occupied by either nation: but to such points neither party should resort unless by permission: and while it provided that neither power should make *settlements beyond* the line of 54°, yet the ships of either party were allowed during ten years reciprocally to frequent the *interior seas and harbors on the coast just* mentioned for the purpose of fishing or trading with the natives.

The expiration of the ten years was the signal for the resumption by Russia of her extreme pretensions—to which a *doubt* founded on a forced construction of the last clause of the treaty gave the only shadow of a pretext.

Following the precedents of its encroaching rapacity, the Russian government—in the teeth of the stipulation for freedom of access to *all points* of the coast not occupied by *Russian settlements*—prohibited our vessels from trading on *any portion* of the *unoccupied* coasts north of 54° 40′. The last clause—which was plainly intended as a temporary suspension of the *prohibition* of the first clause which excluded us from the Russian settlements—was distorted into a limitation of the general right accorded, of landing on any part not actually occupied by a settlement.

Against this assumption our government protested—but Russia still pertinaciously declined to yield her exclusive pretensions: and any day may bring us into collision by her assertion of this unsocial claim. Our fishermen pursue their calling in the north Pacific and on the north-west coast—by the sufferance and at the pleasure of the Czar:—and the sword of the Republic is their only security.

Russia is therefore an *American power*—the jealous neighbor of this Republic—as insolent, aggressive, and tenacious as she has always proved herself on the opposite continent.

We cannot escape the conflict by turning our attention westward, and, abandoning Europe to her dictation, indemnify ourselves by engrossing the commerce of eastern Asia. We do not escape, but directly encounter her universal and engrossing ambition.

From her Asiatic possessions, from the Kurile and the Aleutian Islands, she overlooks the natural and necessary course of our Asiatic trade—now by the occupation of California grown to stupendous magnitude, and soon destined to equal that of the Atlantic states. Her naval stations can command effectually the whole intercourse of California and Oregon with the chief seats of Chinese commerce, and render our communications unsecure at any moment. She can transfer troops and munitions of war to the coast of Oregon more rapidly than we can from the Atlantic seaboard. She is a military power in direct contact with China; and her influence can stir up the Mongol tribes, and pour them like a hail storm on the feeble and effeminate Celestials. She can now in a great measure balance the influence of England at Pekin; her emissaries speak with almost as much authority there as at Constantinople; and a few years must give her the decided predominance.—How that control would bear on our commerce with that empire in the events which have been indicated, it takes no prophet to foretell. We should be excluded from those markets, or subjected to burthens which would strip off the profits, impede the activity, and finally destroy our Chinese trade—or we should be forced to maintain our position against Russian armies, on the spot, across the tracks of Russian navies, and at an expense and sacrifice which the most lucrative returns would scarcely compensate.

Our interests are as directly opposed as our institutions, policy, and principles. Russia is the great wheat country of Europe. To her belong the plains of the Vistula and the vast fields which pour their produce into the lap of Odessa. From these two sources come nearly all the wheat which competes with ours in the European market. She is not a manufacturing power and shews no signs of becoming such. Her whole population are divided between the plough and the sword: and to cut off or to cripple the commerce of the United States, is to rid herself of her chief, and only dangerous competitor.

Her interest, her ambition, her hate, the principles of her Czar, the proud hope of taming Europe to the yoke of absolute power, all combine to impel her into active hostility against this republic. Her territorial possessions, the condition of our neighbors, the relations of our own territory, all afford the utmost facilities not merely for annoyance, but for injury, serious and abiding. She only waits the auspicious solution of the European problem, to seize the first invitation of internal discord or foreign embarrassment, to begin the plot that is to end with our ruin. Her peaceful and friendly tone is politic—but hollow. She would encounter one enemy at a time. She avoids sedulously the roused and combined wrath of the two great free powers of the earth: and she willingly postpones the assault till the blow can be fatal, and securely dealt. If she triumph in Europe, not many years will roll along ere we shall feel the influence of her diplomacy, and be called on to encounter her arms. In ordinary war she is invulnerable to us,—while we are exposed at a thousand points. She can cut off our commerce and fritter away our resources—exempted by her position from the evils of retaliation. She encounters only half the risks of war—holding in her hands the chances of success in attack, the certainty of safe and unassailable asylum in retreat after discomfiture. Like some robber knight, she pounces from her den on the honest and exposed way-farer, and retreats in safety to her hold ere the arm of vengeance can overtake her.

It is, then, the part of wisdom and foresight, for the free nations of the world—the only two whose towers still lift themselves above the flood—to see and provide against these threatening calamities now, while they are yet at a distance and allies are left, rather than to meet them singly after a few years of treacherous peace bearing all the fruits of the most disastrous war.

SECTION VIII.

THE AMERICAN REPUBLIC

AND THE

LAST WAR OF FREEDOM AND DESPOTISM.

THE AMERICAN REPUBLIC

AND THE

LAST WAR OF FREEDOM AND DESPOTISM.

THE policy which this Republic should pursue in consequence of the recent events in Europe has become the subject of vivid discussion and varied views.

I maintain it to be the dictate of high policy, when ever the battle shall be joined in earnest in that final conflict between freedom and despotism, which is unavoidable and may not be remote, to display the banner of the Republic in the cause of the rights of nations and of man, for our own defence.

A wise precaution spontaneously suggests the opening of diplomatic conferences with England, that the two free nations of the world may face together their common foe in that day of trial.

They who stand with their backs to the future and their faces to the past, wise only after the event, and refusing to believe in dangers they have not felt, clamorously invoke the name of Washington in their protest against interference in the concerns of Europe. With such it is useless to argue—till they learn the meaning of the language they repeat.

The opinions of a great statesman who on other grounds reaches the same conclusion are entitled to more respectful consideration. On their side—but not of them—rises the majestic form of Henry Clay—for forty years accustomed to guide the foreign and domestic policy of the republic. His venerable name outweighs the arguments of other men. His wide experience and practical sagacity give, with the men of his day, to his divinations of the future the weight of history. His voice also is for peaceful indifference. Yet the counsels of his youth were in a different tone. His life is now a thing of the past. His country remembers that he is passing away. His eye from the brink of the grave looks keenly into the future, and draws prophetic forebodings of things which shall happen when he will not be an actor on the stage. The marble shaft will point from the place of his ashes to the repose of his soul, long ere she shall summon her sons who follow him to deal with the great crisis which so deeply concerns *them* and *their* posterity. They are to be the actors in those scenes of high import: theirs will be the terrible duty of treading the field where Mars might quake to step: and on them will fall, as the penalty of their failure, the fragments of the crumbling republic—and the curses of posterity. They are entitled to decide for themselves the questions that concern their political salvation.

Forgetting the name, it is fit that the judgment and the reasons of a great statesman be gravely and respectfully considered.

In the memorable interview with the illustrious Hungarian, Mr. Clay—after depicting the difficulties and the futility of military operations by this country against Russia—thus expressed himself—

"Thus, sir, after effecting nothing in such a war, after abandoning our ancient policy of amity and non-intervention in the affairs of other nations, and thus justifying them in abandoning the terms of forbearance and non-interference which they have hitherto preserved towards us—after the downfall perhaps of the friends of liberal institutions in Europe—her despots, imitating and provoked by our fatal example, may turn upon us in our hour of weakness and exhaustion, and, with an almost irresistible force of reason and of arms, they may say to us—You have set us the example, you have quit your own to stand on foreign ground, you have abandoned the policy you professed in the day of your weakness, to interfere in the affairs of the people of this continent, in behalf of those principles, the supremacy of which you say is necessary to your prosperity, to your existence. We, in our turn, believing that your anarchical doctrines are destructive of, and that our monarchical principles are essential to the peace, security and happiness of our subjects, will obliterate the bed which has nourished such noxious weeds: we will crush you as the propagandists of doctrines so destructive to the peace and good order of the world. The indomitable spirit of our people might, and would be equal to the emergency, and we might remain unsubdued even by so tremendous a combination—but the consequences to us would be terrible enough."

This solemn and parting opinion is worthy of the most profound and respectful consideration. He spoke to a great leader in a great but unfortunate struggle: and he spoke on a topic of practical moment to his country. The solemn tone which pervades his remarks bespeaks no light and transient topic of indifferent interest, but one which might in its decision involve the peace, the happiness, the very being of the Republic.

The terrible power of a combination of European despots against our liberties was keenly felt. He indulged no boastful confidence of impunity: nor could the leader in the war with England so far forget his experience as to speak lightly of a collision with a league mightier far than that power, detachments of whose navy dealt us such stunning blows. The greatness of the danger was felt and admitted. The problem was, how to avoid or how to repel it.

He does not treat such a combination as a chimerical terror—but as a real substantial danger, fully within the range of political calculation. He only contemplates it as a retribution for our armed intermeddling in European affairs. His only refuge from its power is in "the indomitable spirit of our people," which, he thinks, "might and would be equal to the emergency." And after the passage of the storm, his eye looks on the ruins in its track, and confesses that "we might remain unsubdued even by so tremendous a combination—but the consequences to us would be terrible enough"—even in our victory.

But there are some serious omissions and some inadmissible assumptions which require to be noticed.

If the combination be so dangerous when directed against our united strength, it must be overwhelming in the day of our factious division, or of civil discord, or servile rebellion.

If this combination be possible, and if despots triumphant in Europe could have any inducement to turn their arms against us, we are not entitled to suppose a pretext will ever be wanting. The inducements will not be those of a just retaliation. To suppose that immunity is to be purchased by peace—is entirely to forget the history of the last thirty years. If it is to shut the eye to the motives of aggression and the fruits of victory. If attack followed only as retaliation, then peace might be safety; but if the war be waged against liberty and its pleading example, then peace is the surest provocation. The assumption that if we let them alone they will let us alone is belied by the whole history of Europe in this century. It vitiates the whole reasoning. It was faith in this which cost Spain her constitution. It was trust in that rotten reed which pierced Hungary through with many sorrows. It is this faith which made every revolution of modern Europe—except that Great Deliverance which put faith only in its sword—the grave of its authors. It is a blind faith, involving deadly error—and utterly oblivious of the events of our own day.

In no one instance in the nineteenth century has the free movement been arrested by armed intervention as a penalty for its meddlesome aggression. Moderation, abstinence from revolutionary excesses at home, rigid refusal of armed propagation abroad, even the denial of all sympathy and countenance to the revolutionary disturbances existing in neighboring countries, have never in a single instance proved a protection:—but that policy has always been the precursor of ruin, the invitation to attack.

The coalition against revolutionary France was formed before she had meddled with other nations: and always under pretexts which left rational liberty free play. Her propaganda was a retaliation—converted by her enemies into a crime, and elevated to the chief dignity among the causes of their hostility. Spain did not seek to propagate her liberal ideas: yet her innocence was no protection. France executed a traitor who wore her crown; and despots yelled with madness at the sight. Spain left a viler tyrant untouched: yet they rushed on and overwhelmed her. The coalition turned pale at the blood of the reign of terror. Spain kept her hands unspotted with blood: yet the Holy Allies imitated and surpassed those cruel days in their triumph. The constitution of Louis XVI. had been tolerated: the Spanish Cortes therefore indulged the hope that theirs would not be assailed—if they refrained from exciting the revolutionary spirit by appeals, or disturbing their neighbor's peace by invasion, or imbruing their hands in blood at home. They did none of these things, and they trusted in their purity for their protection. But in the eyes of the Holy Allies they were miserable sinners—rebels against the divine right of despotism: and they paid the penalty of their confidence. Naples trusted in a similar purity—even more inoffensive: she refrained from appealing to all Italy in the name of liberty, till it was too late: and her infant freedom was set on and vilely done to death. Hungary tried to wash her hands in innocency—and met the fate of her predecessors. Her constitution was of old—outdating the house of her kings. Her reforms were the legal process of this constitution, conceded by her sovereign freely and without any sort of coercion, tumult, or clamor. She dared to take arms to defend herself against his usurpations, clear and confessed. She made no new claims, she foolishly abstained from revolutionary sympathies, she anxiously kept away from the tempting and decisive field of Polish agitation. Yet she was stricken down: for she had asserted a right in the *nation* against the *sovereign.*

If we are to provide against a danger, we must estimate its character, the law of its motion, the orbit of its course, as well as its magnitude, and the spirit of the power which presides over its activity. Its professions are of no worth. Its acts are alone trustworthy.

If the Holy Allies have hitherto not confined their assaults to retaliation, it is a baseless assumption to suppose they will do so in future. They have, always, whenever and wherever the right of the people to control their own affairs has been asserted as a practical principle, under all circumstances, under every pretext, so far as their power has extended, armed for its overthrow. The object of their hostility is—the source of their danger:—and that is—not any particular form of liberty, not its origin in revolutionary violence, not its active and armed propagation, but—liberty simply in itself and for itself—in its own inherent nature their enemy—a propagandist principle by the necessity of its being—one that shines by its own light and spreads in spite of laws and barriers and limits. Its existence is the danger: its extinction is the only safety.

The sin and the danger therefore of this Republic are—its freedom, the silent and powerful influence of its example, that its name is the watchword, its light the hope of the millions of Europe. It is not harmless because it is peaceful; it is for that very reason more potent in its influence. Its pure light would be obscured by the clouds of war. Its peacefulness makes it more worthy of extinction.

Mr. Clay glories in the power of the example; but he fails to draw the inference it involves.

He says "by the policy of Washington we have done more for the cause of liberty in the world than arms could effect: we have shown to other nations the way to greatness and happiness. And if we continue united as one people and persevere in the policy which our experience has so clearly and triumphantly vindicated we may in another quarter of a century furnish an example which the reason of the world cannot resist."

But if this policy have done more for the cause of liberty than arms could effect, then to persevere in this policy is the surest way to bring down on us the enemies of the liberty it has promoted. If in a quarter of a century our example, if unmolested, is to triumph over the reason of the world—and *that triumph* involve the triumph of *liberty* over despotism—then the despotic powers will anticipate their destruction by our ruin. They will not leave us that quarter of a century of deadly example. They will—on Mr. Clay's reasoning—at the expiration of that time, inevitably fall victims to our example. They would be pusillanimous if they sat down in despair rather than try the fate of arms, when failure would only impose the inevitable penalty of inactivity, while success would relieve them forever of the evil—the hateful unquiet spirit of liberty. If peaceful example be the most influential advocacy of liberty, it is *therefore* the surest way to invoke on our heads the hatred and the hostilities of the enemies of liberty. It were curious indeed to tolerate the greater and only to war upon the less of the two dangers. If our union as one people be so dangerous, the despotic powers will avail themselves of every art of fraud or force to dissolve that union. If the peaceful example be more dangerous than arms, they will obscure it by clouds of war. If the reason of the world cannot resist it, they will not wait for it to be convinced, but will protect it from our influence by the bayonet unreasoning and unconvincible. It is a bitter mockery to show people the way to greatness and happiness only that in the pursuit of it they may find a grave. Men will curse the example which lures them into rebellion, and looks idly on till it be extinguished in blood. Kings, radiant with triumph over the effects of our example, will eagerly turn to rid themselves of the fruitful cause. When order reigns in Europe, its restorers will not be wise as serpents if they do not visit their wrath on the cause of the disturbances. It is iniquitous—nay more—it is a blunder to punish the deceived and misled enthusiast, and leave the corrupter and the instigator to go unscathed. To despots, liberty is itself an evil example, fruitful in all political disorders: they will persecute and punish it and root it out—as they would any other contagion. The Republic of America is the embodiment of that spirit in its most deadly form. Its peaceful example is its deadliest sin. Its demerit is its existence. Its only safety is in arms; and refusal to use them is no protection against them. To stand still and see despots root out freedom from Europe—is—not to avoid war, but—only to wait till our allies fall that we may be an easy prey. I do not greatly value the Ulyssean privilege of being last devoured.

If therefore it be possible so to aid the cause of European freedom that it may be crowned with success and grasp the sceptre of rule—it is the plainest dictate of sound policy, quite level to the comprehension of common sense, to let no opportunity slip, effectually, earnestly, boldly, at whatever expense of men or money, to secure its triumph as the best and only safe defence of our security. Though the stars and stripes float on a thousand fields of Europe, we shall incur no more hate, no more danger, no greater certainty of that "tremendous combination," than now hang over us as the inevitable consequence of the final triumph of despotism in Europe. The policy of indifference is the only fatal one; the leaving our own to stand on foreign ground is merely meeting the invader at his own thresh-hold—and it is our only safety.—

Henry Clay declares *this* contrary to the policy of President Washington—the hereditary national policy; and his voice is multiplied by echoes from every quarter of heaven. But is this not putting in the mouth of the illustrious statesman and warrior principles which he never expressed, and which he would be the first to repudiate and abandon?—

I do not hesitate to assert, that no word of Washington indicates any such policy as has been imputed to him; but on the contrary the policy here advocated is the hereditary policy of this government applied to every new practical case as it arose; and that it is in conflict neither with the letter nor with the spirit of the advice of that sagacious statesman. That policy is declared in the following passages of his farewell Address. I adhere to every word of them.

"The great rule for us in regard to foreign nations is, in extending our commercial relations, to have with them *as little political connexion as possible.* So far as we have already formed engagements let them be fulfilled with perfect good faith. Here let us stop.

"Europe has a set of *primary interests* which to us have none or a very remote relation. Hence she must be engaged in frequent controversies, the causes of which are essentially foreign to our concerns. *Hence therefore,* it must be unwise in us to implicate ourselves by artificial ties in the *ordinary vicissitudes* of her politics, or the *ordinary* combinations and collisions of her friendships or enmities.

"Our detached and distant situation invites and enables us to pursue a different course. If we remain one people under an efficient government, the period is not far off when we may defy material injury from external annoyance; when we may take such an attitude as will cause the neutrality we may at any time resolve upon, to be scrupulously respected; when belligerent nations, under the impossibility of making acquisitions upon us, will not lightly hazard the giving us provocation; when we may choose peace or war as our interests guided by justice shall counsel.

"Why forego the advantages of so peculiar a situation? Why quit our own to stand on foreign ground? Why, by interweaving our destiny with that of any part of Europe, entangle our peace and prosperity in the toils of European ambition, rivalship, interest, humor or caprice?

"It is our true policy to steer clear of *permanent alliances* with any portion of the foreign world, *so far I mean as we are now at liberty to do it;* for let me not be understood as capable of patronising infidelity to existing engagements. I hold the maxim no less applicable to public than to private affairs that honesty is always the best policy. I repeat therefore let those engagements be observed in their genuine sense. But in my opinion it is unnecessary and would be unwise to extend them.

"Taking care always to keep ourselves by suitable establishments on a respectable defensive posture *we may safely trust to temporary alliances for extraordinary emergencies.*"

It is not a little difficult to trace the connection between the text of Washington and the interpretation of his commentators. The policy he recommends is that of a great man: it has been expounded into the folly of children. The sagacity of the advice is not more remarkable in its appreciation of the advantages of our peculiar position, than in the careful and precise limitations of the extent and nature of those advantages.

When he warned us against "permanent alliances" he was careful to assure us that we might safely trust to "temporary alliances" for extraordinary emergencies. He felt the galling shackles of the French treaty of 1778 which bound the United States for ever to guarantee her American possessions, and threatened daily to endanger our peaceful relations with all the world by the restless caprices of her ambition; and he justly thought it unwise to multiply such entanglements.

But he felt no superstitious horror of alliances with European powers for the declaration of principles of commercial or political intercourse in which we had an interest, and for their maintenance by arms when assailed in the persons of either of the parties.

The mission of Mr. Jay to London was for the purpose of procuring the recognition by England of certain great principles of maritime law for the protection of neutral commerce against the impartial outrages of the parties to the furious war that then desolated the world. But if England refused to stay her robber hand, Washington had no scruples against an alliance to compel her. The armed neutrality of 1780 between Russia, Denmark, and Sweden embodied the most essential of those principles, and *bound the parties with united forces to punish their violation in the person of either.* President Washington contemplated acceding to it. His instructions to Mr. Jay were—"You will have no difficulty in gaining access to the ministers of Russia, Denmark and Sweden, at the court of London. The principles of the armed neutrality would abundantly cover our neutral rights. If, therefore, the situation of things with respect to Great Britain should dictate the necessity of taking the precaution of *foreign co-operation* upon this head, if no prospect of accommodation should be thwarted by the danger of such a measure being known to the British cabinet, and an entire view of all our political relations shall in your judgment permit the step, *you will sound those ministers upon the probability of an alliance with their nations to support those principles.*"

Washington contemplated an alliance, not to redress *past grievances*, but to repel *future encroachments*, to maintain principles of intercourse new to Europe, to compel their incorporation in her public law. He thus directly contemplated pledging our arms to European powers, to meet the "extraordinary emergencies" of his day, under stipulations which would have required us to defend the commerce of Russia against the aggression of France. He did so, because we were interested in maintaining the same principles which Russia, Sweden, and Denmark had united to defend; we could not defend them alone: and we could obtain their aid only by tendering them our support.

This case suffices to rescue the statesmanship of President Washington from the eulogies of his commentators.

Our great rule has undoubtedly been, while extending our commercial relations, to have "as little political connexion as possible" with other nations. But Washington did not contemplate the possibility of exemption from all political connexions. Nor are we to suppose that by "as little as possible" he meant us to judge of what was possible by any metaphysical measure of possibility. He designated no Japanese policy of political isolation—for he knew it to be impossible. He was not talking at random of Utopian seclusion, nor advising either a selfish abandonment of the duties, or the cowardly retreat from the responsibilities of civilized nations. He was careful to reduce his meaning to certainty—by pointing to the *object* expressed by his language.

"Europe"—he says—"has a set of *primary interests, which to us have none or a very remote relation.* Hence she must be engaged in frequent controversies the *causes* of which are *essentially foreign to our concerns.*"

From this he does not reason against our having any interest in the controversies of European nations. He does not hint that there may not arise combinations among them in which it may be important for us to join. He is careful to guard against any such folly. He only says, "Hence therefore, it must be unwise in us—to implicate ourselves by *artificial* ties in the *ordinary vicissitudes* of her politics or the *ordinary combinations and collisions* of her friendships or enmities."

When these words were published to the world on the 17th of September 1796, George Washington had for more than forty years been an actor of history in no mean part. His country had been a colony of a great European power, ambitious, active, and grasping—mingling in every struggle—and dragging her colonies with her into the vortex. In these wars Washington developed his youthful genius. He was not ignorant of their origin and causes. He knew what had passed on the theatre of Europe within his century, before he was in existence or called into active life. With the result of these events he was called to deal: and their relation to his country was the point of view in which he was required to regard them. On them his eye was turned when he spoke of "primary interests" of European states having only a remote relation to us, and of those "*ordinary vicissitudes* of her politics," and "ordinary combinations" of friendships and enmities, with which he pronounced it unwise to implicate ourselves by *artificial ties.* The eighteenth century from its commencement to its close was one unbroken series of those "ordinary combinations" relative to those primary interests, in which we could not for the future have any sort of interest.

The great wars of opinion which sprung from the reformation had burnt out before the middle of the seventeenth century; and the treaty of Westphalia settled the balance of power and the public law of Europe.

The eighteenth century opened with the war of the Spanish succession—a fierce contest of high ambition and high policy between Austria, France, and England, for the possession or partition of the

Spanish monarchy. It was important to England, that France should not be unduly aggrandised. It was important for France to exclude the house of Austria from the possessions of Spain. But to this Republic, as an independent power, such interests—primary to France, Austria, and England—had "none or a very remote relation." No principle was involved or asserted which would have extended to us; nor was there any imminent danger of the absolute subjection of all Europe to any one power—however inconvenient to England or Austria might be the possession of the Spanish monarchy entire, by a prince of France. The treaty of Utrecht of 1713 settled the territorial partition of Europe, and divided the spoils of Spain.

The second war of the eighteenth century, was that of the Austrian succession—a heartless, spiritless, despicable attempt to wrest from a woman the inheritance of her father, secured by solemn treaties, and guaranteed by every power which drew a sword in the unholy contest. To the United States, it would have been absolutely unimportant whether Maria Theresa maintained the integrity of her dominions, or Charles, Elector of Bavaria stripped her of half her dominions, or Frederick of Prussia robbed her of Silesia, on lying pretexts. The flames of war spread round the world, blazed fiercely on the confines of Hindoostan, and lighted the forests and the lakes of America; but the *issue* was the integrity of the Austrian dominions, invaded and depredated on by crowned freebooters. This was a "primary interest" to Prussia, to France, to Bavaria, to England, to

Austria; but to this Republic it could bear no relation or a very remote one only. The treaty of Aix la Chapelle of 1748 interposed a truce and a breathing spell between the war of the succession, and its offspring—the war of the seven years.

Maria Theresa meditated revenge on the despoiler of Silesia, and nursed her wrath till the day of vengeance. She stirred up all Europe to arms in her cause. The hate of Elizabeth and the hereditary policy of Russia, Saxony, bought with promises of rich spoils, France, inveigled by the arts of Pompadour from her ancient policy—all conspired to crush the king, whose arms or tongue or pen had wounded the vanity or humbled the pride of half the kings and queens of Christendom. But, however important to Europe, surely to *us* it could be of no moment whether Silesia belonged to Frederick, or Maria Theresa blotted his kingdom from the map of Europe. It was one of the "ordinary combinations and collisions of her friendships and enmities," in which only the most artificial ties could possibly implicate us.

Though it spread from Germany to India and America, and the supremacy of English arms and policy expanded her commercial empire to the ends of the earth, it still remained a war about European interests, and one foreign to our concerns. Americans bled to plant the banner of England on Quebec and to wipe out from her escutcheon the stain of Braddock's defeat—in a war for a German principality.

But at the date of the Address, all Europe was wrapped in the smoke of a war of stupendous magnitude—and which history has shewn to have been pregnant with consequences of vital moment to us. At its outbreak, President Washington led the policy of this country. In the midst of no small vituperation and clamor he proclaimed and maintained our neutrality. The advocates of peaceful indifference invoke this proclamation as an exemplification of the principles of the Address. They strenuously argue that it was the war of despots against liberty—equally dangerous to us as any since existing: and, therefore, the example of Washington has declared that even the tremendous combination of European despots against the freedom of the world is no exception to his warning against intermeddling in European concerns. That is the strongest statement the argument will bear.

It is unfortunate that it derives its plausibility from considering the events of the war in 1796 in the light of its future progress; in giving a meaning to those events which it took fifty years to develope, but which they then did not import: and in utterly forgetting the condition of this country, and the reasons for that neutrality which, even under those circumstances, Washington declared to have been predominant in causing its adoption.

We were then a people of only three millions—sparsely scattered over the seaboard from Maine to Georgia—with no army which could be felt in an European contest—with no fleet adequate to protect our neutral commerce from daily depredations by both belligerents—and utterly powerless in a war against the English fleets which swept those of France and Spain from the ocean. Our armed intervention would then have been fruitless to our ally—ruinous to ourselves. Our commerce would have been driven from the ocean and our seaports laid in ashes—for the barren honor of proclaiming ourselves the friends of liberty.

Our constitution of government was not seven years old. The country still resounded with the debate between its friends and opponents: and the very question of peace or war took the line which divided those constitutional combatants. To plunge into the war must sharpen the hostility and embitter the contest of these factions: and the recoil of our own attack might have prostrated our own constitution in the Quixotic effort to aid another people more able to help themselves.

These motives pressed on President Washington: and he declares in his address when referring to his neutrality—"with me, a predominant motive has been to endeavor to gain time to our country to settle and mature its yet recent institutions, and to progress without interruption to that degree of strength and constancy which is necessary to give it, humanly speaking, the command of its own fortune."

Has not this country reached that point *now?*

These reasons would have sufficed to vindicate the neutrality in the French revolutionary wars at the time of his administration—even had the Holy Alliance then existed in full vigor, pursuing with high-handed audacity the extermination of liberty from the world, and illustrating their principles by such deeds as the Spanish, the Neapolitan, the Hungarian assassinations.

But that was not either the avowed, the pretended, or the real cause of the war at the date of the Address. The right to dictate a constitution to France was only like any other illegal outrage—it could be repeated any where: but there was no reason for its extension: and the pretexts and the real objects of the war, the avowals and the acts of the parties up to the date of the Address, developed no marked distinction between this war and all those which had filled the earlier part of the century. It did not appear to be one which immediately or even remotely threatened our security.

Louis XVI. had convoked the States General. That body felt the wants of the times, and presented a constitution to the King, which he sanctioned and swore to observe. He was weak and insincere in the presence of ambitious and desperate factions which he could neither control nor conciliate. They encroached on his constitutional prerogatives. He was imbued with the monarchical idea of the nullity of royal promises—and not unnaturally sought foreign help. Austria and Prussia negotiated treaties for his protection, and prescribed to the people of France the terms of accommodation. Outraged at this insolence, and eager to bring the matter to an issue, the Assembly compelled the King to declare war against the allies: and then justly suspicious of his sincerity, and feeling the impossibility of his conducting with vigor a war waged by their enemies for his liberation, they imprisoned, deposed, and finally executed him. Up to *this* point the war had been professedly for the liberty and safety of the King, *and the restoration of a constitution more free and liberal than that of England.* It was doubtless a gross insult to France to dictate her government. It was a gross outrage on the law of nations to enforce the dictation by arms. But it was a question of European interest only.

The French retaliated the insolent demand by proclaiming the rights of man at the head of her legions, and organizing revolutionary republics wherever she pitched her camps. But this was not the object of the war: it was merely one of the means and weapons for waging it. The French republic became an armed propagandist forcing liberty on reluctant millions as a fitting reply to the effort to force on France a constitution she repudiated and a king she knew to be a traitor. It remained a question of European politics.

The death of the king in 1793 was the occasion for the accession of England and Russia to the coalition. They disavowed any intention of imposing any government on France. They only deprecated her aggressive policy, the rebellion she preached and supported, the anarchy that she suffered and propagated. They professed their willingness to make peace whenever any stable and responsible government should be installed. They renounced all ideas of conquest. England, the only free constitutional government was armed against France; the war was not therefore one directed against all free institutions. All parties would gladly have acquiesced in the constitution sworn to by the king. The revolutionary madness was the object of their terror, their hate, and their hostility. They considered it a temporary madness. They did not aim at the freedom which animated it—but the fanatical and cruel phrenzy which deluged the world in blood in the holy name of liberty. Such were the pretexts—justified by the apparent facts—beneath which the allied powers disguised their ambitious projects.

Their real object was conquest. In less than a month the proclamation of moderation was withdrawn—conquests made were claimed in France for Austria—England detached her troops for the destruction of Dunkirk—and while Austria strove to dismember France, Russia did dismember Poland. The crusade for the safety of kings and the suppression of an ambitious faction was converted into an alliance to plunder France of her territory. It had sunk to the level of a war of aggression and conquest on the one side, as it was charged to be on the other. France waged a war with ideas as well as with arms; but they were the mere instruments for the conduct of the war—not avowedly nor apparently its causes or its objects.

People might well doubt if that were liberty which in its name defiled itself with innocent blood, mocked at the religion of the world, and denied the God of Heaven; which Burke the friend of America execrated, and England the only free power of Europe could be prevailed on to attack. It was liberty—but in its maddest and least amiable mood, goaded to phrenzy by persecution, and wielding the maniac's might for defence. Washington followed the struggle with his prayers. But he feared its fiery contact quite as much as he deprecated its fall before the arms of the coalition.

Nor was the balance of fortune so decided as to leave open any very serious apprehensions of any great change in the relative power of nations. The campaign of 1793 terminated by the rout of France at the camp of Cæsar. The campaign of 1794 saw the allies driven over the Rhine. The close of 1795, after various changes of fortune, left the contending armies marshalled on the Rhine—in balanced power. Spain and Prussia had withdrawn from the contest. England and Austria were no more than a match for France. Russia was digesting her Polish spoliations.

The campaign of 1796 opened brilliantly for the Republic. Moreau and Jourdan carried terror into the centre of Germany and threatened to form the coveted connection with the army of Italy. But the fate of war drove them to the Rhine while Napoleon was crushing the successive armies which Austria poured into Italy—that nothing might be wanting to elevate his victories into miracles. Moreau and Jourdan were beaten *before the address was written;* and *Napoleon was yet between Lodi and Arcola* when it was published.

The war up to the day of the address was a war about European interests. It was an outrage on the independence of France—but she was more than able to protect herself. It was waged under false pretexts for ambitious ends—but the pretexts had more of justification than those under which Frederick seized Silesia and Russia divided Poland.

The coalition was formidable—but incomparably inferior in relative powers and actual conduct to that which in the seven years war menaced the existence of Prussia.

The sovereigns of Europe felt a deep sympathy for their cousin. They sought to quiet internal discontents or to prevent revolutionary agitations, by extinguishing the portentous conflagration which raged in France. They felt and treated it as a temporary fury—dangerous if left unchained, but not as necessarily connected with the idea or the reality of constitutional liberty, nor inconsistent with the forms of monarchical government. They were not then aware of the ultimate and irreconcilable hostility between liberty and despotism. The incompatibility was not yet developed so as to sink into their minds as a principle. They did not yet attack it on principle, from policy, in every phase, regardless of place and time and origin and duration. They professed to be the friends of reasonable, well balanced, constitutional liberty. It was the fashion of the age in courts, in the salons, in the schools.

Its fortune was that of early christianity. It was a novelty—and that attracted. Its scarching penetrating exclusive power and pretensions were unknown or unheeded. It was hated by a few bigots. It was admired by philosophic curiosity, or tolerated by philosophic disdain. It was left to herd with the superstitions that swarmed over the Empire. Its purity and simplicity even attracted Imperial notice; and the statue of Christ shared with those of Abraham, Apollonius, and Orpheus, the imperial devotions.

Its tenets were permitted to spread in obscurity and almost without opposition. But when it shrank with horror from the profane contact of idolatry, proclaimed the purity of its principles as the imperative rule of life, and anathematised as iniquity what the law called religion—asserting exclusive empire where it was only tolerated as an associate, and commanding obedience to the curious and idle enquirer, whose pleasant vices it denounced—it was *then* that Imperial despotism united with private bigotry, by fire and sword, the wild beast and the torturing rack, to exterminate a spirit whose existence was felt to be incompatible with the "*existing order*" of the Roman world.

So it was with modern despots and the spirit of liberty. It took thirty years of war and rebellion, of concession and of retraction, to impress the dullness of royal minds with the incompatibility of popular power and monarchical absolutism. They were long in learning that popular *power* involved *popular sovereignty:* and that there could not be two sovereignties in the same state. They were then forced to choose between the retention or the surrender of their *absolute* power. Any recognition of popular power involved by inevitable sequence their subordination: they were driven, therefore, to deny *all* participation to the people in affairs of government, and to war down every effort to obtain it. They then saw that liberty worked by example, and was as dangerous when peacefully operating in a neighboring state as if it were in their own. They therefore consistently associated themselves to extinguish it in every place whence its light could shine into their darkened realms. This was not the case at the date of the address. It is a new thing in the world. It is the peculiar product of the nineteenth century. It has given a significance to the liberal cause and its contest with despotism which it never had before—and which takes it from the category of those "primary interests" of Europe which have no relation to us.

The combination for the suppression of liberty is not an ordinary combination of her politics, or an ordinary combination of her friendships and enmities. It is a novel, extraordinary, and dangerous conspiracy to suppress liberty as dangerous to despotic power and utterly incompatible with its quiet existence.

It requires no "artificial ties" to implicate ourselves with the fate of the free nations of Europe. Our fate is bound up with theirs. Their fall removes the only hindrance to our fall. The principle of the conspiracy, the consistency of the policy, the influence of this Republic, the impossibility of quiet to despotism so long as it exists, all unite to compel the despotic *powers to elect between our ruin and their own.*

To seize the first opportunity by suitable alliances to meet and overthrow them, to divide their power, to substitute free for despotic governments, to support by money and arms nations which by our aid with that of England can maintain themselves, is therefore the plainest dictate of common sense. Washington would have been the first to see and provide for the coming storm. If he could not avoid it, he would have hastened to dispel it ere it reached maturity. He would not have been so simple as to call alliances for such a purpose "leaving our own to stand on foreign ground." He would rather have said, it is leaving our own that we may meet and repel our foes from the sacred home of our liberties. He would not have called this the "entangling our peace in the toils of European ambition, rivalship, interest, humor or caprice." He meant those words for such wars as filled the eighteenth century.

For emergencies such as the events of the last thirty years have developed, he would have been the last to recommend a temporising policy. The last day of weakness would have been the last of inactivity. He would have seen in the steady march of despotic power from east to west in its unholy crusade against liberty the foreshadowing of a terrible day which procrastination might hasten, but could never shun. He would have regarded the advent of 1848 and the great crisis it developed as a blessed opportunity which Providence might not repeat. He would have considered the adjournment of our fate as a deadly artifice, which secured easy success by a little patience. He would have seen in the triumph of the despotic powers all over Europe, and in the events now there transpiring, one of those "extraordinary emergencies" which his knowledge of human affairs led him to foresee must arise. "*We may safely trust to temporary alliances for extraordinary emergencies*" are the words which indicate his policy in such contingencies. He would not let a day pass without entering on negotiations with England to meet and provide for events which are on the wing—and which this generation may see face to face, involving the integrity, the very existence of the Republic.

The policy of Washington in the hands of its recent interpreters has come to mean a short-sighted indifference to external events if they happen to occur at a distance, blindly disregarding their character and their necessary consequences. His policy is made to mean—indifference to every thing occurring beyond the American continent not inflicting some direct and tangible injury on us.

That great man measured his policy by other rules. Distance was only one element of his calculation. The event, its meaning, and its consequences were what he regarded. Whether near or remote, he was ready to meet and ward off danger by any alliances which would answer the purpose. He had no horror of mingling in European contests: he merely said the system of *permanent* alliances with any power was an evil one, and that meddling in the *ordinary* combinations of European politics relating to interests primary to her but remotely related to us, was unwise. But he never advised indifference to the machinations and the arms of a coalition of European despots of great magnitude, permanence, and power—on a principle which involves our government peculiarly—and hitherto so victorious that all Europe is now subject to its will.

On the contrary, the first steps of that iniquitous alliance mis-called the Holy attracted the attention, excited the fears, and elicited the most emphatic protest of President Monroe. His declaration has ever been regarded as the basis of our foreign policy.

That declaration rests on the wisest principles of statesmanship, which anticipates and meets danger in the distance. It was never reputed a departure from the policy of President Washington; yet it is as far removed as heaven and earth from the puerile trifling put into the mouth of that great man by his expounders.—

That declaration flowed from the independence of the Spanish provinces—and the dangers which threatened them.

Prior to the Spanish revolution, the Holy Allies had offered Ferdinand "an amicable intervention to restore for him—*on solid bases*—the authority of the mother country." The Neapolitan expedition was the best exposition of their interpretation of *amicable;* nor could they have expected that republics in arms would yield to persuasion after having repelled force. The "fatal example" of the revolution at home strengthened the hands of the revolted colonies; and the Allies postponed their reduction till they had restored despotic power to the throne of Spain.

But the independence of the colonies totally altered our relations to them. We hastened to acknowledge them, to form treaties of commerce with them, to open the freest and most intimate intercourse with them. We hailed the blessed vision of freedom and peace which their success seemed to assure. We rejoiced that our borders were freed from the dangerous contact with the vassal colonies of despotic powers; and we indulged few scruples as to the measures we should take to prevent their reduction by foreign force.

The triumphs of the Allies in Spain was the natural precursor of the resumption of their postponed but not abandoned interference in South America. It was natural that Ferdinand, restored to half his empire, should invoke the Holy League to lay at his feet the other half. The example of the rebellious colonies was equally pernicious—the outrage on his divine rights equally atrocious—and conciliation impossible but by the persuasion of the bayonet.

So plainly was this the next step in the drama—that in October 1823 George Canning distinctly warned the minister of France that any interference by force or menace between Spain and the colonies would be the signal for the acknowledgment of their independence by England.

Their independence had been already recognized by this Republic—which greeted with overflowing heart and disinterested exultation the birth of her sisters of the western world. But the impending danger to their infant freedom from the blood-thirsty tyrants of the Holy League called for something more than acknowledgment by this Republic. The first to shatter the chains of despotism, her only title to existence was the right to defy the Lord's anointed. To crush the southern republics because they had not asked leave to be free was to impeach our liberty, and by implication to affirm the right to reduce us beneath the sceptre of England. President Monroe felt the danger and met it in advance. His declaration was based on the triumph of the allies in

Spain, and his conviction that it must be followed up by an attack on the republics of America. His message of December 1823 *pledged this Republic to repel by force of arms any attempt on the part of the Holy Allies to apply their system of compulsory reconciliation to the South American republics.* He did this by way of anticipation; and the event proved that audacity was wisdom. The same month of December 1823 which gave his message to the world witnessed a formal demand by Spain on his Holy Restorers to meet at Paris to devise measures for reinstating his despotic power in America. The *plan* comprehended only the *restoration of the colonies* in America. Yet to subject *them* to Spain was no *wrong* done to *us*. We expressly and repeatedly declared our neutrality between them and Spain. That was to declare their existence must depend on their ability to maintain themselves. If they fell before the arms of Spain we might pity but would not aid them. But had not Spain a right to invoke the aid of other powers in the war? And if so, was it not inconsistent to make the exercise of that clear right the criterion of peace or war with all Europe? Was not that within the policy of Washington according to the new lights of modern commentators? Assuredly it was no aggression on *us* to restore the colonies of South America to their allegiance to Spain. Why then did Monroe and the great men of the Washingtonian era, his friends and disciples, brought up at his feet and worshipping his memory, so promptly declare their readiness in *that* contingency to fly in the face of what we now are taught to believe was the very pith and substance of his teaching?

The reason was—that they knew a little more about the policy of their master. It is plainly as much in the teeth of the policy of the address to mingle in controversies between European and American nations *having little or no relation* to our peculiar interests, as to intervene in struggles between European powers having only the *same degree* of relation to us. When the address was written, *all America beyond our limits was colonial.* No independent flag waved from the north pole to Cape Horn but our own. The Viceroys of European monarchs ruled at their will the whole continent beyond our limits; and those limits did not stretch across the Mississippi, nor reach the Gulf of Mexico. Every European war must therefore spread to this continent and blaze all round our borders. If every such contest was to form an exception to Washington's rule of isolation, the rule itself would have no case left to operate upon. It did not therefore draw the line of distinction between European and American affairs to which his commentators now delight to refer. He did not contemplate our intermeddling in all American contests, as European nations are apt to do in contests touching the territory of Europe. America was no exception to his rule: but it was embraced in it—as dependent on Europe and following the ordinary vicissitudes of its politics. He had seen more than half of North America change hands within his own day: and a reversal of the event was no improbable contingency. Yet he made no exception of such a case. He was not basing his policy on the *theatre* of contest, but on its *objects*, its *principles*, its *relation near or remote* to our safety and independence. Whether the threatening cloud arose in Europe or America was not the question: but—was it likely to burst on us.

President Monroe took this view of the policy of this country, and he acted on it. He had watched with keen interest the struggle of Spain. He greeted with joy her free constitution, and it consoled his benevolent mind "to see the extraordinary moderation with which it has been conducted." His message of December 1822 was filled with the fairest anticipations; and though the atmosphere of Europe boded a storm which led him to advise instant preparation, nothing indicated the blow which followed. Between that time and the message of December 1823 the Holy Alliance had developed their policy, illustrated it by a terrible example, and stood ready to follow it up in another hemisphere. They had prostrated Spanish freedom: they prepared and threatened to coerce the obedience of her rebellious colonies. They professed no hostility to the United States; and their intervention was as the ally of Spain, a principal party in a legitimate contest in which we had formally declared and scrupulously maintained our neutrality. But President Monroe was no inexperienced political trifler—but a practical statesman, bred in a great school, conversant with affairs, versed in the logic of political sequences, and perfectly conscious of what must follow the reduction of the Spanish colonies. The pretexts were transparent: and he did not refuse to see through them; nor would he believe we were safe because the first blow fell on our neighbors.

He saw for the first time the policy of the Holy Allies assume a definite shape. Still affecting the disguise of hostility to revolutionary violence and excess, which had disgraced, discredited, and overthrown the first French revolution, their assault on the liberties of Naples and Spain revealed the real purpose of the alliance, the real object of their hostility. It was not the excesses of revolution, nor the danger of an armed propaganda, but peaceful, quiet, legal, constitutional liberty, guarded by armed freemen against the encroachments of perfidious despots—which they banded to overthrow. President Monroe saw that this principle included our Republic—as Henry Brougham saw it was applicable to England—and that the subjection of the Spanish colonies was only the preliminary step to intrigues, intermeddlings, aggressions, and combinations against us. He therefore met the distant threat by a timely warning. Our strength was not great enough *then* to be felt on the continent of Europe. Alone we could there effect nothing, while France was the slave of the Holy Allies, and England was paralyzed with terror or halting between two opinions, disgusted with her former allies, startled at the development of principles she had sanctioned by her example, yet not resolved to meet their pretensions in arms. He therefore measured his declaration by our strength: and with a boldness which still startles us when we regard the disproportion of the parties and the enormous power he engaged to meet, he laid down the line beyond which the Holy Allies should not march westward without crossing swords with the American Republic.

President Monroe and his cabinet were not troubled by many scruples about leaving "our own to stand on foreign ground," when they declared in the face of the assembled and allied tyrants of Europe that an attack on Chili was an attack on them. Alluding in the message of December 1823 to the recent events in Spain, the President said:

"It need scarcely be remarked that the result has been far different from what was then anticipated. Of events in that quarter of the globe with which we have so much intercourse and from which we derive our origin, we have always been anxious and interested spectators. The citizens of the United States cherish sentiments the most friendly in favor of the liberty and happiness of their fellow men on that side of the Atlantic. In the wars of European powers *in matters relating to themselves*, we have never taken any part, nor does it comport with our policy so to do. It is only when our rights are invaded or *seriously menaced*, that we resent injuries or make preparations for our defence. With the movements in this hemisphere we are of necessity more immediately connected, and by causes which must be obvious to all enlightened and impartial observers. *The political system of the allied Powers is essentially different in this respect from that of America.* This difference proceeds from that which exists in their respective governments. And to the defence of our own which has been achieved by the loss of so much blood and treasure and matured by the wisdom of our most enlightened citizens, the whole nation is devoted. We owe it therefore to candor and to the amicable relations existing between the United States and those powers, to declare that we *should consider any attempt on their part to extend their system to any portion of this hemisphere as dangerous to our peace and safety.* With the colonies or dependencies of any European power we have not interfered and shall not interfere. But with the governments who have declared their independence and maintain it, and whose independence we have on great considerations and on just principles acknowledged, we could not *view any interposition for the purpose of oppressing them or controlling in any other manner their destiny, by any European power, in any other light than as the manifestation of an unfriendly disposition towards the United States.*

"The late events in Spain and Portugal, show that Europe is still unsettled. Of this important fact no stronger proof can be adduced than that the allied powers should have thought proper, on a principle satisfactory to themselves, to have interposed by force in the internal concerns of Spain. *To what extent such interposition may be carried on the same principle is a question in which all independent powers, whose governments differ from theirs, are interested; even those most remote, and surely none more* SO THAN THE UNITED STATES. Our policy in regard to Europe, which was adopted at an early stage of the wars which have so long agitated that quarter of the globe, nevertheless, remains the same, which is, not to interfere in the *internal concerns* of any of its powers, to consider the government de facto as the legitimate government for us, &c. &c. But in regard to these continents, the circumstances are eminently and conspicuously different. It is impossible that the Allied Powers should extend their political system *to any portion of either continent without endangering our peace and happiness: nor can any one believe that our southern brethren if left to themselves would adopt it of their own accord. It is equally impossible, therefore, that we should behold such interposition in any form with indifference.*"

This declaration—if any thing but empty gasconade—is the formal adoption of the policy it has been my purpose to advocate. I desire to apply its principle to a case clearly within the contemplation of its author, but not then so developed as to justify or require more active precautions.

It reiterates the policy of Washington, that "in the wars of European powers *in matters relating to themselves*, we have never taken any part, nor does it comport with our policy to do so." But if our rights be "*invaded or seriously menaced*,"—no matter how or where, by what nation or combination of powers,—it is our policy to prepare to repel aggression.

But by "seriously menaced" he does not mean any formal declaration of hostile intents, nor any actual movement directed against us. Any act whose principle and whose tendency is to implicate our peace and happiness *with the system of the Holy Allies* he considers as a serious menace. "*Any attempt to extend their system to any portion of this hemisphere,*" he pronounces "*dangerous to our peace and safety.*" "Any interposition for the purpose of oppressing" the South American governments, or *controlling in any other manner their destiny,* by any European power," he viewed as a manifestation of an unfriendly disposition to us. He did not wait for a direct assault; he treated the intermeddling with *any* of the governments of this hemisphere as an act of hostility. It was not the fact of the assault, but the principle involved in it which woke his apprehensions. He did not mean to propose a partition of the world with the European powers; and yielding to them the old world, engross to ourselves the new. But he was ready to repel their assault on the smallest and most distant republic of South America—though vastly more distant than Europe—because "*to what extent such interposition may be carried on the same principle, is a question in which all independent powers whose governments are different from theirs are interested, and none more so than the United States:*" because "*their system could not be extended to any portion of either continent without endangering our peace and happiness;*" because he recognized the citizens of the most remote of the American governments as "our southern brethren," and regarded any attack on them as only the prelude to an attack on us. He did not make the intermeddling a cause of war because it took place in *this hemisphere.* We have no more rights in America beyond our borders, than in Europe or Asia. But he denounced war as the penalty of interference—

because it was considered a manifestation of an unfriendly disposition towards *us:* because the *principle* on which such interference would rest must embrace our government, be as applicable to us as to them, and directly involve the assertion of a right, whenever the opportunity might invite, to deal with us as they dealt with them. President Monroe, therefore, met the danger in the distance with ready defiance. He did not measure our danger by leagues. He regarded the significance of the acts. The Rio de la Plata is farther from us than London or Paris. Our trade and connexion with Brazil are not near so great as with several European powers: and Rio Janeiro is more distant from Washington than Washington is from Madrid. The republics of the western coast, Chili and Peru—by the ordinary route of commercial intercourse—are vastly more distant than any part of Europe; and our own possessions in Oregon, by the same route, more distant still. It was not geographical relations therefore which dictated the declaration. It was the principle involved in the intervention, its applicability to ourselves, *and the disposition such an intervention would manifest on the part of the Allied Powers to make their power the only limit of their hostile assaults on the liberties of nations.* The principle of the intervention in Spain might consistently justify like intervention under similar pretexts for the suppression of free institutions in any other country. President Monroe saw the extent of the principle; and declared no nation more interested in its extension than the United States. He watched for the spirit which was to guide its application. The assertion of a right was nothing till it assumed a practical shape. But when an act was done involving a principle applicable to us, he thought it the part of a wise statesman to look out for the first *indications of an intention so to apply it.*

The declarations of the allies in their Spanish expedition did not distinctly declare their object to be the destruction of all free institutions. They confined it to the particular case. They covered it up under special pretexts which however unjustifiable did not make it manifest that they intended to extend the system beyond the particular circumstances. If it rested *there,* we were not directly and materially interested to fight against an example. Nor were we able to war against combined Europe.

But whatever act indicated an intention of applying the rule of intervention to the United States, President Monroe considered ground of hostility. He declared that any act against any American government, on any part of either of the American continents, however remote, however insignificant—*was evidence shewing an intent to make the principle involved in the Spanish expedition a practical one all over the world,* whenever power and opportunity would permit. He therefore pronounced such an act an aggression on us—incompatible with our peace and happiness—and just cause of war.

But was President Monroe so little of a practical statesman as to make one *act* the only evidence of an unfriendly disposition, and to exclude all other evidence? Did he mean to be guilty of the folly of saying that an actual assault on some American government is the only evidence he would regard as valid of a disposition to assail liberty in its western home? Would no declarations, no preparations, no hate, no open and avowed system of policy pursued for a series of years over the ruins of independent governments, written in characters of blood on a thousand fields and always pointing westward as its aim and goal, supply the place of the one single act of overt hostility to some insignificant American government? Such assuredly was not his view. He felt and avowed that no nation was more interested than the United States, in the question which the ambiguous and oracular declaration of the allies had left doubtful—whether the principle was to be extended to all cases within their power and its reach—or was to be confined to the case of Spain and other cases in circumstances alleged to distinguish it. If the allies meant the principle of that case to be applied where it could be done, to all governments, Monroe felt that we were interested in opposing it every where—especially should it be actually applied in America—but not less in Europe, if opportunity and ability existed to settle the question ere it should reach our shores. Had Monroe lived in 1848 and 1849, consistency and sound policy would have driven him to urge on England an alliance to break the power and humble the insolence of the allied despots. Should God in his providence open such another opportunity, on us and on our children will rest the bloody consequences of neglecting it.

The same spirited and expanded policy inspired another celebrated declaration of that immortal message—which the arrogant claims of Russia to the north Pacific and north-western coast provoked and justified. It was a part of the same policy which proclaimed the readiness of the United States to repel with arms any attempt to oppress any of their American sisters, that closed the American continents to European colonization—the source and the pretext of political intrigue, and the ready cover for insidious assaults where open hostility would be dangerous.

In the discussion of the pretensions of Russia, President Monroe stated to Congress—"the occasion has been deemed proper for asserting as a principle in which the rights and the interests of the United States are involved, that the American continent, by the free and independent condition which they have assumed and maintain, are henceforth not to be considered as subjects for future colonization by any European powers."—

That declaration breathes little of indifference to affairs not immediately touching our own concerns. It was not confined to the north-western coast then in discussion, nor to any territory which we then claimed, or to which we might in the future set up a pretence. It did not rest at our confines and relate only to territory on our borders, nor did it contemplate the islands of the Gulf which lie across the channel of our southern trade. It did not stay its sweep within the range of territory peculiarly related to the United States in any manner. It was as long and as broad as the continents of America. It covered them—every foot—with our arms. It pledged this Government not merely to protest against but to repel, as an aggression dangerously involving our rights and interests, any attempt at colonization within or without our territory on either continent. From Greenland to Patagonia by that declaration Europe stood excluded, or if she entered, it could only be over our prostrate arms or tarnished honor.

But *this* is something very different from the Washington policy of the new school. This declaration was no tangling alliance—it was no needless political connexion with any foreign power. It left us free as before to fight or forbear as our interests or honor might require. But it did pledge us to the world to sustain by arms that declaration in its full and substantial width whenever and wherever it was substantially violated. No body could demand our aid against our will; but our dignity was at stake if we failed to make good our word.

This therefore, settled the policy of this country in all foreign affairs. It forever repels and refutes the foul aspersion that our foreign policy is selfish, unsocial, narrow-minded, or short-sighted. To be indifferent to affairs going on around us is no part of our national policy or national character. This declaration is the embodiment of our far-sighted policy—and of the fearless readiness of our statesmen to proclaim candidly to the world what we consider as dangerous to our interests or our security. It declared that we could recognize no newly acquired colonial rights—for we regarded all the territory of America now finally partitioned between independent powers—however wild, uncultivated, or remote might be its situation—however fairly the subject of colonization before the recent elevation of the Spanish colonies to the dignity of free nations. It was as wide as the principle of the Holy Allies, which refuses to recognize any right to create a new dynasty in Europe. It was more sweeping than the treaties of 1815 settling the territorial partition of Europe. It was not a treaty whose execution could be exacted—but it was the formal and spontaneous expression of the central principle of our own independent policy. It was based upon a wide estimate of the dangers which new colonial settlements must entail on any of the new republics within whose territories they might grow up—upon the inconveniencies our commerce must sustain from the vexatious regulations of powers inimical yet distant and irresponsible—upon the deep interest we took in the integrity, the peace, and the purity of our southern sisters. Recent experience had taught that colonization might be the cover or the pretext for aggression; and all the nation with one acclaim exulted in that manly and open pledge of our influence in the cause of liberty.

But if such a policy were fit to be pursued, it was expedient that all interested in its maintenance should concur in giving it effect. Permanent alliances might be inexpedient, but consultations for common purposes to be pursued by common methods, securing unity of plan and binding closer the bonds of sympathy by declarations of principles which should rule the actions of the parties in designated contingencies—these were equally expedient and important. The community of interest and fate was a better bond than the frail language of treaties which ingenuity can always evade. Each party remained at liberty to pursue her course free from any right of another to implicate her in wars she might not approve. Europe had her congresses of Vienna, of Laybach, of Verona, to provide for her common interests, and for the suppression of liberty: it was fit that the free republics of America, threatened by that hostile combination, should pledge themselves by their solemn declarations not to tolerate its armed intermeddling on this side the Atlantic. Having many and grave common interests, commercial and political, of primary moment to them, and having little or no relation to the affairs of Europe, it was fit that they should have their congress of Panama, to consult and provide for the maintenance of their rights, and the promotion of their peculiar interests.

At the instance of several of the South American republics, the states of America were invited to meet in diplomatic congress, at Panama; and the representatives of Peru, Mexico, Central America and Colombia, met on the 22d of June 1826.

President Adams, inspired by the wise and manly policy of his predecessor—shaped by himself as Secretary of State—now as President recommended the appointment of ministers to that congress. Strong opposition arose in the Senate and House of Representatives. The resources of Daniel Webster's statesmanship were marshalled in defence of the wisdom of the measure—in opposition to and to the confusion of the let alone men of that day. The President, at the call of Congress, explained the purposes contemplated by the mission. After the most elaborate consideration, the Senate and the House approved that policy. This is the most authoritative exposition ever given of our foreign policy by all branches of the government. It settles definitively that policy to be not one of timid neutrality or of selfish and unsocial isolation, or of mean pursuit of filthy lucre, while the world is in arms struggling for the triumph of truth. But it declared that in our sphere, and in our day and according to our measure, and so far as is compatible with our safety, we are on the side of liberty, not merely in word, but in deed—not merely in the cabinet, but in the field.

The message—affirmed by the votes of both houses of congress—is the best exposition of the policy it proposed, and they espoused.

The President first considered whether the course proposed had any tendency to change the policy of the country, which sedulously avoided "entangling alliances;" and "unnecessary political connexions." He came to the conclusion that time had changed the condition of affairs, and introduced new elements requiring consideration. Our situation was no longer "detached and distant;" but we were the central, the oldest, the most powerful and experienced member of a new system of independent republics. This system had interests primary to its members and only remotely related to the nations of Europe. Their change from colonial vassalage to independence multiplied our relations with them as well of interest as of sympathy. As colonies, they were a sealed book. As free nations, we delighted to read in them the transcript and impress of our own glorious institutions working by example. With them, we not only then had, but must necessarily continue to have—whether we wished it or not—numerous and complex political relations, which must increase with their growth. He affirmed that the time foretold by Washington, when our augmented strength would enable us "to defy material injury from external annoyance and with reference to belligerent nations we might choose peace or war, as our interests guided by justice should counsel"—had arrived. He declared, that "*America* had a set of primary interests, which have none or a very remote relation to Europe: that the interference of Europe, therefore, in those concerns, should be spontaneously withheld by her upon the same principles that we have never interfered with hers: and that if she should interfere, as she may, by measures which may have a great and dangerous recoil upon ourselves, we might be called in defence of our altars and firesides, to take an attitude which would cause our neutrality to be respected, and choose peace or war as our interest, guided by justice shall counsel. The acceptance of this invitation, therefore, *far from conflicting with the counsel or the policy of Washington, is directly deducible from and conformable to it.*"

To what contingencies these words related he proceeds to shew, by invoking the authority of his predecessor, and incorporating in his message the celebrated declaration of defiance flung by him in the face of the banded tyrants and peacemakers of Europe. They both held the same policy, and concurred in regarding it as the just development of the counsels of the father of his country addressed to the manhood of his offspring.

To the suggestion that such consultations might prove distasteful to the Holy League or to Spain, he loftily replied—

"Our attendance at Panama can give no *just cause* of umbrage or offence to either; and that the United States will stipulate nothing there which can give *any such cause*. Here the right of inquiry into our purposes and measures must stop. The Holy League of Europe itself was formed without inquiring of the United States whether it would or would not give umbrage to them. The fear of giving umbrage to the Holy League of Europe was urged as a motive for denying to the American nations the acknowledgment of their independence. That it would be viewed by Spain as hostility to her was not only urged but directly declared by herself. The Congress and Administration of that day consulted their *rights* and *duties*, and not *their fears*. Fully determined to give no *needless* displeasure to any foreign power, the United States can estimate the probability of their giving it only by the right which any foreign state could have to take it from their measures. Neither the representation of the United States at Panama, nor any measure to which their assent may be yielded there, will give to the Holy League or any of its members, nor to Spain, the right to take offence: *for the rest, the* United States *must still as heretofore take counsel from their duties rather than their fears.*"

There were several objects of that Congress at Panama. It was benevolently hoped that private war might be banished from the ocean, and piracy cease to be the ally of civilized nations—that neutral property covered by the flag and protected by the bottom might sail unscorched through the flames of war—that our counsels and experience might aid our younger and less tried sisters in treading the thorny path of political life. But these were not all, nor its chief objects. The main purpose of that congress, in the view of President Adams, was to arrange a common plan to protect by arms, if protests proved vain, the rights of republican America from the armed pacificators of Europe. Whether in the shape of a treaty, or a declaration of common purpose, or an understanding, tacit, but clear, was matter of secondary consideration. The time, the mode, the extent of aid, were to be defined. The field of action was not necessarily to be confined to this continent. The purpose was the protection of the liberty and independence of this western world, whether questioned on the Amazon, the Atlantic, or the Rhine.

Mr. Adams expressly declared the purpose of that congress to be—to give effect to Monroe's declarations that these continents were not the subjects of European colonization. He declared that "most of the American nations have declared their entire assent to them; and they now propose among the subjects of consultation at Panama, *to take into con-*

sideration the means of making effectual the assertion of this principle, as well as the means of resisting interference from abroad with the domestic concerns of the American governments."

At that very time there lay in the Russian archives the records of a consultation held on the importance of reducing the South American republics under the dominion of Spain. It formed a part of that scheme that *the United States should be subjugated.* The memoir containing this startling proposal emanated in the year 1817 from the pen of Pozzo de Borgo—one of the most eminent of the remarkable corps of diplomatists by whom Russia prepares the march of her armies. They do not impertinently volunteer their advice unasked upon their government. That memoir was therefore on a subject then under consideration by the Russian Government, and its language gives the confirmation of history to the logic of this work—which deduced from the principles of the Holy Alliance the necessity of their attempting to overthrow this Republic as their crowning labor. Pozzo de Borgo rests his opinion on that very incompatibility between our institutions and those of the allies and the effect of our example, which it has been my purpose to develope. He said—

"Founded on the *sovereignty of the people, the republic of the United States of America was a fire, of which the daily contact with Europe threatened the latter with conflagration;* that *as an asylum for all innovators,* it gave them the means of disseminating at a distance, *by their writings and by the authority of their example, a poison of which the communication could not be questioned*, as it was well known that the French revolution had its origin in the United States; that *already* troublesome effects were felt from the presence of the French refugees in the United States." He then proceeded to argue that our reduction would be an *easy enterprise*, while our augmenting power made us objects of fear to *European monarchical* governments.

Russia therefore had been meditating our subjugation—as matter of sound policy—on the principle of the inherent incompatibility of our system and hers—prior to the Spanish and Neapolitan revolutions, and before the congresses of Laybach and Verona had proclaimed her principles to the world or elicited the warning protest of President Monroe. This fact gives the confirmation of history to the prophetic penetration of Monroe and Adams, and properly appreciated, it flings a terrible light on the path we have been trying to explore.*

In the face of this peril we are proud to reflect that President Adams in his message did not confine himself to our own domestic concerns. He did not contemplate a selfish repose amid the troubles of our neighbors, nor the resting secure in our own strength for our own protection. He did not contemplate turning a deaf ear to the cry of the feeble for help against the mighty, nor leaving them to perish so

* For this important document, I am indebted to the profound and statesman-like speech of Senator Soule—which was not delivered till after these pages were written, and which I was so unfortunate as not to see until they were in the printer's hands. Otherwise, I should have been most happy to extend my obligations to its comprehensive researches. 7 July, 1852.

that we only might be safe. But heartily concurring in Monroe's two declarations of principle, feeling that we were aimed at by the Holy Conspiracy of Europe, confident that division, inaction, and timidity would only hasten the inevitable day, he resolved to organize a plan of united resistance to any encroachments near or remote by the allied sovereigns.

The congress of Panama was therefore intended as a counterpoise to the congress of Verona. Its purpose was to elevate the protest of the United States to the dignity of the universal policy of republican America. It aspired to unite in one unbroken front the republics of these continents for the conservation of liberty in this its last asylum against those who, having strangled its infant energies in Europe, were hasting to follow with bloody hands its flourishing offspring beyond the ocean.

On this ground it was placed by the message, and defended in congress; and while much opposition was there felt and expressed against any entangling alliances, yet the voting the appropriation by the House of Representatives, and the approval by the Senate of the mission and the ministers, after this message and a full discussion of its principles, can be considered in no other light than the deliberate affirmation by all departments of the government that the policy of the message was the policy of the country.

We stand, therefore, committed to the principle of united opposition to any development of the principles of the Holy Alliance threatening the cause of free government in this western world. No man is entitled to say, it is our policy to be patient and inactive while our allies and natural friends are falling around us so long as we are untouched. The fathers of the Republic did not deem so meanly of its destiny and power. They feared ambitions and entangling alliances, they deprecated needless political connexions, they repudiated the folly of national attachments or antipathies, of hereditary devotion or hostility. They felt that their first duty was to their nation; but their second duty was to liberty and humanity. They would not sacrifice the former to the latter; but they were quick to see that the one was closely allied to the other, and our safety was wrapped up in the freedom of our neighbors. They were prudent not to draw the sword till it might be felt—nor then till it was required: but they fearlessly proclaimed to the world the limits of patience, the principle of peace or war: and they left to the future and the hereditary spirit of their children to redeem the gage of their plighted honor. They did not condemn this mighty Republic to silence in the great debate of nations. They did not place the sword in the hands of the President as an idle bauble, or to be drawn only in the cause of Mammon; nor did they ever dream that this people, silent and inactive amid the clang of arms where the destiny of nations was being decided, should play sutler to the camp and fatten on the blood of the martyrs of freedom—pursuing like the jackall with creeping and stealthy pace the low hunt for prey over the field of the weltering dead—but stained by no blood of theirs.

They would have recoiled with disgust at the picture of their descendants playing the Jew among the nations—in the world but not of it—with no voice in its affairs and no weight in its destinies—careful only of gain and ready to fight only for gold—holding the sacrilegious love of lucre the only religion elevating the spirit to martyrdom, and liberty valueless save as its security. Had such been their spirit, we had been no nation. Had such been their legacy of dishonor to us, their children, we might have started on the humiliating mission—but we should have caught inspiration at the sight of arms. We might have gone, like the son of Jesse, to the field of battle laden with parched corn and cheeses for our elder and heroic brethren: but he mistakes the spirit of this Republic who supposes that her children could calmly listen to the Goliath of despots defying the hosts of liberty without taking up that challenge and testing in arms the might of that uncircumcised Philistine.

Much rather, when I contemplate their youthful daring and matured might, do I recognise the lineaments of the offspring in Milton's painting of our English ancestors—

"Methinks I see in my mind a noble and puissant nation rousing herself like a strong man after sleep, and shaking her invincible locks: Methinks I see her as an Eagle muing her mighty youth, and kindling her undazl'd eyes at the full midday beam; purging and unscaling her long abused sight at the fountain itself of heav'nly radiance; while the whole noise of timorous and flocking birds, with those also that love the twilight, flutter about, amaz'd at what she means, and in their envious gabble would prognosticat a year of sects and schisms."

So stood the Republic of that day—lofty and defying.

But we owe our escape from a collision with the despotic powers to other terrors than our protests.

Thrice have the European revolutionists diverted the lightning from our heads to their own.

In 1815, the wars of the giants closed. Napoleon was chained to the rock of St. Helena; and the European system was reconstructed at Vienna.

Allowing themselves small breathing space, in 1817 the allied despots prepared to restore to the crown of Spain the sceptre of the American Indies, and audaciously debated our subjugation as a disturber of the public peace of the world.

The explosion in Spain and Naples diverted their arms and their thoughts from conquest to defence from 1819 to the end of 1823.

Restored to his absolute throne, Ferdinand in December 1823 urged on his allies the resumption of the American expedition.

Our protest may have had some weight. But just then the smouldering fires blazed up in Greece, and the Ottoman empire seemed crumbling to pieces.

The Czar eagerly turned from the certain perils and doubtful fruits of a western crusade; and the day of Navarino and the passage of the Balkan employed in the rich and tempting field of Turkish conquest till 1829, the arms we otherwise might have felt.

The shock of 1830 followed swiftly on the treaty of Adrianople: the army of the Balkan was recalled to the plains of Poland: and France having once more broken prison fixed the eye and roused the fears and the hate of the Czar. Europe for eighteen years continued too unsettled to allow the thought of western conquests. The despotic powers were busy with the work of compression—ignorantly preparing from afar the era of 1848.

Prostrate for a moment by that explosion, they regained their feet; and now the liberal cause lies crushed beneath the ruins of its shattered fortress: while Russia, confidently grasping the dictatorship of Europe, is ready for any enterprise to expand or consolidate her empire.

The cycle of time has brought us back to the circumstances, and in face of the dangers which occasioned the declarations of President Monroe, and the wise precautions of President Adams. The insolence of an Austrian Minister has provoked Secretary Webster's indignant rebuke. In language such as this government has not held since the lofty message of President Adams, he reminded the Imperial despots that this Republic had a voice and might take a hand in the affairs of the world. The time is not far distant when we shall be called on to redeem those pledges, or stand recreant before the world. It is now time that we consider of our course ere we be required to take it.

The American Republic in the face of every danger will adhere to her ancient, wise, and liberal policy—varying her measures to meet the shifting of events—but holding fast to the unity of the principle amid the variety of the means by which she pursues it.

Her policy is that of the Father of his Country—applied to circumstances within his foresight and covered by his words.

It is still her "policy to steer clear of *permanent alliances* with any portion of the foreign world;"—but it is also still her policy—now in the face of a great crisis—"to trust to *temporary alliances* for extraordinary emergencies."

The country has *now* progressed "to that degree of strength and constancy, which is necessary to give it, humanely speaking, the command of its own fortune."

The time has come "when we may choose peace or war, as our interests guided by justice shall counsel."

"Our detached and distant situation," has ceased to be a fact—by the creation of the Spanish American republics on our borders. We form the centre of a new and peculiar system—at war with the principles which are being enforced on Europe, and which can only triumph finally by our overthrow.

This change enabled and compelled Mr. Monroe to deduce from the policy of Washington his declaration to the Holy Allies, "that we should consider any attempt on their part to extend their system to any portion of this hemisphere as dangerous to our peace and safety."

He meant by those words that in such event "our interest guided by justice" would counsel us to choose *war*.

The impending danger of the extension of the system of the Holy League to American affairs induced Mr. Adams to send ministers to Panama "to take into consideration the means of making effectual the assertion of that principle, as well as the means of *resisting* interference from abroad with the domestic concerns of the American governments."

It is now matter not of conjecture but of history, that the object of our fears was no phantom. We know that the allied despots stood prepared to apply their system of armed intervention on this side the Atlantic; that our subjugation was within the range of their views; that the assault on our southern neighbors which must have implicated us was turned aside by European revolutions; and that they who made them are now there prostrate and disarmed. We know that the same necessity of policy requires our subjugation for the peace of European despots: and the plan which once existed we do not know to have been abandoned.

Recent events have renewed and increased the dangers which President Adams sought to obviate at the congress of Panama. The triumph of Russia in 1848 has left her free to pursue the principle of her policy consistently to its most distant results. The Holy Alliance, reduced to a unit by the dictatorship of the Czar, scornfully repudiates the political events of thirty years, and refuses to recognize a crown of France save on the head of a legitimate Bourbon. It turns its scowl of open hate on the popular freedom of England and America, and denounces war on the very foundations of their constitutions—as organized disturbers of the peace of the world, whose overthrow only abides the fullness of time. Steam has added wings to its might, exempted naval war from the vicissitudes of the winds and the waves, and leaves New York more exposed to Nicholas than was London to Napoleon.

If therefore the congress of Panama were a fit precaution against that of Verona—a congress of London speaking the will of England and America will be a fit response to the diplomatic notes of Vienna.

Confiding in the assurance of Washington that "we may safely trust to temporary alliances for extraordinary emergencies," I point to the "extraordinary emergencies" impending over us; and insist that now as "heretofore, taking counsel from our duties rather than from our fears," we should construct such "temporary alliances" as may be requisite to enable us to surmount them.

This policy which I propose is no wild crusade to force freedom on reluctant nations. It is no propagandist policy made available for self-defence. It does not propose to enforce liberty by the bayonet or to preach it from the camp. It is no proclamation of the rights of man to people in contented or in discontented slavery. No institutions accepted or acquiesced in are proposed to be overthrown—still less is any hostility felt or avowed or recommended against kings and monarchical government. The principle is defensive, not propagandist. The history of forty years is its justification. The safety of our own freedom is its object. We are threatened with the success of a scheme of policy which has consistently pursued its course through thirty years of triumph—which now is on the point of being crowned as the arbiter of Europe—and which we have reason to know can and will make itself felt on this side of the Atlantic. We would defend ourselves by aiding those who are our natural allies; who with our aid may be victorious: who without it run great risk of failure: for if they fail our only hope is—in a successful contest single handed with the power before which they fell.

Neither is it recommended that the Republic declare itself the guarantor of the independence of nations. The power of this Republic is not equal to such a declaration: and its settled policy disclaims it. We have the right to aid any nation unjustly assailed. It is our duty to regard our own interests in the exercise of that right. To conquer San Marino or to occupy Cracow are acts of outrage equal to the partition of Poland or the conquest of Hungary: yet to defy Russia and Austria in the cause of the former would be senseless; while self-preservation might under some circumstances require us to espouse the cause of the latter. The right is the same in each case: the reasons of policy must decide on the exercise or the forbearance of our right.

Many outrages may even now be committed in Europe in the name and in the cause of despotic power which nevertheless we should be foolish to resent. Nothing is more possible than the occupation of Switzerland by France and Austria; but if no other power interpose to aid Switzerland, if no revolutionary outbreak shake the continent—our intervention would be equally impolitic and nugatory.

But if England be assailed with deadly hostility by the combined despots of Europe, aiming to extinguish the glories of her arts and commerce, the light of her example and her liberty, the mighty refuge of hunted freedom, then—in spite of her monarchical head and aristocratic decorations—I see the vile attempt of despots to crush the spirit of liberty which alone renders her powerful, terrible and hated: and in my judgment, the time would have come when the sword of the republic should be drawn to defend in the person of England the rights of freedom and our own independence.

If God shall put it again in the hearts of the people to rise with simultaneous resolution against their oppressors as in 1848, and shall bless their efforts by again placing their rulers at their mercy and liberty within their grasp, then this Republic should not stand still and see them overborne by combinations of foreign arms and domestic treachery. She should not hesitate to improve the precious opportunity which Providence affords. She should display the banner of freedom in aid of our struggling brethren, and fling her sword into the trembling scale which weighs the destiny of the world.

We must be ready to make costly sacrifices of blood and treasure. Despotism will deliver terrible battle ere it loose its gripe on the neck of man: and the next battle will be the final and decisive one. It will be no passing cloud; but neither sun nor stars shall appear for many days after its fury bursts over the world: and they who love fair weather and smooth seas should pray that that day be put far from them.

But our contribution will be of our abundance to the necessities of the weak and destitute. Their wants will determine the shape of our aid. We shall be called on for no army for the invasion of Europe. The cause of liberty *now* numbers her soldiers by the million; it can command more men than it can arm, support, or officer. The spirit of liberty—like that of religion—makes her abode in the hearts and homes of the poor and the powerless. Their blood is the only libation they can pour on her altars—but that is ever ready at her call. We shall be called on for liberal and unceasing supplies of provisions—for the hand that wields the musket must abandon the plough. Our coffers must stand open—that men willing to contribute their life to the cause may not become a fruitless sacrifice. Arms must be placed in the outstretched hands of her devotees—for despotism has been careful to leave them defenceless. The military monarchies of Europe will yield to no arguments but steel and lead,—and they must be made to feel the bayonets they are so ready to inflict. Military science may be needed to marshal the willing but ill-instructed recruits,—and our youths at West Point and her splendid alumni eagerly expect their country's call to the field of glory. Our fleet—augmented so as to be less scandalously unequal to the resources and the wants of the country—combined with that of England can sweep our enemies from the face of the ocean—

and its high duty will be to pour in the supplies we furnish through every seaport of the continent, while it vigilantly intercepts all assaults on our domestic peace. From invasion by European armies we have nothing to fear; they will be employed at home, or if they venture the rash experiment, the luckless force which lands will melt away before the flood of armed men our teeming population will enable us to pour around it. Our only danger is from our southern neighbors, and they can only be driven into the arms of the despots by our selfish, grasping, unsocial policy.

Hungary fell—not for lack of men or heroism or science, but—because destitute of arms for the hands of her sons and of food for their mouths. She had no friendly flag, no La Fayette and Kosciusko, no French money, arms, or hearts. No French fleet poured its stores into her ports or kept them free to neutral commerce. But for such aid vain had been the devotion of Washington. He would have been buried in a month beneath the masses of disciplined soldiers whose march trampled out Hungarian freedom. His name would have been branded as that of a traitor—or enrolled among the martyrs of liberty—leaving no offspring to bless him with the name of father.

The principle therefore of our aid must be—to supply the deficiencies of the liberal men of Europe—to place them on even terms with their foes—and then trust to their courage and devotion to win for themselves what no one can give them—the priceless blessings of deserved and appreciated liberty.

The grievous fault of 1848 should not be repeated by England and America. They then threw away by sloth and indifference, by timidity and selfishness, the greatest opportunity ever afforded to settle the war between freedom and slavery. France is equally to blame; but she has paid the penalty of her folly by bitter humiliation beneath the heel of her tyrant. She has her own salvation to work out, and not till that is done can her glorious legions be counted amid the hosts of freedom. In the presence of her great agony let the tongue of censure be silent—yet let not the eye which provides for the future fail to mark the costly errors of the past.

Things would be very different in Europe now, had France and England and America acted with unity, energy, and devotion.

The men of the Provisional government reversed the precedents of the great revolution in order to rescue the cause of the republic from the stain of blood and the imputation of ambition. They proclaimed peace as their policy and refused to mingle in the strife of neighboring people lest they should bring on their cause the charge of propagandism. History looking on the event pronounces that policy a blunder. It could be right only on condition that all other powers acted on it also. The northern powers had been canting of peace for thirty years—yet never failed to make war under pretext of its preservation. It was contrary to experience to anticipate any change of their policy or of their conduct. It was a blunder to act on so baseless a supposition. It should have been assumed that their moderation was only a calm policy waiting the time to strike; that their only restraint is coercion that the first blow might decide the combat; that no faith could bind the enemies of freedom; and that disability to do harm was the only assurance of safety.

Had France and England acted on this theory—treated the cause of the people as theirs, wherever it was contested, and manfully afforded it the support of their name and their arms—Europe would now be free and at peace, and the dictatorship of Russia a thin shadow of the past.

Had France crossed the Alps and supported the cause of Charles Albert, an inconsiderable force would have driven Austria, distracted and enfeebled by an universal revolt, from Lombardy—put to flight the incubus which oppressed the breathing of Italy—and secured its entire independence.

Had England remembered her greatest moment—when Ferdinand anxious to repay his debt to despotism, prepared to crush the Portuguese constitution whose freedom he hated and whose contact he feared, and George Canning electrified Parliament by the memorable words—

"The precise information on which alone we could act arrived only on Friday last. On Saturday the decision of the government was taken. On Sunday we obtained the sanction of his majesty. On Monday we came down to Parliament.—And at this very hour—while I have now the honor of addressing this House—British troops are on their way to Portugal"—and had she acted in that spirit—Europe would not now be at the feet of the Czar.

Had Palmerston the liberal breathed the free spirit of Canning the tory—and when Russia crossed the Carpathians, sent British troops to Hungary—as Canning did to Portugal—Hungary had now been free.

Had he firmly supported the struggling nations of Italy whose revolts he countenanced and encouraged only to desert, English statesmen would not now be estimating her power to wage single-handed a war against the spiritual and temporal despots of combined Europe.

Had England met the menace of Russian intervention in the affairs of Hungary with her armed protest, it probably would never have taken place—and Hungary was master of her own destiny so long as she had to deal with Austria alone. If Russia disregarded that protest and England had given effect to her declaration by such support of Hungary as she bestowed on Spain against Napoleon, there can be no sort of question of the result. She would have been aiding a martial and heroic people, so absolutely united in their cause that the enemy could not buy spies, so devoted that thousands were turned away in tears because there were not arms to put in their hands, with a government resting on the affections of the people and wielded by the only man equal to the crisis of 1848. She need have sent no army to rally a people animated, united, and in arms. All they needed was her countenance, her commerce, her supplies of arms, her fleet to sweep the seas. With no other aid Hungary could have turned the tide of Russian invasion and set the very heart of the empire in a flame by an appeal to the fiery Pole. This Republic could have aided in this cause: alone she could have turned the scale: with England it would have been an easy game. They were both blind and indifferent: and with the fall of Hungary all the precious blood of the revolutions of 1848 sunk fruitless into the earth.

Should the fires of revolution again blaze up—should any such combination of propitious events again occur—it is the true policy as it is the bounden duty of the two only free and powerful governments of the world, with united arms, to dare the worst in the great cause of freedom—unswayed by any prejudices about forms of government, socialist theories, the rights of rival classes—but firmly holding to the conviction that the people of every nation, when freed from the oppression and terror of external domination, will wisely, calmly, and peacefully settle their own affairs on a basis satisfactory to themselves. No temporary excesses of the outraged people should chill their ardor or relax their efforts; for every battle is with confusion and garments rolled in blood: and liberty is worth the costly excesses which accompany the conflict. We should lay aside the arrogant boast that however the genus *human being* may prevail in Europe the species *man* flourishes only in America. We leave to despots as the only defence of their iniquities the humbling suggestion of the unfitness of the people of Europe for the blessings and securities of liberty. It would be well to seek in the wisdom and moderation of their legislative proceedings the proofs of their capacity; and to look for the causes of their overthrow in the combination of external violence and internal treachery. It might moderate our scorn for the humiliation of France by Louis Napoleon to reflect what would have been our fate had Washington accepted the crown his officers pressed him to assume; and how far the necessity of a standing army of three hundred thousand men would place our institutions at the mercy of our President. It may be worth while to reflect how long our revolutionary fathers could have stood before such armies as invaded Hungary; and that we achieved our independence with three thousand miles of ocean rolling between us and our foes only by the gold and arms of France without which we must have failed. It will throw light on the question to remember that a standing army of ten thousand men would have saved Charles I. his head, and secured England for the cause of legitimate monarchy. We join in the scandal of our enemies when we thus confound the capacity to govern with the ability to repel overwhelming violence or to insure exemption from internal treachery. We should rather stand amazed at the stupendous successes of the friends of liberty in the face of such obstacles than scandalized at their overthrow. Their heroism is worthy of our sympathy not of our scorn; and if they fell we are guilty of their blood which flowed because we failed to repay the aid we received. When the people of Europe are relieved from the fears of external and despotic violence those great armies—so dangerous to free institutions—will melt away from the face of the earth; and with security and freedom will come peace, moderation, and repose. We hold fast to the faith—that the wildest theorist, the most licentious socialist, the fiercest jacobin is less dangerous, less deadly, less bloody and proscriptive, than is the soft tongued and treacherous hearted, the crowned and anointed, the legalized and legitimate pirate against human freedom; and turning from the red republic to the redder despotism, we remember that one is a passing fury, the other a perpetual scourge breathing poison and dealing death, and dwelling in darkness which is rendered doubly terrible by the blacker demons of spiritual despotism which flit around its throne the obsequious ministers of its will.

The contest is not between *republicanism* and *monarchy:* but between *freedom* and *slavery:* the *power of the despot* and the *power of the people.* It is matter of serious doubt whether a hereditary head—if one can be found with an honest heart—be not the safest for the present necessities of some parts of Europe. Whether best or worst, it is entirely compatible with free institutions: and its adoption or rejection should not be permitted for a moment to divide the friends of freedom in the face of their common and deadly foe—who can be conciliated by no form of government where popular power is honestly recognized. It is folly for the friends of the people to insure their common ruin, because they cannot agree on the form in which they will enjoy the liberty they have not yet acquired. The strongest freest best government of the world—after our own—

is the popular monarchy of England. The crowned head of Victoria is infinitely dearer to us than the crownless despot who mocks the world with the nickname of *Prince* President of the French Republic. It is true that royalty ancient and modern has defiled every word which man has invented to designate it. Despot, tyrant, king—what of iniquity do not the very words import? Yet it is the *use* alone which has soiled them. In their origin they were simple and honest names for high offices—as respectable as that of president: and that venerable title will contract similar contamination if worn much longer by the despot of France. There is something cold and heartless, selfish and inhuman, at the very core of royal natures. Lifted—like lofty mountains—far into the regions of the air, their approach to the heavens makes them only colder than their fellows of the earth. The light of the sun pours without its warmth on their heads—illuminating the distant paths of ambition, but not softening the heart so that it can relent in its inexorable purposes. Human sympathies perish in the eternal snows which wrap them round. They embody and represent the cold malignity of Satan, treacherous, cunning, and cruel, unmoved in their purposes by any soft emotion, wise in the light of reason to pursue their deeds of iniquity, and infinitely removed from the reach of pity or remorse for the blood that they shed or the hearts that they break. Such is the curse with which despotic power blights its possessor: and its blackest traits have been exemplified on the thrones of Europe in the middle of the nineteenth century.

Still a hereditary crown, surrounded and limited by the people from whom it emanates and to whom it is responsible, may comport with freedom of no mean grade: and they who unite in that great cause must tolerate the prejudices, the weaknesses, the necessities, the waywardness and perversity of each.

The existing repose of Europe is transitory. What shall be the next scene of that drama there is no prophet to tell; but whatever be the shape events may take, we know the chief actors and the parts they will play. We know that the Czar will lead the crusade of despotism: and that he will be opposed by the hosts of freedom—but who shall be their leader, or who their allies, or when that day shall come, it is not given us to know. It may be at the threshhold—or half a generation off. It may be that France will shake off the domination of Louis Napoleon and Russia may march in the cause of kings under the name of the Bourbons. It may be that Louis Napoleon may acquiesce in her dictation, consent to rule on her terms and by her aid, and postpone till his death the decisive conflict. It may be that he will appeal to the pride of France, and array her against the northern league in the name of national sovereignty, for the benefit of his personal ambition: or that allied with his masters he may purchase his peace by services against freedom. Germany may once again draw the sword and clutch it with a firmer and more resolute grasp. Some unknown and unanticipated event may open the flood-gates of revolutionary war. But however and whenever the general peace is disturbed the parties to the contest will be the servants of light and of darkness—and the latter will be led by the Czar of Russia.

The problem we have to solve is—by what arms he may best be met and overthrown.

Europe is quiet on the surface—but boiling beneath. It is a crust covering molten lava—which any day may stir into the resistless fury of the earthquake, engulfing every throne in its fiery chasms. Russia is the only power of Europe seated on ground not undermined by the volcanic fires of revolution—the sole and the last refuge of despotism. She is powerful to protect; but she is not invulnerable. In wars of ordinary ambition she can be assailed in no vital part. She can repel invasion and retaliate it with impunity. Experience has shewn that with her on their side the monarchs of Europe are too strong for their subjects. But to the fires of revolution she is obnoxious. Her Polish provinces are exposed so that she cannot protect them. Their indomitable spirit supported from abroad will roll back the tide of Russian invasion, dam up the resources of the princes of western Europe, and deliver them naked and defenceless to the fiery indignation of their outraged people. Thus only can Russia be assailed. Thus only can the cause of freedom be emancipated from her deadly power.

This is the only possible mode—but it is sure and effectual. Every foot of territory gained by freedom is the frontier of a new campaign of advance. Its light now shines over all Poland—where the whole people worship its beams. Its grey dawn spreads even beyond the limits of her provinces, foretelling the approach of the light still below the horizon. If Germany be free, and the Polish provinces of Prussia and Austria, speaking the same language and having the same national traditions with those of Russia, once obtain national institutions, the whole power of Russia cannot keep their brethren in darkness or in sleep. An imaginary line of posts and sentinels alone marks the division. The frontier seems movable and unsettled. Russia has hopes of a westward march. It seems as if Providence prepared the eastward spread of liberty and light. With Prussian and Austrian Poland free, it would be a war of extermination alone which could suppress the Poles whom Russia holds enslaved. It is the certainty of this consequence which causes Russia so anxiously to watch and to ward off a danger she sees to be fatal if once fastened on her. The problem of the age is—to establish a free government on the Russian frontier and maintain it there. To prevent it Russia has hitherto lavished her blood and treasure—and she is ready to lavish more. The evil would not be so deadly if it could be stayed at the inner boundary of the Polish provinces. But once securely seated in Poland, even though she continued faithful to the Russian crown, its despotic power must fade away before it. Its example would gradually wake the idea, the desire, the resolution of obtaining free institutions. The progress of cultivation, the habits of forethought, the examples of Polish debates, the impossibility of excluding Polish newspapers, would force the imperial government to a change of policy under penalty of being swept away in case of obstinate refusal. The idea of equality, the central idea of justice and the very foundation of the democratic theory, would render it impossible for Russia long to continue the mild, legal, public, and constitutional rule of a popular government in Poland—side by side with the iron despotism however paternal which now reigns in Russia. The people of the central provinces now are quiet, devoted, and loyal subjects: but they are so because they do not desire political privileges. If that desire be at all diffused it breeds opposition to the despotic power of the Emperor, discontent, murmurs, conspiracies, and rebellions; and these necessarily engender military law, bloody executions, jealous inquisitions, and judicial murders. The despotic power is at once converted into a tyranny, and civil discord consumes the resources of the land till despotism or liberty sit on an unquestioned throne. It was to prevent this evil that Russia abrogated the Polish constitution after the rebellion of 1831, and invaded Hungary in 1849.

But failure in either of those struggles would have permanently settled the triumph of free principles. The same danger revives at every resurrection of the revolutionary spirit—and it must always be met by Russia in the same manner, promptly, energetically, and successfully. The despotic power of her Autocrats is at issue in every revolutionary struggle in any part of Germany.

If therefore Russia can be made to abstain from interference—or if her power can be balanced by the counteracting influence of free governments—the success of the liberal cause seems certain.

We know the utmost power we have to meet—even in the absence of a Polish propaganda and a Polish revolt. Russia with all her vast military resources for defence against military aggression is by no means more powerful in foreign war than several other governments of Europe. Her military power is not greater for foreign invasion than that of France. All Germany united under a federal constitution such as ours would have nothing to fear from her utmost might. Her population of sixty millions is sparsely scattered over an immense territory, in a low state of civilization, and of little intelligence; her pecuniary resources are limited like those of all merely agricultural and pastoral states; and the single campaign of Hungary drove her to solicit loans in the English market. The compact territory, the intelligence, the military aptitudes, the central position of Germany, if united under one government, fully compensate for the excess of the heterogeneous population of Russia in a direct contest of military power. Russia has never been able to send half of her nominal army of European operation across her frontiers. She could contribute only one hundred and twenty thousand men in 1814 to march beyond her limits; and the hundred and eighty thousand who entered Hungary were not only much the largest force ever sent beyond her frontier, but that body taxed to the utmost her military resources and was all she could spare for foreign aggression. Her power lies not in its preponderance, but in its unity, its promptness, and the unhesitating resolution with which it is put in motion when the time for action has arrived. If therefore the spirit of the revolution once again awake all Germany, and her people put not their faith in princes but seize the moment of success to consolidate their power in the shape of formal governments, taking the sword from hands interested to abuse it and placing it in hands honest and able, Germany would be mistress of her own fate. If Russia offer to interfere, the free governments of the world should draw the sword in her defence, and proclaim at the head of their armies the restoration of Poland among the nations of the world.

We condescend to debate no question of international law with Russia on this point. She has long since made her sword the measure of her rights, and we are content to accept the rule.

If she may intervene at the call of despots in the cause of the existing social order, we may do so at the cry of suffering liberty in the cause of human rights.

We rely on the "modern instances" of the Russian chancery for our right to rebuild what she has destroyed.

If Russian impudence plead the right of nations freely and unmolested to dispose of their internal affairs we concur in the assertion of the principle—and seeking her interpretation of it on the plains of Poland and Hungary, in the divan of the Turk, and among the principalities of the Danube, we turn to the shattered walls of the Polish fortress and to the broken columns of the Hungarian temple, and claim with restoring zeal to raise in renewed glory those ancient structures.

To the murmurs of Russian diplomacy we deign no other reply than the scornful interrogatory, "Quis tulerit Gracchos de seditione querentes?"—

But watchman—what of the night? What of hope is there that light shall break from the darkness of Europe, that the murky calm of triumphant despotism is the harbinger of the bursting storm of revolution? Shall the waters stagnate into green and loathsome corruption, fertile in slimy reptiles which the sunshine of despotism breeds; or will the breath of the tempest waking them into life, restore them to sparkling purity and freedom?

The extremity of the despair of Europe is the surest trust that the day of her redemption draws nigh. Assuredly her condition has never been worse; her people are in that lowest deep below which there is no lower: and that is the best assurance that they will venture a contest which can change their fate only for the better. Flight is now no refuge for the persecuted children of liberty in Europe. All the despots unite in menacing their last retreats. Switzerland and England alone remain above the flood whereon their feet can rest: and even there the long arm of despotism is stretched out after them. Russia has remonstrated with England on her hospitality—Austria has grumbled at the reception of Kossuth. France has united with her in threatening Switzerland with the consequences of indiscreet hospitality: and both would delight in an opportunity of dividing her mountain barriers as an indemnity and security against the emigrant machinations which disturb their repose—like the whispers of an evil conscience. The miserable find no refuge in Europe; their sole safety is beneath the ægis of this Republic. Already the Austrian minister has muttered his master's anathemas at the free spirit of our people who rose up as one man before the persecuted exile whom the nation delighted to honor: and no man can say how long it will be ere imperial blood hounds will hunt the fugitives to our shores. Since the empire of Nero and Caligula sunk before the northern barbarians Europe has felt no such night as that which now wraps her. No incubus in her darkest night has pressed so heavily on her breast. Her Kings are the jailors or the madhouse keepers—her people are convicts or maniacs, chained to the oar, or cramped in the straight jacket, watched with the jealous eye of suspicious tyranny, and chastised by the lash of inexorable power. Genius, virtue, patriotism, are crimes: the only virtues are obsequious submission, or active and zealous oppression. Gladstone has removed the rags from the running and loathsome sores that afflict Italian justice—and Europe has groaned aloud at the horrible recital. The days of Robespierre grow mild in comparison. Seem justified as a passing phrenzy in the presence of these cold-blooded, refined, and endless persecutions of the virtuous and the patriotic. The sharp madness of the revolutionary tribunal is virtue beside the cunning, cool, and deliberate villainy of the Neapolitan judges. The guillotine is mercy compared to the rotting away of life and limb piecemeal in the damp and filthy dungeons of Naples. Incivism is more a crime and more a pretext for judicial murder than honest devotion to liberty and the confessed constitution of the land. The twenty thousand prisoners for political offences in the small Kingdom of Naples throw into the shade the blackest excesses of the iniquitous leaders of the revolution. The murderous revenge of Austria on prostrate Hungary has filled the world with execration: and the very draymen of London constituted themselves the avengers of innocence on the vile Haynau. Martial law has superceded the criminal tribunals of Germany; and political sins are judged before courts constituted for the extermination of liberty in the persons of its friends. The voice of public discussion is hushed in her legislative bodies and the public press is silent in its great appeal. Sharp scrutiny scans the traveller for traces of his country: and the American or the Briton gets scanty courtesy and grudging leave to cross the prison bars of the Austrian frontier—lest his national costume and tongue might awaken the memory of a happier land. Light hearted France sighs beneath a despotism such as she has never known. Her protector has sharpened his sword against her, annihilated her constitution, scattered or imprisoned her legislative assembly, exiled her most illustrious citizens, banished to deadly climes her honorable men—marching them in long lines of thousands like felons to the gallows. He has placed vile creatures tools of his perfidious ambition in the dignities of the government, and murdered by the hundred, in open day, in the streets of Paris, by French soldiers, their fellow-citizens who dared prefer to him the constitution he had sworn to protect yet ventured to destroy. He has seized the press and stifled the voice of public complaint. By a mock election he has added fraud to his violence—and caused the tongue-tied press to speak lies for his justification. The heart of France will burst—or she will fling off the perjured usurper who apes Napoleon's tyranny and suppresses his greatest crimes without his immortal services which indemnified France for her sufferings: and then, as her legions arm for the rescue of the liberty she loved, her voice will be—as the shout of Achilles from the rampart.

The simultaneous agitations of 1848 were the breath of the angel troubling the waters: but the people had none to carry them to their healing touch.—If God shall once more send his angel to trouble those waters now so stagnant: if he shall inspire the people of Europe to rise in this great cause: if he shall endue them with wisdom, moderation, and union: if he shall raise up to lead them men who will fling to the winds all hopes of favor, all fear of death, all thoughts of compromise, strong to wrest the sword from their rulers and powerful to smite with it in the cause of liberty, who quail on no path however bloody, and once seated at the summit of power look undazzled from their height to the still higher cause—honest in their triumph as in their obscurity, and adjourning till the common foes of mankind are humbled the question how they will secure the trophies and fruits of victory—then the day of final judgment is at hand. These things will cry aloud to the free of all the earth to be up and doing. It will be the voice of God declaring the work his inspiration—and calling on those he has made free to prove themselves worthy of the blessing.

But when shall these things be, and what is the sign of their coming—say they who will fear no storm on the morrow because the sky is bright to-day.

God vouchsafes no prophecy to man in these days—but the prophecy of history.

Shall the Muse of history ever stand—a prophetic Cassandra, pale with the vigils of the past but glowing with the light of the future and her eye glittering with prescience of that which shall be—in vain warning the nations on their march to ruin, with her finger pointing to the open gulf before and the power pressing them into it from behind? Shall no voice ever attest her truth save the cry of despair or the groan of the lost?

God does not mark the future on the face of the heavens or of the earth. The sun will not be veiled in blackness nor will the moon be turned to blood that we may be warned of the coming desolation. The day of our death is in no wise different from the day of our birth. The heavens do not frown when the earth is stained with crime, nor are they illumined with unusual splendor when liberty and virtue are triumphant. The flood rushed over an astonished world invading the nuptial couch and the festive board. The amphitheatre resounded with the gladiator's groan and the wild beasts yell while the Lord of Peace lay meekly in the manger. The great convulsion of modern times broke—like the trump of the final day—on the ear of the thoughtless revellers: and the earthquake which lately covered Europe with ruins came unheralded save by the preternatural calm. One moment the waters were as glass—the next all foam and fury, kings' hearts failing them for fear, and the fountains of the great deep broken up to overwhelm them.

No man can say what a day may bring forth. No man is a safe counsellor in the affairs of this Republic who is willing to trust its fate to the treacherous and shifting chances of the morrow. Let us be as they who watch for the morning.

Whenever the trumpet shall sound for that judgment day, I look to see the stars and stripes of the Republic—the tri-color of the west—streaming in matchless splendor over the banners of freedom. Her youthful maturity has waxed strong by the blessings of freedom—till now her power surpasses that of France when she followed Napoleon to Moscow. Her children bless with grateful voices the God of their fathers who gave them liberty to enjoy, to protect, to transmit, and to spread. They hail the day which summons them to the field, and cheerfully recognize the duty they owe to the world they have roused. By their example has Europe been waked out of sleep; at their voice have her sons grasped the sword and died the death of the free; on them has God conferred the precious guardianship of the sacred fire; and on them as on the priests of a holy religion rests the high duty of its propagation. They have lured man from the quiet and safe repose in patriarchal despotism to the knowledge of his high destiny, and inspired him with the resolution to enjoy its precious fruits. On them rests the great privilege of succoring their offspring in the day of its need; of adding the power of arms to the resistless power of their example: of proving that the magnanimous spirit of liberty is equal to its pacific blessings; of maintaining in the face of fiercest despots the rights of mankind. Rather let the pillars of the Republic shake to their foundations, and her lofty battlements be overwhelmed bearing with them the last hope of Liberty on earth, than that she should falter in the terrible hour, or swerve from the bloodiest path she may be called to tread. Let her sun set—if it so please God—not the pale shadow of its early splendor, dimly shining through a long and languid twilight, accompanied to its rest by the requiem of the night birds that succeed to its realm—not thus be thy fall, Oh my Country!—but rather let her sun shining in meridian splendor, blazing at the zenith in its high calling, suddenly, in the twinkling of an eye—when the world may no more be free—plunge in midday to endless night.

So shall men remembering thy greatness say that thy fall was worthy of thy glory!

THE END.

ERRATA.

READ,

Page 305, line 9, defying, for defiant.

Page 432, line 2, coercion ; that, for coercion that.

Page 445, line 26, comparison—seem, for comparison. Seem.

Page 447, line 10, surpasses, for suppresses.

www.ingramcontent.com/pod-product-compliance
Lightning Source LLC
LaVergne TN
LVHW021130110826
845150LV00005B/979

* 9 7 8 1 4 2 5 5 5 0 3 6 3 *